An Extreme Event

UPDATED EDITION

DEBBIE WHITMONT

RANDOM HOUSE AUSTRALIA

Random House Australia Pty Ltd
20 Alfred Street, Milsons Point, NSW 2061
http://www.randomhouse.com.au

Sydney New York Toronto
London Auckland Johannesburg

First published by Random House Australia 1999

National Library of Australia
Cataloguing-in-Publication Entry

Whitmont, Debbie.
An extreme event.

Updated ed.
Bibliography.

ISBN 1 74051 049 6.

1. Sydney–Hobart Yacht Race (54th : 1998). 2. Search and rescue operations - Tasman Sea.
3. Yachting accidents - Tasman Sea. 4. Survival after airplane accidents, shipwrecks, etc. I. Title.

797.140994

Cover photograph by The Photo Library
Cover design by Greendot Design
Typeset in 11.5/15 Garamond Adobe by Midland Typesetters, Maryborough, Victoria
Printed and bound by Griffin Press, Netley, South Australia

10 9 8 7 6 5 4 3 2 1

To Jessica and Billy

ACKNOWLEDGMENTS

In all, 115 yachts and 1135 sailors took part in the 1998 Sydney to Hobart race. It's estimated that nearly 1000 people were involved in the rescue effort. This account, which grew from a television documentary made for the ABC's *Four Corners* program and screened in Australia in February 1999, tells some of their stories. Wherever possible, I have used direct quotes from interviews done either for the original program or for the book. Additional material is from newspaper and magazine accounts at the time as well as my own library research.

So many people helped with this book that it is impossible to thank all of them. Firstly my thanks go to more than 120 people who were involved with the race and gave up their time to talk about it later. Many of them were generous and patient enough to put up with being interviewed on a number of occasions over a period of months. I would especially like to thank Roger Badham, Tom Bibby, Peter Davidson, Brian Emerson, Alan Gifford, David Gray, Geoff Hill, Ollie Hreinisson, Peter Joubert, Peter Keats, David Key, Rob Kothe, Steve Kulmar, Tanzi Lea, Andy Marriette, Locky and Kass Marshall, Mike Marshman, Peter Miekle, Iain Moray, Drew Murray, Wacka Payne, Joe Pirello, Geoff Ross, Gary Shanks, Peter Sinclair, John Stanley, Gary Ticehurst and Steve Walker. I hope I have done justice to their stories. I am particularly grateful to Rob Matthews, who not only spent many hours talking to me but also read the manuscript and made a number of helpful suggestions. I owe special thanks to Tracy Pillamer for her excellent research and additional interviews.

In researching both this book and the documentary before it, I made a deliberate decision to avoid dwelling on the private pain of those who lost loved ones in the Sydney to Hobart. They have already been through enough. No words can express the grief of losing a father, husband, son, brother or dear friend. I hope that for the family and friends of those who died, this book will serve as a faithful account of some events during the race. The stories of those who survived the storm are tribute to the courage of all those who experienced nature's worst.

The book would never have been written without the original TV documentary. For that, my thanks go to everyone at *Four Corners* and many others at the ABC, but particularly to Michelle Baddiley, Adelaide Beavis, Tami Bokey, Matt Brown, John Budd, Ross Byrne, Kerry Christie, Ann Connor, Julie Costello, Anne Delaney, Michelle Gibson, Greg Heap, Sharnelle Magee, Geoff Krix, Gavin Marsh, Michol Marsh, Rosemary Meares, Jessica Momberg, Michael Nettleship, Margot O'Neill, Mario Pelligrino, Bronwen Reid, Liz Scott, Anthea Stewart and Duncan White. Above all, I want to thank producer Lisa McGregor, who not only contributed her considerable skills as a journalist and producer but also took the time to read the manuscript and make valuable suggestions.

Thanks, too, to Lyndsay Brown and to all at Random House who put their faith in an untried author, in particular Jane Palfreyman, Belinda Yuille, James Mills-Hicks and Hazel Flynn. Hazel Flynn was a source of constant encouragement and worked far beyond the call of duty to help me finish the book on time. I am grateful not only for her many helpful suggestions, but also for her friendship throughout.

Last, but far from least, I want to thank Peter McEvoy for his love and encouragement—for keeping me going, finding time to read drafts and improve them, and for changing more than his share of nappies when the deadline loomed. Special thanks, too, to my friend Helen Kiel.

Some people who saw the original TV documentary complained that it tried to lay blame for a tragedy that couldn't be avoided. I don't believe that is true. After any disaster, it's natural to ask questions. And it's natural to hope that, if any mistakes were made, the same mistakes won't be made in the future. There will always be storms. And some of them will always be fatal. It can only be hoped that, when they occur, lessons learnt in the past will mean that some unnecessary tragedy might be avoided.

Books about sailing are usually written by sailors. This one is written by a journalist. My only direct contact with the yacht race came on its first night, when I stood on the coast south of Sydney and watched as a spectacular electrical storm broke out over the ocean. I didn't know, then, that a few kilometres out to sea hundreds of sailors were hauling in their spinnakers, less than one day away from the maelstrom. I certainly didn't realise that many months later I would still be fascinated and moved by their experiences.

Finally, this book is written for anyone who longs for adventure and is inspired by those who still go out of their way to find it. Without adventure, and without risk-taking, the world would be a dull and limited place. This book is dedicated to my mother, who has always let me have my adventures. And to my son, who I hope will have many of his own.

Sydney
August 1999

Sunday, 27 December 1998
Bass Strait

Tom Bibby sees the distress flares a few minutes after midnight. They must have been fired upward into the air, but the howling wind forces them down and across till they barely skim the highest waves. Bibby watches the red sparks fizz out to sea in a sweeping arc. On the fishing trawler Moira Elizabeth *he's picking up wind speeds of 40 knots (more than 70 kilometres an hour). Whoever fired the flares must be in trouble, and they aren't far from the trawler. But Bibby hopes someone else is looking out for them. By now, he has enough troubles of his own.*

Early that morning, knowing the weather would get bad, he'd given up fishing and gone to shelter. But then he got the message that seventeen people on a disabled yacht were missing. At four-thirty in the afternoon, Bibby turned the Moira Elizabeth *and headed out into one of the worst storms either of them had ever experienced. Seven and a half hours and more than a hundred dangerous and frustrating kilometres later, the storm is still raging and Tom Bibby still can't find the yacht that he's looking for.*

Three times the yacht's crew has given its position, but on each occasion when the Moira Elizabeth *battles to the given coordinates it finds nothing and no-one. Now Bibby is wondering why. Maybe something's wrong with the yacht's positioning system. Maybe the sea is just too wild to get a proper fix. Either way, the* Moira Elizabeth *is still ploughing back and forth, often at the worst possible angle to the wind and the seas. The 26-metre,*

179-tonne trawler has already been tipped on its side twice. The whole business is beginning to look more like a wild goose chase than a rescue.

Now Tom Bibby is trying to figure out which way the yacht is drifting. He's heading north when he sees the flares and reaches for the radio. It hasn't helped that, for most of the night, the trawler's radio has refused to work. An hour ago he finally got it back on air and now at least if he can't find the yacht he can talk to its crew. They call him back on the radio and report they've also just seen red flashes. So the trawler and the yacht must be very close to each other. Somewhere in between them someone else is in trouble.

Earlier that night the skies above Bass Strait erupted in distress flares, like a macabre display of New Year's Eve fireworks. The fifty-fourth annual Sydney to Hobart yacht race had become one of Australia's worst sporting disasters. By nightfall on the race's second day, sixteen yachts and more than 150 sailors were missing.

Tom Bibby is convinced that someone else must be responding to the distress flares he's just seen. But no-one is. Just a few kilometres from the Moira Elizabeth *and the yacht* Bibby *is searching for, another smaller yacht is half-full of water. In the dark and the storm, and with its radio broken, the yacht* Business Post Naiad, *might as well be on another planet. On board, two men lie dead. Seven others are doing what they can to bail water.*

As they bail, they see the reflection of a light thrown up on the clouds. They know that a boat, maybe a trawler, must be nearby. They try to attract its attention by firing off flares. But it's too windy for the flares to work properly. They watch them fly low and shoot out to sea.

As the flares fade, Business Post Naiad*'s seven survivors carry on bailing. They stuff pillows in the broken windows of their yacht and prepare the life rafts. They don't have a proper sea anchor, so they stream a jib and a spinnaker from the yacht's bow to try and make it point into the seas. It doesn't work very well and the boat may roll again, but there's nothing more they can do. They go below; down into a foot of water, spilt diesel, and a storm-flung chaos of food, equipment and nine men's possessions. By the light of two torches they sit and wait till morning.*

ONE

*The fishing community in Eden have just about had
enough of rescuing yachts.*

—Joe Pirello, *fisherman*

*Over the years, we've been called on to bring yachts in
tow after being damaged by various storms and
southerly busters. Eden's become pretty aware of what
can happen and these days we have a 'Nautical Night'
down at the harbour, knowing there'll be a lot of yachts
arriving in distress. We capitalise, for commercial
reasons.*

—Locky Marshall, *fisherman*

Sunday, 27 December 1998

In Eden's harbour the clouds hang low and grey. Past the wharves, the
odd wave is breaking over the lowest of the concrete blocks piled up
into an ugly breakwater. Along the pier, old nylon fishing nets laid out
long ago for repairs that never happened are blowing into multicoloured
tangles.

Halfway between Sydney and Melbourne, and the safest natural
harbour on the south-eastern coastline, Eden is as beautiful as its name-
sake. One hundred and fifty years ago its founders predicted that it
would become one of the world's great ports. But it didn't. A safe haven
in the days of sail, and a whaling town in the days of whales, Eden was
bypassed as ships grew sturdier and the last whales were slaughtered.

Instead of thriving as a halfway point between two big cities, its port, Twofold Bay, fell into neglect. It was too far away from either of the big centres to matter.

In recent decades Eden's main claim to fame has been a skeleton, carefully cleaned, reconstructed and proudly displayed in the town's Killer Whale Museum. The skeleton is the remains of Old Tom, the last of a pack of killer whales that visited Twofold Bay for more than a century. One day in 1930 Old Tom floated into Eden's harbour, already very dead and more than a little on the nose. It was the end of an era.

By late 1998 Eden's once controversial woodchip mill is faltering and its tuna cannery is on the brink of closure. Just about the only industries left to employ people are fishing and tourism, and even they are struggling. Two days after Christmas, at the height of the holiday season, the jetty cafe is open but deserted.

From the deck of his yacht *Trident IV*, Drew Murray glances over to the jetty and thinks about walking over for a coffee. It doesn't look as inviting as he'd hoped. The two wharves are lined with trawlers but there isn't a person in sight. The sheltered harbour is still relatively calm, but the weather's turning bad. Everything is unusually deserted, as if the whole town is suffering some kind of silent post-Christmas hangover.

Instead of going ashore, Murray goes below and turns on the jug. He's already decided to spend a quiet day in the harbour. He's on his way home to Launceston in northern Tasmania. There's no hurry to get there.

Spooning out coffee, Murray's thoughts wander to Launceston, the small town he grew up in. He still has a house and some of his closest friends there, but these days he spends more time away from Launceston than in it. When he does go home, the friends he catches up with are sailors, like Rob Matthews. Drew Murray and Rob Matthews both spent childhoods sailing on the river. Then they swapped their dinghies for yachts and began racing in Bass Strait and the ocean around Tasmania. The two probably wouldn't have become friends if it hadn't been for yacht racing. Twenty years ago, Drew thought Rob was too loud; Rob thought Drew was too wild. But two decades smooths off a lot of rough edges. Now, a professional seaman himself, Drew Murray rates Rob Matthews as a skilled helmsman, a sailor he'd trust anywhere, and one of his closest friends. Even so, in everything but their shared love of sailing, the two men couldn't be more different. Matthews is a public servant, married with two children. Murray is a wanderer, happily unsettled and more at home on the water than anywhere on land. He spends most of his time on *Trident IV*. Matthews still loves ocean racing but Murray sails cruisers. Murray hasn't entered a serious yacht race since he won the Melbourne to Hobart race with Matthews fourteen years ago. Murray gave up yacht racing the way other people have to give up drink or cigarettes. He realised it was bad for his health.

Now, as Drew Murray makes coffee in Eden, Rob Matthews is barrelling down the coast, racing in the Sydney to Hobart on *Business Post Naiad*. It's a tough trip, one of the few long ocean races left in the world, and Murray knows his friend will be tired, cold and wet, and loving every minute of it. He wonders how far south the boat would be by now. The race started yesterday afternoon and it usually takes at least a full day to make Eden from Sydney. But there was a lot of wind last night. The water boils. No point yet, Murray thinks, but in a little while he'll try turning on the radio to find out what's happening in the race.

≪   ≫

Above the harbour, on the hill behind the wharves, Locky Marshall looks out the glass doors leading onto his verandah. The fishermen who work for him always joke that once they are in the bay they can't get away with slacking off. Marshall can see everything they're doing without even leaving his lounge-room.

Marshall's original business was butcher shops. A thorough and organised man, he learnt all he could about meat: how to cut it, pack it and get it to market in the best possible condition. Then, twenty-six years ago, maybe because he'd learnt all he could, he took up fishing. By the time the government brought in fishing quotas, Locky Marshall had meticulous records of every fish his boat had ever caught. In the whole of New South Wales, he was the only fisherman able to give concrete proof of his claim for a quota. He'd always told his wife, Kass, that one day those records would come in handy.

Now Marshall has two boats, a share in two others, a Master's Class Four seaman's ticket and a big house overlooking Eden's harbour. On the ground floor, next to his office, a huge party-room with a juke-box, pool table and colour photos of massive hauls of fish has become a de facto club for local fishermen.

This morning, Locky Marshall is thinking about weather. The afternoon before, the Bureau of Meteorology issued a storm warning for coastal waters near Eden and Bass Strait. He wonders whether the trawlers in the harbour should be double moored. The forecast is for winds of 45 to 55 knots and he figures that could mean 10-metre seas. One of his boats, the *Josephine Jean*, is fishing close to shore. If they have any luck, it will be a useful catch. Between Christmas and New Year, a lot of fishermen take time off and prices are sky high.

Marshall isn't particularly worried about the *Josephine Jean*. Her skipper, Ollie Hreinisson, is an Icelander and knows what he's doing. If the weather turns bad Hreinisson will go 'dodgem', lifting his trawl and heading into the waves. If it gets too bad, the *Josephine Jean* will probably come home. Just the same, Marshall thinks he might give the skipper a call on the mobile.

In the Marshalls' kitchen, Kass is chatting to some friends about costumes for Eden's annual wharf party. Over the next few days, the harbour that history passed by will fill up with visitors. At least once a year, thanks to the Sydney to Hobart, the safest haven between the race's start and its finish swarms with sailors. Some have simply given up the race and decided to take it easy. Others have damaged their yachts, or their crews are too seasick to continue.

Over the years, Eden has learned to take advantage of the influx. Now it puts on 'Nautical Night', an annual fancy-dress party. Kass and the others are joking that this year the same old costumes will be dragged out yet again. There'll be the pirates and the castaways and, as usual, the old man who comes as King Neptune and brings a coffin to lie in. It's always a big night. Or, as hungover sailors say the next morning, 'a bit of a high tide'.

As Marshall goes downstairs to his office it crosses his mind that the storm warning might make for a record crowd, and not just for 'Nautical

Night'. Eden's shopkeepers will be rubbing their hands together. Over in the harbour, listening to the latest weather forecast, Drew Murray is thinking much the same.

Marshall calls Ollie Hreinisson. The *Josephine Jean* is trawling in shallow water just east of town. The wind is about 25 knots. Perfectly safe for a 200-tonne steel-hulled fishing boat.

Across town Eden's police sergeant, Keith Tillman, is leaving his house, next door to the police station. He crosses his drive, opens up the station, and starts making phone calls. Budget cutbacks mean the Eden station often has to be left unstaffed, but today he wants all his officers on standby. The Sydney to Hobart is on and there's a storm warning. Keith Tillman has a suspicion the police station might get busy.

A few hours later Sergeant Tillman leaves the station, jumps into the police car and drives to Locky Marshall's house. It is 2.10 p.m. when he knocks on the door. The local coastguard has just passed on a distress call from a boat in the Sydney to Hobart yacht race. It will be the first of many. Opening his front door, and seeing the police sergeant, Marshall has one thought: *Here we go again.*

TWO

In today's society, people need an escape and the Sydney to Hobart race is an adventurous thing to do in the sailing scene. It's just a matter of how the ocean appeals to you, what enjoyment you get out of it.
—John Stanley, helmsman, Winston Churchill

There's a lot of tradition about the Sydney to Hobart. And there's the challenge of the race. It's always unpredictable in terms of what sort of weather you're going to get. And that adds to the mystique and the appeal of it.
—Hugo van Kretschmar, commodore, Cruising Yacht
Club of Australia

Saturday, 26 December 1998
Sydney Harbour
At Rushcutters Bay in Sydney's eastern suburbs it's a warm summer morning. The Harbour sparkles. The usually quiet bay is home to the Cruising Yacht Club of Australia and the day after Christmas—the start of the Sydney to Hobart—is the busiest day of the year. The band starts playing at breakfast time. By mid-morning, onlookers crowd the nearby park and the club's marina swarms with sailors, would-be sailors and well-wishers. The club's bar is pumping out beer and bloody marys. Its cash registers are humming.

But that morning, amid the last minute race preparations, there is one small, yet puzzling, incident. A few days later, Geoff Bascombe will remember it. And it will worry him.

Bascombe has flown to Sydney for the start of the Sydney to Hobart. He's a former Navy diver and in his home state, South Australia, everyone knows him as Mega. One of his many skills is maintaining yachts and helping them prepare for big races. And, as a diver, part of his job is to get into the water and check and clean his clients' boats just before the start.

On race day, Mega's job begins early. He puts on his dive gear, gets in the water and works on the boats owned by three of his clients. But swimming back from the last one, something odd on another boat catches his attention. He swims over to the yacht, an old-style wooden plank boat, to have a closer look. Right on the water line, near the stem post at the boat's bow and at the end of one of the planks, some paint is missing. And where the paint is missing, there is a black line. To Mega's eye, the line is about five-sixteenths of an inch wide. The black colour is the caulking—the compound used to plug up seams in a wooden boat. And it's showing. It's not necessarily a problem in itself, but it could be the sign of one. 'Once the caulking is out, it means there could have been some kind of movement inside,' he explains later. It's obvious, that in a few hours time, the boat will be setting off for Hobart. Says Mega: 'If the boat were under a lot of stress, more caulking could fall out. I thought the crew should know about it.'

There are three men around the wooden boat. As Mega remembers it later, one, or maybe two, of them are on board. The other one, or maybe two, are close by, on the jetty. 'I told them and they acknowledged it,' says Mega. 'They said something like, "Yeah, well, we'll let the boss know about it."'

The yacht Mega has been looking at is the Sydney to Hobart's oldest and most beautiful competitor. Three days later a photo of it, taken just before the race, will be published in a Sydney newspaper. The boat's deck gleams in the sun and its crew match the bright mood in bold black and white striped shirts and floppy white sunhats. The headline above the picture reads: 'SYDNEY CREW LOST AT SEA'. The yacht's name is *Winston Churchill*.

Winston Churchill is owned and skippered by Richard Winning, from the third generation of a wealthy Sydney family known for its large, successful whitegoods business. The family is also known for sailing. 'We look at it as a bit of recreation,' Winning is reported as saying some months before the Sydney to Hobart. 'Gentlemen's ocean racing—that's our game.' Exceptionally proud of his yacht, Winning makes no secret of the fact that Sir Winston Churchill is one of his heroes. Since he bought the boat, Winning has had it extensively refurbished. The most recent refit, overseen by Winning's chief helmsman, John 'Steamer' Stanley, has cost more than $250,000. Among the crew for the Sydney to Hobart are Stanley and two of Winning's boyhood sailing friends, John Dean and Michael Bannister. Dean plans to celebrate his forty-seventh birthday on the way to Hobart.

On the morning of the race, Richard Winning remembers arriving at the marina at about 9.00 a.m. 'I think I was the first one there,' he recalls, 'because I live the closest.' But Winning doesn't know Mega and he doesn't remember a diver. That morning, says Winning, no-one mentioned caulking, or a problem with the boat's hull, to him.

So who did Mega talk to and warn? 'It was early in the morning,' Mega recalls. 'I had done three boats. It could have been 8.30. It could have been nine. I wasn't keeping track of the time.' It is possible that the three men Mega saw and spoke to weren't even part of *Winston Churchill*'s crew. But if they weren't crewmembers, who were they? And why was at least one of them on the boat? A few hours later, everyone on the boat is wearing the boldly striped black and white crew shirts. But that fact doesn't help. Mega can't remember what the three men were wearing. At the time, it wasn't important. 'You get used to seeing a lot of loud shirts around yacht races,' he says later. 'I have a lot of loud shirts myself.'

'There was nothing wrong with that boat, or at least nothing that money couldn't fix,' says Winning. 'I saw it up on the slips two days before the race and there was nothing wrong then. After that, the yacht was motored across the Harbour to the marina. I didn't examine it on the day but I certainly wasn't aware of any untoward damage. I'm not famous for going to sea on damaged boats. Ask anyone. That boat was mollycoddled. If any boat was going to make it to Hobart, it was that one.'

If Mega did warn some of the crew about a possible problem, the message didn't get through to the man who knows the veteran *Winston Churchill* better than anybody. John Stanley has spent months working on the boat at a marina owned by Richard Winning. Like Winning, Stanley doesn't remember any conversation with a diver. And, like the rest of the crew, he's already focused on *Winston Churchill*'s trip south. As a young boy, Stanley fell in love with boats the first time he saw one. When his parents first took him to the local yacht club, he sat on a ramp, stared at the yachts and knew he wanted to sail. 'Ever since,' he says, 'I chased trying to be on the best boats with the best guys, until I got a name for myself as being pretty good.' Now in his early fifties and a builder by trade, Stanley is on his fifteenth or sixteenth (even he has trouble remembering) Sydney to Hobart. But *Winston Churchill* should know the way to Hobart even better than he does. The oldest boat in the race, *Winston Churchill* has sailed the course seventeen times. Often among the first boats over the line in its heyday, these days *Winston Churchill* races more for pleasure than competition. Stanley's feeling pretty relaxed. *Winston Churchill* doesn't head straight for the starting line. First, she hoists her sails and takes a run up the Harbour.

'The *Winston Churchill* was built for the ocean,' says Stanley. 'At the start of the race in a boat like the *Winston Churchill*, you've just gotta go for clear air and not get too involved. Boats, a lot of boats, can go past a boat like that—it's a slow-tacking boat so you just keep your nose clean. You just get out the Heads.'

Across the water, a line of sails is beginning to form for the start. Sailboats have raced on Sydney Harbour since the earliest days of the colony. Back then everyone started at anchor with their sails down. Now, after a ten-minute warning gun, they hover behind the line in a kind of suspended animation. For serious contenders, the start—manoeuvring into the front row, choosing the best breeze and picking up speed as quickly as possible—is a race in itself. A year's preparation might be wasted by a collision on the starting line. A minute lost in the beginning could cost overall victory. The Sydney to Hobart yacht race covers 630 nautical miles (1000 kilometres). It usually takes three or four days to finish. But in 1982, it was won by just a few seconds.

In 1998, just before one o'clock, 115 yachts line up for the fifty-fourth race to Hobart. Sydneysiders can't have a white Christmas, but they can have a ringside seat for the beginning of one of the world's great ocean races. Every year thousands watch the start from spectator boats on the Harbour, picnics on the foreshores or on televisions at home. Two hundred years ago, stranded in an island colony, they might have watched just as keenly for sailing ships bringing news or desperately needed supplies from the other side of the world.

At a distance, the race boats look deceptively still; up close, the crews are frenzied. People shout; loose sails flap. The wind from the nor'east turns more easterly. At the last minute a couple of the bigger yachts change places and head for the leeward end of the line, betting on getting ahead before they'll have to give way on the tack up the Harbour. Then, in the wide angle panorama filmed from helicopters and shown live all over Australia, the strip of sails explodes forward. With three small puffs of smoke and the bang of a toy cannon, 1135 sailors start racing to Hobart.

Since the first Sydney to Hobart fifty-three years earlier men have walked on the moon and built computers the size of pinheads. The only thing that hasn't changed is the ocean. It's just as fickle—and all powerful—as it was in 1945 when nine yachts weighed anchor, set their sails and headed out to sea.

THREE

Apart from the storm, the voyage was uneventful. The repairs to the mainsail occupied twenty-four hours of hard stitching. We tried to keep regular watches at night, but we could not get quite enough sleep. The water came on board during the southerly blow; nevertheless we kept the Primus going and managed to get hot meals of a kind.
   —Captain John Illingworth, after winning the first Sydney to Hobart race in 1945

They say a yacht race is what happens as soon as one boat crew is close enough to see another. It's as basic as going faster than someone else, and as complex as astronomy. It's about how to squeeze out that extra edge, to sail closer to the wind, to concentrate harder and longer than another helmsman and another crew. It's about yacht design and technology, skill and experience. And most of all, it's about luck. Ocean racers talk about being thrown around by a gale in the morning, then speeding 'downhill' in the sunshine or lying becalmed under flapping sails by afternoon. They talk about floundering helplessly while a tiny gust of wind pushes someone else's boat ahead. They talk about being cold, exhausted and seasick, and about how they'll never do it again. Then, the next year, or the next weekend, they do.

Australia's earliest white settlers were all migrants. By the middle of the nineteenth century, when the white population passed a million, most settlers had spent a good while on sailing ships just getting to their new colonial home. It isn't surprising that after they arrived many took up sailing as a pastime. The taste for boat racing grew after the first narrow-beamed and speedy Yankee clippers pulled into Sydney. Soon, the clippers were racing each other to and from the colony. Passenger ships rushed eager fortune hunters to the goldfields. Merchants sped the Australian woolclip to the markets in England. And more Australians took up racing for fun. In 1896, the first man to sail single-handedly around the world, Joshua Slocum, was startled by Sydney's appetite for sailing:

> Everybody owned a boat. If a boy in Australia has not the means to buy him a boat, he builds one, and it is usually not one to be ashamed of. The typical Sydney boat is a handy sloop of great beam and enormous sail-carrying power; but a capsize is not uncommon, for they carry sail like Vikings.

For all that, Sydney's earliest boat races were better known for post-race drinking binges than skill, and it didn't take long for the colony's first sailing club to sink itself into bankruptcy over a drinks bill. It was only with the arrival of a Scottish merchant, William Walker, that Sydney yacht racing became somewhat more organised. Walker belonged to the Royal Thames Yacht Club in London. Within a year of his arrival in Sydney, he had organised royal patronage for a club and became commodore of the Royal Sydney Yacht Squadron. The Squadron's first officially organised ocean race was a two-boat challenge from Sydney to Newcastle and back. Fought out between Walker and another of the Squadron's founding members, the contest soon became a duel between favourite and underdog—on one side, Walker's prestigious English yacht *Chance*; on the other, a small Sydney-built boat, *Xarifa*. A good deal of pride and money (much of both belonging to William Walker) rode on the outcome.

At first it seemed *Chance* was unbeatable. *Xarifa* was barely out of the Heads when it was hit by a southerly gale, broke its topmast and wrecked its rig. The frustrated crew watched *Chance* disappear ahead in the distance, while they sailed on with what was left of the rigging and made desperate repairs. Despondently, they finally rounded the mark, headed back in the darkness and ran into a furious storm. Everyone on *Xarifa* assumed *Chance* was miles ahead, and the crew of *Chance*, though they overshot the turn and almost wrecked their own boat on a reef, thought the same. But throughout the race neither boat ever saw the other one. It was only the next day, as he came through Sydney Heads cracking open a bottle of champagne, that William Walker discovered *Xarifa* had pulled in four hours ahead of him. He sent *Chance* to the Pacific Islands to be sold; he didn't want to see it again. The race was a victory for the underdog. And it showed that even a two-boat race is never over till the finish.

By the turn of the century the first Australian yachtsmen were racing farther afield. In 1907 the American yachting magazine *Rudder* offered a trophy for the winner of a race across Bass Strait. Four boats competed in what was supposed to be the first race in an annual challenge. The race was won by a yacht called *Thistle*. But the boats were hit by such a ferocious gale that the winner's wife (who'd sailed with her husband) hid the trophy, hoping to discourage anyone from racing again. Her ploy almost worked. There wasn't another officially organised Bass Strait race until 1929. In that one, with 10-metre seas and hurricane-force winds, only three of the six starters made it to the finish. Bass Strait yacht racing then went into lull until the 1930s.

If it hadn't been for a fluke of bad weather and good timing, the first Sydney to Hobart yacht race would probably by now have been almost forgotten. But the race came at an opportune moment. For years there'd been nothing but grim news from the Second World War. By late 1945, with the war over, the escapist appeal of a boat race to Hobart, billed as the longest ever sailed out of Sydney, proved irresistible.

A year earlier, in 1944, a few yachtsmen had combined their hobby with the war effort by patrolling the coast around Sydney Harbour. Patrolling soon turned to racing and the beginnings of a small yacht club. At first the nine members of the Cruising Yacht Club of Australia met in a photographic studio and then in a cafe after closing time. Before long, they were hiring a hall. At one meeting a guest speaker threw down the challenge that would eventually make the club world-famous.

The speaker was an Englishman then in charge of the Garden Island Naval Dockyard, Commander John Illingworth. He was a keen ocean racer. When someone at the meeting invited him to cruise to Hobart, he agreed to go, as long as they were racing.

For the first race to Hobart, Illingworth bought a small yacht called *Rani* and did a few of his own alterations. It turned out that he took racing extremely seriously. Yacht handicapping even then was so complex that few yachtsmen understood it. But Illingworth did. He worked out handicaps for all nine competitors, by the formula used for British ocean races. The fact that he knew how to do it should have been a clue to his chances.

The first Sydney to Hobart followed the same course the race follows today—south down the New South Wales coast, across Bass Strait, down the Tasmanian coast, across Storm Bay and up the Derwent River to Hobart. Since 1996 the race record has been just over two and a half days. In 1945 even the fastest boats were expected to take at least a week.

The first race started, as it would fifty-three years later, with a trademark Sydney Harbour nor'easter. The favourite was a Hobart boat skippered by its designer, Percy Coverdale. With wartime solidarity, the British prime minister had given the nod to naming the yacht *Winston Churchill*. Like most of the others who'd originally planned a simple cruise to Hobart, Coverdale got more than he expected. On the second day out of Sydney, it was reported that a strong south to south-west gale had 'scattered' the fleet.

But gales didn't just scatter the fleet, they came close to devastating it. A 52-foot boat called *Archina* stopped racing and tried to wait out the storm for nearly forty hours before giving up and pulling out. Her owner phoned home from Jervis Bay and said most of the crew had never seen worse seas or been more violently seasick. Another yacht, *Saltair*, was forced into shelter behind Montague Island. The crew spent a day ashore, shooting rabbits and cooking them. The crew of *Horizon* battened hatches and waited below for twenty-four hours, and another boat, *Wayfarer*, lost its mainsail and jib. In between two gales that hit the race, the airforce sent out a plane to check on the damage. Two yachts couldn't be found. One, *Horizon*, was finally spotted 50 miles from Tasmania. But Captain Illingworth's *Rani* had simply disappeared.

Then, six days, fourteen hours and twenty-two minutes after the race began, *Rani* sailed into Hobart. Earlier that morning she'd popped out of the mist near Tasman Island, almost in the home stretch. No-one except Illingworth (who won a private bet on it) thought the race would take less than a week. When *Rani* ripped its mainsail in the storm, Illingworth set his crew to stitching it. When the boat flooded, he set them to bailing. The only reason the planes didn't see *Rani* was because they didn't fly far enough south to find her. Cheered home up the Derwent River, Illingworth kept asking how many yachts were ahead of his. Everyone just laughed in reply.

The next day the *Hobart Mercury* carried the banner, 'RANI TRIUMPHS IN OCEAN YACHT RACE. "MISSING" FOR FOUR DAYS. CROSSED FINISHING LINE AT 1.22 A.M. TODAY'. Starved for copy over the Christmas holidays, the Sydney *Daily Telegraph*, which was edited by a yachtsman, put the story on its front page. Other newspapers followed. By the time it was over, the race that began as a one-off cruise from Sydney to Hobart was set to become a national institution.

Captain John Illingworth took the victory in his stride and described the race as 'uneventful'.

The last boat home was *Wayfarer*, which had hit the worst of the weather. Her skipper, Peter Luke, said they'd had gales every second day. And when it wasn't blowing a gale, it was almost a flat calm. It took *Wayfarer* eleven days to finish.

According to the newspapers, the three hundred people lining Hobart's Constitution Dock for the finish had only one disappointment—that the winner wasn't the sentimental favourite, *Winston Churchill*. The boat arrived seventeen hours after *Rani*, having survived the gale by sheltering behind Babel Island in Bass Strait, only to then be trapped in a calm. The crew spent half a day fishing. The skipper, who'd been hurt in the gale, finished the race with his arm in a sling.

Neither Captain John Illingworth nor his winning yacht, *Rani*, ever raced to Hobart again. But *Winston Churchill* did.

In 1998, fifty-three years after its first trip down the coast, once again in a nor'easter, *Winston Churchill* rounds the sea mark outside Sydney for the eighteenth time. The yacht doesn't get a great start but for a veteran it's in a good enough position. Nearby is another old campaigner, *Canon Maris*, sailed by two of John Stanley's long-time friends, Ian Kiernan and Richard 'Sightie' Hammond. Hammond is the true veteran of the Sydney to Hobart. The 1998 race is his fortieth.

< >

It's simple to write off the Sydney to Hobart as a few rich businessmen trying to outdo each other with money-guzzling yachts and too much technology. But though the big boats fighting for line honours get the most attention, for every yachting billionaire there are dozens of builders, engineers, salesmen and weekend sailors. Yachts of different sizes race each other on handicap, friends compete against friends, yacht clubs against yacht clubs, veterans against veterans. And though the winners are usually professionals, there's never any shortage of amateurs and optimistic outsiders who think that maybe this time they'll pull off the big one.

In 1998 the runaway favourite for line honours is the 1995 winner, *Sayonara*, owned by American high roller Larry Ellison. The $5 million *Sayonara* towers over the Sydney to Hobart fleet in much the same way Ellison's $7 billion Oracle Corporation stands tall in the world of computer software. *Sayonara* is built to come first and Ellison's twenty-two man, mostly professional, crew (Ellison makes twenty-three) is there to make sure it does. For the race, *Sayonara* is transported from San Francisco to Sydney on a container ship.

It's later reported that even before the start Ellison has mixed feelings about the Sydney to Hobart. To begin with, his arch rival, another software tycoon, Hasso Plattner, hasn't even entered his yacht *Morning Glory*. (In 1996 *Morning Glory* won the Sydney to Hobart's only cash prize—$300,000—for setting a new race record. As proof, if any is needed, that a yachtsman with a boat big enough to break the record couldn't possibly need the money, Plattner said at the time that $300,000 wouldn't pay for the mast he damaged during the race.) Without *Morning Glory* competing, Ellison can't have the pleasure of defeating his rival. But even worse, two days before the start, flying into Sydney on the Oracle jet, his girlfriend begs him to give the whole thing a miss. Maybe she was put off by the 1995 race, when one of Ellison's celebrity crewmen, the chairman of News Limited, Rupert Murdoch, lost the tip of a finger. Whatever it is that worries his girlfriend, Ellison ignores her. Later he tells a reporter it's because he wanted to find out how good a sailor he's become. 'The Sydney–Hobart is a little like childbirth. It takes a while to suppress the pain and then you're ready to do it again.' This time, filling his father's boatshoes, Rupert Murdoch's son Lachlan is sailing with Ellison. As expected, *Sayonara* is the first boat out the Heads, just ahead of another maxi yacht, *Brindabella*.

On *Winston Churchill*, John Stanley is waiting for the afternoon breeze to turn into a southerly buster later that evening. Before leaving Sydney, he sat down with Bureau of Meteorology forecaster Ken Batt and read through the outlook. But Stanley doesn't put a great deal of faith in weather forecasts, even if they come from old friends like Batt. 'There were obviously a few ifs with what the weather was going to do,' he explains later. 'In years gone by there wasn't all this technology. You've just got to look at it and say to yourself, "Well, are these guys right or are they wrong? I mean, how many times have they been wrong and how many times have they been right?" Sometimes you can have too much technology and miss the basic things. So you take it, you find it interesting and you go with it. But once you're in the ocean, what you get is what you get and you've just gotta deal with it.' To John Stanley it all looks pretty much like any other Sydney to Hobart. The forecast says the winds could get up to 50 knots on Sunday. It sounds manageable.

Shortly after 1 p.m., John Stanley takes a last look back at the glittering Harbour. The *Winston Churchill* reaches the red-and-black marker at the Heads, turns right and hoists a spinnaker for a beautiful run south. It will be her last voyage.

FOUR

It looked pretty grim and I was quite concerned. I figured there'd probably be a fair bit of carnage among the fleet.

— Roger 'Clouds' Badham, yachting meteorologist

The Sydney to Hobart's a tough race, a very tough race. I don't think there's a tougher ocean race in the world and you've got to say that generally the weather information isn't up to standard. Firstly, it's a matter for the crew and the boat. Then the yacht club should work hard to see that the most accurate information is available. And the Bureau should be able to supply accurate and detailed information. It's a matter for all three.

— Steve Kulmar, helmsman, Sword of Orion

Saturday, 26 December 1998
Early Afternoon

Most long-term weather forecasts have their genesis in programs run on one, or all, of the world's main weather supercomputers. Australian forecasts are usually influenced by computers in England, America and Australia. Every twelve hours, Australian forecasters download the computer-generated models and use them in the risky business of trying to predict what the weather will do up to a week in the future. In Australia, one run of models is available at around 11.00 a.m., and the next is available twelve hours later, at around 11.00 p.m.

Twice a day, at the Bureau of Meteorology in Sydney, the duty fore-caster logs on to the computer and checks the latest runs. Another regional computer model gives more detailed predictions for a shorter timescale, about thirty-six hours ahead. On the first day of the Sydney to Hobart the forecaster on duty, Peter Dunda, logs on as usual. It's about one-thirty in the afternoon, half an hour after the race has started. What shows up on the Australian Regional computer model surprises him. So does the new run from America. Early in the morning the bureau predicted a cold front with gale-force winds for waters off New South Wales's far south coast. But now the models are suggesting some-thing more serious. The computers show the cold front tightening into a deep low-pressure system. And, if they are right, the low-pressure system will develop quickly.

Dunda's phone rings. It's the bureau's Melbourne office. The fore-caster there has seen the same models. At 1.58 p.m. Melbourne issues a storm warning. At 2.14 p.m. Dunda does the same. It's a relatively unusual thing to do. After more than a year working with computer models, he has never issued a storm warning before. In the past year the Sydney office has only issued one other storm warning for coastal waters, and that was in the middle of winter. This one's in high summer and, as Dunda knows, right at the time the bureau's supposed to be providing special forecasts for the Sydney to Hobart. So, after he upgrades the warning, he picks up the phone again. He calls the Australian Maritime Safety Authority, the Eden Royal Volunteer Coastal Patrol and the Sydney to Hobart race media centre.

Most yachtsmen who race across oceans know something about the com-puter models forecasters use to predict long-term weather. But the majority take them with a fair few grains of salt. Some put them only a few steps ahead of reading entrails when it comes to the accuracy of prediction. But the development of computers has revolutionised weather prediction. Before computers, forecasting was more art than science, a thankless combination of guesswork, intuition and experience.

But in the early 1960s, when computers made it possible to do vast numbers of complex and tedious calculations relatively quickly, an American research meteorologist, Edward Lorenz, realised that modelling weather was an ideal way to use them. Soon Lorenz was programming-in data on temperature, air pressure and wind speed and applying the laws of physics. His computer spat out a pattern of imaginary storms, blizzards and heatwaves.

Lorenz's imaginary weather system was the beginning of all computer modelling. Within twenty-five years, programmers were taking all kinds of information and feeding it into computers that could do millions of calculations per second. They didn't only try to predict weather. Some used social and economic data to come up with predictions for the future development of whole countries.

The predictions weren't always accurate but they were better than nothing. But even at the beginning, Lorenz's colleagues and students, who used to place bets on what his computer's imaginary weather would do next, noticed that the models never followed exactly the same pattern. Lorenz discovered why when he tried to repeat the development of one of his weather systems. For the re-run, he used the same data but, because he was hurrying, he copied it to three decimal places rather than the six the computer stored in its memory. Instead of repeating its previous model the computer produced a new pattern that was radically different. Lorenz was surprised. But what happened is now well recognised. It's called the Butterfly Effect. Based on the idea that everything is interrelated, the Butterfly Effect suggests that seemingly insignificant events, such as the flitting of a butterfly's wing in an Amazonian rainforest, might have complex and significant results somewhere else. Eventually a small change, like the flitting of the wing, can escalate into a massive event, such as a hurricane on the other side of the planet.

Lorenz noticed the Butterfly Effect because, in his highly complex weather system, even a slight variation to the input changed the output results completely. The more complex the model, the tinier the change that will affect it. That's the problem with weather. It's so complex that no model can hope to imitate the reality. The wind speeds, temperatures and air-pressure readings that go into computer models are never perfectly accurate; each one is an average, a summary of readings over time. To recreate the world's weather exactly, a computer would have to plot every molecule in the atmosphere. Even if it could do that, no computer yet built could move fast enough to keep up with each molecule's movement. So no computer yet can recreate the world's weather before it happens. In a sense, the earth itself is the smallest possible model for the planet's weather. Only the earth itself can factor in all the variables.

It all means that computers can't predict weather, they can only give hints about how conditions might develop. The real job of predicting still lies with forecasters, who have to piece together the clues and inter-pret the models the best way they can.

Two days before the Sydney to Hobart, on Christmas Eve, about 250 yachtsmen have a first-hand experience of how even meteorologists can find computer models confusing. The yachtsmen are at the Cruising Yacht Club for the annual, and compulsory, pre-race briefing. The segment on weather is run by Ken Batt, a forecaster with the Bureau of Meteorology in Sydney and a veteran of several Sydney to Hobarts. In keeping with the season, Batt is wearing a red Santa hat topped with a white pompom.

But that day even the Santa hat can't help Batt explain what the computer models are saying. Two days before the race, each of the world computers is showing a knot of concentric circles somewhere near Tas-mania. Each is predicting the formation of a low-pressure system, but none agrees on where or when it will happen. It doesn't make life easy for Batt. For about twenty minutes, he describes every kind of weather that could possibly develop between Sydney and Hobart. Then he notes that the models disagree, but he doesn't discuss them in detail. He suggests everyone will just have to wait until the morning of the race.

Despite the Christmas spirit, a number of yachtsmen leave the briefing frustrated and cranky. Many find it next to useless. One, Steve Kulmar, calls it a circus. Kulmar has raced in sixteen Sydney to Hobarts and competed in the Admiral's Cup. He leaves the meeting with the impres-sion that the race would be hit by a southerly: 'The southerly would probably abate in about twelve hours, probably not getting above 30 to 35 knots. Then it may get confusing as we make our way down the Tasmanian coast. That was the out-take that most people took from the weather briefing. There was certainly no indication that the breeze would strengthen considerably and an intense low-pressure system would form in Bass Strait.'

A handful of yachtsmen have a fair bit more information, or at least a fair bit more background. Some yachts, either because they're hellbent on winning or just because they can afford it, employ private forecasters to brief them on weather. For the Sydney to Hobart, a number, including *Sayonara* and *Wild Thing*, have been working with freelance ocean weather expert Roger Badham. In the yachting world, Badham is so well known he usually doesn't need a surname. He doesn't even need a first name. Everyone just calls him Clouds. He has a PhD in meteorology, has worked with the Bureau of Meteorology, lectured at university, done time as a TV weatherman, and has forecast for yachts in the Sydney to Hobart since 1977. In the late 1980s he was the official race forecaster, but when the America's Cup moved to San Diego, he couldn't spare the time and the job fell to the weather bureau. Now he spends part of his time in a forest retreat south of Sydney, and the rest of it travelling the world with a laptop computer. He's consultant to some of the world's most serious ocean racers and some of the craziest. His clients include America's Cup syndicates that demand on board forecasts every ten minutes while they are racing and lone sailors who frequently end up upside down in the middle of nowhere. He enjoys all of them, even if he thinks some of them are 'fruitcakes'. To most yachtsmen, he's a guru.

In the week before the Sydney to Hobart, Clouds and his clients pore over the computer models every day. He tells them the models are pretty good up to three days ahead. The fourth day tends to get fuzzy. He says the fifth and sixth days are sometimes in fairyland. So, even two days before a four-day race, the models can't give much guidance. But Clouds takes his clients through all the models, anyway—not so much to predict what will happen, as to try to get a feel for what *might* happen. He likes to have his clients look at all the possibilities.

On 22 December, Clouds sees the American global model—often the most bullish—predicting a low-pressure system will form in or very close to Bass Strait. 'The other models,' he says, 'had a rather shotgun approach. A low was definitely going to form but was it south of Tasmania, east of Tasmania, or in Bass Strait? That was the big question mark. And how intense would it be? It was going to happen but where and exactly how intense? Not too sure.'

Twelve hours before the start of the race, Clouds checks the latest outputs. At about 2.00 a.m. he sits down in front of his computer to write his final pre-race briefing notes. The American global model shows a cold trough in the upper atmosphere turning into a definite low, smack bang in the middle of Bass Strait. But the other global models are less certain. For the last two weeks, the European model has been the most accurate. Now both it and the Australian model are playing down the low. Clouds usually rates the models A, B and C in order of preference. This time he writes that only a game person would attempt a ranking. Nevertheless, he does it. He figures it's unusual for an intense low to form over Bass Strait in December. Weighing everything up, he decides to go with a regional Australian model, rather than a global one. The regional model puts the low-pressure system to the south of Bass Strait, off the coast of Tasmania. In the middle of the night Clouds writes, 'Over Bass Strait—well it depends exactly where the low develops, how close to Tasmania, but best guess is not too far south, and the forecast at the time of writing this (early hours of 26th) is for quite strong winds across Bass Strait on the 27th.'

The next morning, before the race starts, Clouds is at Rushcutters Bay, giving his clients a last-minute briefing. So is the Bureau of Meteorology. Eighty-seven yachtsmen collect the bureau's weather pack. Inside the pack are wave predictions, tide charts, printouts from the Australian computer models and a forecast for strong to gale-force winds on the south coast over the next forty-eight hours.

Clouds finishes briefing his clients and goes home. Sometime in the early afternoon, he logs on to check the new output from the Australian regional model. What he sees surprises him. Over the last twelve hours the picture has changed radically. Now the regional model is definitely

going for a low-pressure system *inside* Bass Strait; so is the latest run
from the American model. It's clear that whatever is brewing is going
to hit in the strait and not, as it seemed last night, one or two hundred
kilometres further south. Clouds can see the low-pressure system is
winding itself up into a nasty little storm with a circle of 40 to 50 knot
winds spiralling around it. Definitely one notch up on what he imagined. 'The implication,' he says, 'was in terms of the timing and the
severity as it actually moved toward the fleet on the first night out and
then the strength of the winds the next morning. And how they'd build
up during the Sunday afternoon. It looked pretty grim.' It looks so grim
that he begins making phone calls. He calls a yachting journalist, Rob
Mundle. A few hours earlier, during the race start, Mundle and other
commentators have already said they expect 'some pretty savage weather'.
Now Clouds tells Mundle that the low is going to be 'nasty'. That it's
going to be as bad as 1993, when two-thirds of the fleet didn't make it
to Hobart. And that some time on Sunday afternoon there will probably
be quite a bit of damage.

Then Clouds does something he's never done before. He phones one
of the boats he's been working with, *Wild Thing*, via one of the crew's
mobiles. *Wild Thing* is a new boat and Clouds thinks the crew members
ought to know what they are in for. As he expects, they're racing and
only have their voicemail on, so he leaves a message. It was, he says,
along the lines of: 'Hey, look, this is looking really bad. And, you know,
you should think about what you're doing.'

At first, Clouds thinks the storm will hit early on Sunday afternoon.
He figures that means the really big boats will just miss it and the
middle-sized boats will probably cop the worst weather. But later that
night when he downloads the next model run from the computer, he
realises the worst of the storm will take a little longer to catch up with
the fleet. It looks like the full blow will probably cross the race course
late on Sunday afternoon. And that makes it far more dangerous. It
means the nastiest winds and the worst sea conditions will coincide with
the middle-sized yachts—and with the fastest of the small boats that are
racing to Hobart.

FIVE

> *It's uncomfortable, it's wet, it's cold, it's miserable and
> it has to be endured and that's called going to Hobart.*
> —*Rob Kothe, skipper,* Sword of Orion

> *It's a chance for an ordinary person to do something
> great. It's Everyman's Mountain.*
> —*Rob Matthews, helmsman,* Business Post Naiad

Saturday, 26 December 1998
Mid-Afternoon

Outside the Heads, the strong nor'easter sends all the boats flying.
Leading the field, Larry Ellison's *Sayonara* hits more than 26 knots
(about 48 kilometres an hour), the boat's fastest speed ever. For the big
yachts, conditions on the first afternoon could hardly be better—the
1998 race looks like being a record breaker. But Sydney to Hobart race
records aren't made or broken easily. When *Kialoa* set a new time in
1975 (two days, 14 hours, 36 minutes and 56 seconds) its record stayed
on the books for twenty-one years. It wasn't broken until 1996, when
Hasso Plattner's *Morning Glory* came in a mere 30 minutes inside it.
Even so, in 1998 Larry Ellison is eyeing the record set by Plattner. He
thinks *Sayonara* stands a good chance of knocking it over.

Further back in the fleet, *Sword of Orion*'s skipper, Rob Kothe, is out
on the rail, waist-deep in water. (Racing yachts use their crews as human
ballast so they can go faster without tipping over.) A boat's speed is
directly related to its length on the water but even the 13-metre *Sword*

35

of Orion clocks 23 knots. At the helm is English Olympic yachtsman Glyn Charles. A semi-professional sailor and a close friend of *Sword of Orion's* helmsman and sailing master Steve Kulmar, Charles is a last-minute addition to *Sword of Orion's* crew. He is young, well liked and respected as a sailor, and has competed in four Admiral's Cup races and represented Britain at the 1996 Olympics. He was in Australia training English yachtsmen for the Olympics when Kulmar suggested he join *Sword of Orion* for the trip down to Hobart. Charles phoned his mother in England, said he wouldn't make it back home for Christmas, and stayed. Kulmar was delighted. But someone else was bitterly disappointed.

At 23, Tracy Roth had a record of 30,000 sea miles and five Atlantic crossings. The one thing she hadn't done was the Sydney to Hobart. And her heart was set on it. Until the last minute, she planned to do the 1998 race on *Sword of Orion*. But Steve Kulmar's invitation to Glyn Charles ended her chances. A few days before the race, Roth was dumped from the crew to make room for Charles. She says she cried bitterly and swore she'd never go racing again. She was so upset she refused to come to Sydney for the start of the race and, instead, watched it on TV from her home in Wollongong. But by the next night her feelings will have changed. A few days later she tells a reporter, 'I believe in fate but I believe more in God and, in this case, I believe the Lord was probably on my side.'

As *Sword of Orion* hurtles south, two smaller yachts aren't far behind it. Iain Moray, the skipper of one, *Siena*, remembers that first afternoon as one of the best sails of his life. There's a 40-knot nor'easter and a three- or four-metre swell coming from behind. With clouds of spray splashing out each side, *Siena* feels like a huge surfboat. In fact it's one of the smaller yachts in the race, at just over 11 metres. Even so, *Siena* does more than 18 knots. As afternoon turns to evening Moray passes more than twenty other boats. He can't imagine *Siena* will ever again sail faster.

Nearby, the Tasmanian crew of another small yacht, *Business Post Naiad*, is thinking much the same. For skipper Bruce Guy, competing in the Sydney to Hobart is the culmination of a long campaign. Though

Guy's done the race twice before on other boats, he's spent the last two years putting together a crew and preparing *Business Post Naiad* for the ultimate race. One of Tasmania's most dedicated amateur yachtsmen, Guy joked that he should have bought a new kitchen for his wife, Ros, but instead he spent all his money on sails and equipment. A member of the small Port Dalrymple Yacht Club since he was a teenager, Guy has raced dinghies, trained state teams, been vice-commodore of his sailing club and president of both the state and national Sabot associations. (Sabot is a class of sailing dinghy.) As part of the lead-up for the Sydney to Hobart, Guy and his crew entered and won Tasmania's toughest test of endurance, the Three Peaks Race. Dreamed up in the lochs of Scotland, the Three Peaks combines yacht racing with mountain running. Yachts start out from northern Tasmania, sail to Flinders Island and race down the east coast of Tasmania to Hobart. At three stops on the way, teams of runners from the boats race each other up and down mountain peaks.

Business Post Naiad's crew is a group of friends gathered from different parts of northern Tasmania. Among them are Bruce's nephew Tony Guy, Steve Walker, a sail maker, and Peter Keats, an electrician. The boat's most experienced yachtsman and one of its chief helmsmen is Rob Matthews. Matthews has sailed in nine previous Hobarts. Before this one, he wonders if ten—a good round number—is enough for the Sydney to Hobart. After this race, thinks Matthews, he might retire.

The only first-time Hobart racer on *Business Post Naiad* is Phil Skeggs, a locksmith and Bruce Guy's back-fence neighbour. Over the past five years since Guy first took him sailing, Skeggs has become almost as passionate a sailor as Guy himself. Six months before the race, when another regular crewman realised he may not be able to get enough time off work, Skeggs began seriously training with *Business Post Naiad*. Even so, his nine-year-old daughter, Kirsty, didn't want him to go. She didn't want her father to be away for Christmas. Maybe he has second thoughts himself. On Christmas Day, the day before the race starts, he makes nearly a dozen phone calls to his family in Launceston. But if Phil Skeggs was worried, his father wasn't. He knew Bruce Guy. And he knew that Phil couldn't be in better hands.

Bruce Guy is known for his meticulous planning. Six weeks before the race, everyone on the boat knows what they'll be eating for every meal between Sydney and Hobart. Guy has worked out the menu and divided up the shopping list so that everyone can chip in equally. When *Business Post Naiad* leaves Tasmania for Sydney on 10 December 1998, there's only been one small complication in Guy's preparation. Though he applied for it months earlier, a certificate needed to register for the race was delayed in arriving. It seems now that Guy couldn't send it to race organisers until just before he left Hobart.

In the history of ocean racing, the most tragic year on record is 1979. That year, the Fastnet race, then part of the British Admiral's Cup competition, was hit by a storm that left fifteen sailors dead. Of the three hundred starters, more than twenty yachts were abandoned and nearly eighty rolled over. After the race, boat designers argued that racing yachts had become too flimsy to cope with severe weather and that ocean racers had sacrificed safety for speed. Studies of the Fastnet disaster led to the development of rating rules, known as the International Measurement System (IMS), for measuring a yacht's potential speed and safety. Like other world ocean races, the Sydney to Hobart followed the Fastnet recommendations and now requires all entrants to meet minimum IMS standards. Every boat that races has to go through a series of complex measurements and calculations. One of the calculations is called the limit of positive stability (LPS); in very rough terms, the LPS is the angle at which a boat will turn upside down rather than bounce back to its upright position, taking into account wind and waves. The Sydney to Hobart requires an LPS greater than 115 degrees. If a yacht has already competed once, the limit is slightly lower—110 degrees.

Bruce Guy's boat was built in 1984 and originally called *Swuzzlebubble*. *Swuzzlebubble* sailed in the Admiral's Cup and did two Sydney to Hobarts. When Guy bought the boat in 1996 he renamed it *Naiad*, the Greek word for water nymph. Over the next few years he sailed *Naiad* tens of thousands of ocean miles and crossed Bass Strait dozens of times. He also made various alterations to improve the boat's handicap rating. In 1997 when the yacht was measured for stability its LPS was well over the limit needed for the Sydney to Hobart. Six months before the race Guy sent the boat to be measured again—this time, it seems there was some confusion and the new certificate was delayed. He finally sent the certificate to the race organisers in Sydney shortly before leaving Tasmania for the start. None of the crew saw the new certificate which showed *Business Post Naiad*'s limit of stability was less than the required minimum. In fact, it was calculated at just under 105 degrees. The race organisers received the certificate, though they aren't sure when, filed it away and sent off a receipt. But the CYCA didn't pick up the fact that the boat didn't comply, and *Business Post Naiad* was accepted as eligible for entry.

But after the race, the boat's certificate is found to include some confusing inconsistencies. There are inexplicable differences between calculations on the boat's new certificate and one issued beforehand. Somewhere, the measurement process has gone haywire. But by the time all this is finally discovered, it's too late to work out what went wrong with the other calculations. More to the point, it's impossible to know whether any of it would have made a great deal of difference. Now, helmsman Rob Matthews believes Bruce Guy was probably confused by the race entry form. Races in the lead-up to the Sydney to Hobart, the Telstra Cup, have less stringent requirements than the Hobart but the race entry form lists both sets of rules. Matthews thinks Bruce Guy may have misread the entry form and believed his boat complied with it. 'There's no way Bruce would have done it deliberately,' says Matthews. 'He'd spent two years planning for the Sydney to Hobart. Why would he enter an ineligible boat?'

By the time the race starts, paperwork is the last thing on anyone's mind. Speeding south, *Business Post Naiad* is running about tenth in her division. In sailing, the shortest straight line to a destination is called the rhumb line and in the Sydney to Hobart most yachts follow it, staying fairly close to the coast. Other skippers, like Bruce Guy, go about eight kilometres further out to sea to piggy-back on a strong current running south. In summer, warm water runs most of the way down the east coast of Australia. The East Australia Current can be five or six degrees warmer than the ocean around it. Over summer it gradually works its way down the coast. By late summer and autumn it moves far enough south to lure tuna and the fishermen who chase them to Tasmania. But the current runs fastest and strongest around December and January, the time of the Sydney to Hobart. Then, it usually stretches from south-east of Sydney to near Gabo Island, at the northern tip of Bass Strait, and runs at about two or three knots (about 3.5 to 5.5 kilometres an hour). Yachtsmen find the current by sailing where the water is warmest. In the old days, they'd throw a bucket over the side, haul it up and drop in a thermometer. Now, most boats have built-in heat sensors.

When the *Business Post Naiad* crew first check the water temperature just outside Sydney it's about 18 degrees Celsius. Later, when they pick up the current the water's about six degrees warmer, 24 degrees. The current's running at four knots, surprisingly fast. It makes a beeline down the coast and sweeps *Business Post Naiad* along with it. Rob Matthews recalls it as running surprisingly straight, without the usual curls and twists. But further south the warm current is already whirling around a huge cold-water eddy. The whirlpool is just near Bass Strait where the warm current runs headlong into a wall of cold water coming from the opposite direction.

As Rob Matthews heads south on *Business Post Naiad*, in Launceston his wife, Carmel, is philosophical about spending another Christmas without him. She knew what she was in for when the two first met thirty years earlier. Not too long after they were married, Carmel found a job with a yachting supplier. Now, at the end of the race, she's planning to join Rob in Hobart. She booked the hotel about six months earlier. She had to. Leave it much later and there isn't an empty room anywhere in town. At the end of the Sydney to Hobart, the New Year's Eve party on Constitution Dock is the biggest night of the year in Tasmania. Carmel and Rob Matthews don't plan to miss it.

SIX

*We were enjoying the race. We were all pottering down
the coast, a hell of a lot of spectators. There was
certainly a great Sydney farewell to the fleet and I don't
think anyone at that stage would have thought what
was to happen, you know, within the next twenty-eight
hours.*

— *Lew Carter, radio operator on* Young Endeavour

Ask Lew Carter how he became a volunteer radio operator and he'll tell
you about his mentor, Tweetie Thompson. Back in the 1970s, it was
Tweetie who nominated Carter for membership of the Cruising Yacht
Club. A decade later, Carter was doing Tweetie's job on the radio-relay
boat in the Sydney to Hobart. As he tells it himself: 'Tweetie Thompson
used to make sausages. And he was a great seaman—he was at sea during
the war—in the Royal Australian Navy, he was torpedoed on the *Sydney*.
He was a bit of a figurehead to me, Tweetie.'

'For the first fifteen years of my sailing with the CYC, I was on various
yachts on the navigation side. And Tweetie—Tweetie had lost his wife
fairly tragically—and I introduced him to my next door neighbour and
he married her. Unfortunately, two or three years down the track,
Tweetie—he was also a heavy cigar smoker—died of throat cancer. And
it was right on the Christmas period, a few weeks before the Hobart
race. I thought it would be quite fitting, and the CYC thought the same,
if I applied for the position to do it that year.' Lew Carter has been in
the job ever since. These days he does it with the help of a married

couple, Michael and Audrey Brown. (After the race, the CYC will give him an award for his work on the radio. It's called the TWT Thompson Memorial Trophy.)

The radio-relay boat Lew Carter and his team are on is *Young Endeavour*, a 40-metre steel sailing ship, given to Australia by the British Government as a Bicentennial birthday present in 1988. It is run by the Royal Australian Navy and partly crewed by young volunteer trainees. On this trip there are twelve Navy staff, eighteen trainees, Carter and the Browns. Once the race begins, *Young Endeavour* is the key communication point for every yacht. Organisers use it to follow the race and sailors use it to check on other competitors. For many yachts, *Young Endeavour* is the main source of weather information.

During the race, the communication system requires that at three set times every day the whole racing fleet tunes in to the *Young Endeavour* for scheduled briefings, known as 'skeds'. At the skeds, Carter and his team read out a weather report and then the yachts, in alphabetical order, give their positions. This year there are 115 yachts and the whole process takes more than an hour. A boat that misses two consecutive skeds is presumed missing. In between skeds, the radio-relay team picks up bits of weather information and Carter gets a chance to chat on the radio. 'I find the job so great,' he says, 'because it's a direct link with so many people I've actually sailed with or would like to have sailed with. There are quite a lot of fairly famous people that I've only ever met on the radio. Though they don't say it to you directly, you certainly know that at times they need another shoulder to cry on. Especially if it's rough, or early in the race if the weather forecast isn't that good and it's getting dark, it's quite comforting to have someone else to talk to. And I think it's quite an honour too, that the yachties place their trust in me, with their lives.' In its early days the radio-relay boat was known as 'the mother ship'. But, after indignant protests that yachtsmen don't need nursing, the term was dropped. That doesn't bother Lew Carter. He still calls *Young Endeavour* the mother ship. 'I don't know,' he says, 'whether they call me the mother.'

≺ ≻

In the first Sydney to Hobarts, CYCA officials called mid-race progress reports 'heresy' and banned them. But even then they reckoned without newshounds. In 1947, Frank McNulty, a young reporter crewing on the yacht *Moonbi*, went to great lengths to thwart the blackout. Another keen reporter in the race, Lou d'Alpuget, gives this account of McNulty's ingenuity:

'*Moonbi*'s team, encouraged by her watch captain, the young newspaper reporter Frank McNulty, took aboard two baskets of carrier pigeons. McNulty's plan was to get exclusive eye-witness reports of the race back to his newspaper by loosing the pigeons daily with ricepaper messages fastened in capsules on their legs. He got one report through in this way, but the pigeons generally were a disaster. Some were seasick and refused to fly off when the weather was bad. One did a tight circuit of the yacht then swooped back down the main hatch onto its basket. Worst of all, the birds kept everyone awake with their incessant cooing, spilt pigeon peas from one end of the yacht to the other and made the cabin stink like a fowlyard. The crew wanted to make them into a pie, but this McNulty refused to allow. He was rewarded when one of the birds laid an egg on his pillow.'

In 1951, officials saw the light and introduced a radio-relay boat. It was already becoming clear that few other races in the world attracted the same attention as the Sydney to Hobart. The race officials soon realised that publicity was one of its greatest strengths. And with publicity came something else—sponsorship. At first sponsorship was discreet. Then it exploded. In 1991 the race was won by a yacht named after the tobacco company, Rothmans. *Rothmans* crossed the finish line like a floating billboard, with a giant advertising logo on its spinnaker. Ultimately, it was penalised for the stunt and the win was withdrawn. Nowadays, about a quarter of the boats have some kind of corporate backing, ranging from finance for a few sails to full sponsorship. News coverage is a promotional goldmine for the winner, but any high profile is good advertising. By 1998, there are boats named after wines, cars, computing equipment and mobile phones. Some yacht names are such a mouthful that when they call for assistance, rescuers and radio operators don't know whether they are referring to one boat or two.

Far from carrier pigeons, now photographers and TV crews buzz the fleet continously and there are on-board film crews, satellite phones, weather faxes, e-mail and a race web site. Every boat must carry both a high frequency and a very high frequency (HF and VHF) radio. The race's prime sponsor, Australia's major telecommunication company, Telstra, claims it puts about $1 million into the race and its leadup. Telstra boasts that the race brims with the latest technology. One of Telstra's services is SatCom C, an e-mail-like system installed on about twenty yachts and designed to automatically transmit positions. The other is a service called Yachtcoms, set up to link the radio-relay boat, *Young Endeavour*, to race organisers in Sydney and Hobart by a designated phone line. However, not only is SatCom C very expensive, it is not effective in emergencies, because it works by storing information rather than transmitting it immediately. Nor does Telstra point out that Yachtcoms relays messages through an 'antenna farm' more than a thousand kilometres away from the race, in Queensland. Yachtcoms works well in the first section of the race, poorly in the middle of the course, and almost not at all in the final stretch. Ultimately, *Young Endeavour*'s most effective means of communication are its HF and VHF radios and an old-fashioned analogue mobile phone.

≺ ≻

On the first afternoon of the race Lew Carter settles in behind the radio desk on *Young Endeavour* and waits for the southerly change to come through and upset everyone's lunch. At the 8.00 p.m. sked on the first night out of Sydney, *Young Endeavour* broadcasts the Bureau of Meteorology's storm warning and the afternoon forecast the bureau compiled some six hours earlier. The forecast predicts winds to the south of the mainland will increase to 45–55 knots (around 85–100 kilometres an hour) late on Sunday afternoon. Few sailors give it a second thought. The forecast doesn't sound like anything unusual. And anyway, on the first night out, the far south coast could be as much as two days sail away. Between now and then, anything could happen. 'Weather,' says

Carter, 'is one of those things. As we all know, it can be very confusing and sometimes you can listen too much and read the wrong slant on it. I'm not a marvellous weather predictor by any means and I tend to listen as much as I can, but without overdoing it—which, in my opinion, would confuse me.'

What is more, Carter already has a more immediate problem to deal with—the radio-relay boat's HF radio, its most important link to the fleet, is playing up. For all the talk about technology, *Young Endeavour* only has one HF radio. It needs one that works properly, and in a hurry. A replacement has to be rushed out by boat from Wollongong, the first big port south of Sydney.

SEVEN

*There's a list and you can go through and read the
weather conditions in every single race. So you go
through and you'll think about what you'll do in this
scenario and what you'll do in that scenario. But in the
previous fifty-three Hobarts there's only been two sailors
lost. It never occurred to me that in the fifty-fourth
Hobart we'd lose six. At one stage we could have lost
thirty. But it would never have occurred to me in my
wildest nightmares that that could happen to anybody.
Let alone to me as a skipper.*

—*Rob Kothe, skipper,* Sword of Orion

Ocean racing's a crap shoot really.

—*Drew Murray, skipper,* Trident IV

Saturday, 26 December 1998
Evening

On *Sword of Orion*, Rob Kothe is listening to the first sked positions.
It's early in the race, but it looks as if some of the smallest boats in the
fleet might be winning on handicap. Kothe's yacht isn't one of the
smallest, but it is one of the most competitive. Four months earlier, he
surprised everyone by nudging out the favourite to win Race Week at
Hamilton Island. Under a different name, *Sword of Orion* came fifth in
its class in last year's Hobart. Since then Kothe has refitted it. Now that
he has two Admiral's Cup yachtsmen on board, Steve Kulmar and

Andrew Parkes, and the Olympian Glyn Charles, *Sword of Orion* has to be a real contender.

It's a clear summer evening and it stays light till around 9.00 p.m. As it gets dark a number of the boats see lightning in the distance. It's the first sign of the southerly. At Point Perpendicular, to the north of Jervis Bay, *Business Post Naiad*'s crew takes down the spinnaker and gets ready for the change.

More than 200 kilometres further south, Drew Murray and his friend Mary Krieg are on Murray's boat, *Trident IV*, polishing off the remains of a Christmas turkey. They've spent the day anchored in a tiny inlet just south of Eden. Cruising from Queensland to northern Tasmania, the two are on an open-ended holiday. Once they cross Bass Strait, they plan to take the long way home and circumnavigate Tasmania.

Murray isn't quite sure how he turned into a seaman but it seems to suit him. Years ago, he could have done well in the family wine business, but instead he disappeared overseas. Since then, he's seen and done a lot that even his oldest friends don't ask about. By his own account, he used to sail and do everything else like a wild man. Finally he says, fifteen years ago he did something so reckless, he horrified even himself. Back then, his boat, the third in his *Trident* series, was racing from Melbourne to Hobart. At nightfall, with *Trident III* hurtling toward the south-west tip of Tasmania under spinnaker, he knew he was winning the race on handicap. But the weather got worse and the wind built to 50 knots. As the yacht got closer to South West Cape, Murray's navigator told him they were going to hit the rocks if they didn't change course. But Murray couldn't bear to lose time resetting the spinnaker. So he told the helmsman to take another compass reading, add 10 to whatever it was and tell the navigator the earlier reading was a mistake. The helmsman did it and *Trident III* continued on its course. Suddenly, the outline of South West Cape rose out of the darkness. It was almost on top of them. Murray thought if he reached out, he'd be able to touch the cliffs. *Trident III* won the race on handicap, but Murray never raced seriously again. He decided it brought out the worst in him.

These days, Drew Murray leaves racing to his friends. One of the crewmen he tricked in south-west Tasmania is now one of his closest mates—Rob Matthews. Another, Tony Guy, is his brother-in-law. Right now those two are heading south in the Sydney to Hobart on *Business Post Naiad*. Since the race around South West Cape, Drew Murray has become a licensed Commercial Master. He's run cruise boats and paddle steamers and sailed yachts back to Sydney after their owners have raced to Hobart and jumped on planes to go home. His old friends are amazed by the transformation. *Trident III* is long gone and *Trident IV* is a comfortable 15-metre cruising yacht, with its own generator, TV, VCR and a good collection of cookbooks.

After dinner, Murray sits on deck smoking a cigarette. He doesn't like the sound of tomorrow's weather forecast—a storm warning and 55-knot winds in Bass Strait. Mary can see he's fidgety. The two of them are still on deck when the tiny dark bay around them suddenly strobes a blinding white. A bolt of lightning hits a tree on the shore, about ten metres from the boat. Tomorrow, says Drew, they'll pack up, turn around and wait out the storm in Eden harbour.

A couple of days earlier, Hobart residents reported some of the most peculiar weather they had ever seen. Hobart was battered by severe electrical storms and parts of the town were flooded and blacked out. Now, as Murray watches, the unsettled weather is moving into New South Wales. A few hours later, electrical storms light up the skies almost as far as Sydney. Between two and three that morning, the southerly change that comes with them hits the leading small yachts. Around *Business Post Naiad* and *Sword of Orion*, the wind builds to 35 knots and holds there. At the front of the pack, the crew of *Sayonara* is still aiming for a new race record. As the wind picks up, they still think they might pull it off.

EIGHT

◄ ►

*A voyage, expressly taken for discovery in an open boat,
and in which six hundred miles of coast, mostly in a
boisterous climate, was explored, has not perhaps its
equal in the annals of maritime history.*
— *Matthew Flinders, writing about George Bass's
voyage in a whaleboat from Sydney to Westernport*

*While the sea lanes between Melbourne and Sydney are
in operation, and pleasure seekers or adventurers sail
around our stormy coasts, stories of shipwrecks will
continue to unfold.*
—*J.K. Loney,* Victorian Shipwrecks

Near the most south-eastern corner of Australia, just past the border of
New South Wales and Victoria, the low, shrubby mound of Gabo Island
marks the beginning of Bass Strait and the end of any shelter sailors can
expect from the mainland. In 1998, when the Sydney to Hobart fleet
starts poking its nose into Bass Strait, it is 200 years, almost to the
month, since George Bass and Matthew Flinders first proved that Bass
Strait was part of an open ocean and that Tasmania was an island.
Yachtsmen these days call the stretch of water between the mainland's
most south-eastern extremity and the top of Flinders Island 'the
paddock', because there's nothing in it. For nearly 300 kilometres, along
the rhumb line, there are no lighthouses, no oil rigs, and no floating
weather stations. There is nothing but sea, sky and horizon.

It was 1642 when Abel Tasman first saw the west coast of the land he christened Van Diemen's Land. For the next 150 years, ships sailing to the new colonies from the west rounded what's now called Tasmania by going south of the land Tasman had charted. Lieutenant James Cook might have found the shortcut through Bass Strait sooner. In 1770 he landed near the beginning of the strait, at Point Hicks. But, like many after him, Cook fell victim to one of the area's notorious sou'westers. Rather than continuing south, he decided to avoid the gale and head north. So Cook never found Bass Strait. It turned out that he found Botany Bay, and what would later become Sydney, instead.

Towards the end of the eighteenth century George Bass, a surgeon turned explorer, decided to test his suspicion that Tasmania was an island. In a tiny open whaleboat rowed by six oarsmen, Bass followed the coastline all the way from Sydney to Wilsons Promontory at the southern tip of mainland Australia, and as far as Westernport in Victoria. There, as the New South Wales governor, Captain John Hunter, wrote later, Bass found 'an open ocean westward and by the mountainous sea which rolled from that quarter and no land discoverable in that direction we have much reason to conclude that there is an open strait'.

While Bass was in his whaleboat, his friend Matthew Flinders was sailing back from Preservation Island. Up until then it had been thought that Preservation Island lay in a deep coastal inlet. But Flinders was coming to the same conclusion as Bass—that Tasmania was separated from the mainland by a strait. When Bass and Flinders compared their findings, Governor Hunter gave them an 11-metre wooden sail boat, the *Norfolk*, to circumnavigate Tasmania and prove their theory. They did: sailing across the island's north coast, then down the west coast and back up the east. The most north-westerly point left them in no doubt about their discovery. It was so constantly pounded by open ocean and the gales of the Roaring Forties that they called it Cape Grim. When Bass and Flinders returned to Sydney, they reported they'd found an island and, on the way, seen hundreds of seal colonies. The most immediate impact of their voyage was that mobs of sealers invaded the small Bass Strait islands, massacred the animals for their fur and wiped out most of the seal population.

Apart from the slaughter of seals and whales, the maritime history of south-eastern Australia and Bass Strait is largely a story of bad weather. The first time George Bass rounded Cape Howe in his whaleboat he was trapped for nine days, 'without intermission, by a gale'. The wind came from the west-south west, funnelled (as he later discovered) through the strait from the Indian Ocean. Bass went ashore and waited it out, exploring the countryside. Two hundred years later, five sailors retracing his historic voyage around Tasmania were less fortunate. On their way home, about 60 kilometres south-east of Gabo Island, they and their 11-metre replica of the *Norfolk* disappeared. Five aircraft searched for a day and a half until a plane finally picked them up on its radar. They'd been blown out to sea by what they said were 80-knot 'cyclonic winds which had whipped up mountainous waves'.

In the 200 years between that voyage and Bass and Flinders' pioneering journeys, numerous vessels disappeared entirely. J.K. Loney, a passionate shipwreck historian, has documented many of them in a series of books and pamphlets. In 1837, heavy south-westerly gales blew the schooner *Schah* ashore near Cape Howe. Six passengers drowned; the thirteen survivors spent five days walking through bushland to Eden. The next year another schooner was wrecked nearby. A settler on a cattle drive found the bodies and buried them. In the year after that, at Cape Howe, all that turned up on shore from another sailing ship was a dinghy.

The history of wrecks around Gabo Island is even more miserable. A granite block, still on the island, commemorates one of the earliest and worst disasters. In 1853 the steamer *Monumental City* ran aground in the middle of the night. The captain decided to wait till dawn to free the ship but before morning a gale blew up and ripped it apart. Three lifeboats were launched, but each one of them was destroyed or blown away. Finally a seaman grabbed a rope and swam to the shore. As the passengers and crew abandoned the ship it broke up. Thirty-three people died. The remaining fifty-four survived on the bleak island until the weather improved and they salvaged a lifeboat. In the next fifteen years, storms totally destroyed six sailing ships in the same area. Only two wrecks left any survivors. For several more decades gales claimed dozens of vessels and dozens of sailors. The seabed was littered with sunken cargoes of coal, potatoes, wine and pianos.

Eden's trawlermen who fish around Gabo and south to Tasmania know all the old stories and most of the recent ones. Old-timers like Locky Marshall expect two or three storms a year. They explain that after Gabo Island the coast travels west, and the most dominant winds from the south are sou'westers. The winds hit the hills of the mainland and bounce outwards. The stronger they are, the bigger the seas they whip up around Gabo. As Marshall puts it, 'It's treacherous. A storm warning can have a wind strength of 45 knots, into the high fifties and sea conditions can be 10, 12, even 15 metres high. That wouldn't be unusual.'

But it isn't only wind. Just as waves on a beach rise up as they hit shallow water, waves in the shallows of Bass Strait rise higher than they would in deeper water. The waters around Gabo Island are shallow and tangled by strong currents. As another south-coast fisherman, Joe Pirello, describes it, 'It's an area where warm and cold currents meet and you get these whirling currents which can have a bad effect on the waves. If you get a strong wind and huge seas and the current's going against the sea, peaking into the sea, then you get really steep seas. Bass Strait's got some of the most unpredictable weather in the world. It's a funny place. It can be the most beautiful place in the world and the most horrible place in the world. If you're there when it's bad, it's really bad.'

NINE

Several crewmembers have been washed overboard but survived, recovered by their own crew or by another yacht. A couple of sailors have died of heart attacks while many have limped ashore in Hobart with broken ribs, collarbones, arms and shoulders and concussion. Many compete each year despite recurring seasickness.

Then what is the attraction? It is the challenge of the wind and the sea, the comradeship of this adventure, the competitive boat-for-boat tactical encounters and, not the least, the remarkable hospitality that Tasmanians show the crews who have reached their island state. Then, there's the celebrations at Hobart's old waterfront pubs, the Customs House, the Telegraph and others, and then the QLD—the traditional Quiet Little Drink, where the count of beers consumed runs into thousands and thirsty sailors sway to local bands.

—Peter Campbell (media director, Cruising Yacht Club of Australia), 'History of the Sydney Hobart Yacht Race: 1945 to 1997'

There has always been a superstition that the toughest Sydney to Hobarts come in a seven-year cycle. The cycle goes back to 1956, when the race was hit by a 50-knot sou'wester in Bass Strait and a southerly gale in Storm Bay, Tasmania. One yacht nearly sank, another lost its masts and a third was blown more than 350 kilometres out to sea. The story of that 'blow', told by a crewman from the yacht *Renene*, kept the 1956 race alive for decades. It's set out in Murray Davis's book, *Australian Ocean Racing*:

'We had just passed Gabo on Saturday when we sprang a leak which proved impossible to stop. At first we were not worried, but the leak got worse. We started bailing in shifts, three men on buckets, one on the pump. By Monday we were bailing desperately in shifts of thirty minutes. We had given up hope of sailing the boat and were ready to abandon ship when a southerly buster hit us eighty miles east of Eddystone Light-house, and our rubber dinghy and lifebelts went overboard. All our liquor supply had gone into the sea and we were using bottles to bail. Our hands were badly bruised by the buckets and we were deadly tired but there was no time to sleep. On went the bailing as though it would never end and we were in the fourth day of our fight. We were really at the end of our tether when we entered Wineglass Bay. In our fight to beach the yacht, we felt as though we couldn't lift another bucket. Then we saw the most wonderful sight—a fishing boat came alongside and hailed us. He towed us thirty miles into Oyster Bay, while we kept bailing. Most of the crew went to Swansea Hospital for treatment for their hands and minor ail-ments, but we were all right.'

In 1956 the winds hit 74 knots (138 kilometres per hour). Back then, it was thought to be the highest wind speed ever recorded.

Seven years later, in 1963, there was a strong sou'wester in Bass Strait again and 70-knot winds in Storm Bay. One yacht, lost for four days, was towed in by a British submarine. On another, which was knocked down twice, the cabin filled with fuel and the crew starved for four days because they were afraid they'd blow themselves up if they lit a match to start the stove. Seven years after that, in 1970, it's said that a 50-knot wind blew for about seventy hours. That year, one old salt gave the classic description, 'It would make grown men quail. It built up a very large breaking sea, the like of which I have never seen before or since.' He might have said it again seven years later when, in 1977, seventy boats finished but fifty-nine didn't make it. The unluckiest were hit by an 85-knot squall.

Fitting the cycle, the 1984 race was one of the most disastrous ever. For the first time, more boats pulled out (two-thirds of the fleet) than made it to Hobart. It was also the year of the first racing fatality, when a yachtsman was knocked overboard. In 1984 a low-pressure system formed in Bass Strait on Christmas Day. By Boxing Day, when the race started, the low had settled in near Gabo Island. There, it combined with the current to build treacherous seas.

In 1991, the seven-year curse seemed to be lifting. That year the only ill wind came from the economy. After the excesses of the 1980s, even the richest yachtsmen were pinched by recession. Race entries in 1991 were the lowest for fifteen years. In the grand prix division for money-hungry maxi-yachts there wasn't a single entry. Maybe it was enough of a blow in itself. For whatever reason, the weather was fair and the race had one of the lowest retirement rates in more than a decade. But the sea must have been saving its power. The real hiding came two years later. By its second day, the 1993 race outdid 1984 as the worst on record. On the second night, there were four maydays, one man overboard and two yachts sunk. If 1984 had been a year of treacherous seas, 1993 was a year of wild winds. It wasn't till five years later that the two coincided. That happened in 1998, back on the seven-year cycle.

The 1998 race would turn out to be more dangerous than any before it. *Sword of Orion*'s chief helmsman, Steve Kulmar, sailed in both 1984 and 1993, but neither came close to what he experienced in 1998: 'In 1984 I thought, "My God, nothing could be worse than this." On the first night we copped a southerly and as we went further south it blew very hard from the south-west, up around 50 to 55 knots. We had our storm sails up. It was very, very windy, but the real problem was the sea because there was a big sea going south and wind coming north. So the seas were treacherous. But 1984 was controllable because it all happened during the day; it was sunny and visibility was good. And the wind never really got above 55 knots consistently. And then by evening it lightened off to 35 or 40. After that it was a pleasant race. [In] 1993 we knew the wind forecast and we knew we'd be in for it. It was a slog the whole way. Again, we ran into the southerly the first day. The wind freshened and freshened; it was windier than 1984. We sailed the whole race, four and a half days, into windy conditions. As we got to Bass Strait and closer to the low-pressure system, it was very windy but the sea was fairly flat. It was ferociously windy. It got up to 89 knots but not for long, and then it backed down to about 55. I don't think we set a spinnaker till we got to the Derwent River.'

For all its drama, the 1993 race ended safely. Most yachtsmen didn't make it to Hobart but all of them, even the one lost overboard for five hours in Bass Strait, made it home. That success was due largely to one man, a hydrographic surveyor and the volunteer race director, Greg Halls. During the crisis, he directed yachts to assist each other, rescue other crews and search for the man overboard. He organised teams to track more than sixty yachts when they headed back to port. After the race, Halls told a journalist: 'With conditions like they were that night, you know it's going to be bad.'

Five years later, in 1998, Greg Halls will see the conditions, hear the first maydays, and feel concern again. But this time, Halls is no longer the race director. And he isn't the one making the decisions.

TEN

You can have all these safety rules and no-one follows them. I mean, how would you know what someone's wearing a hundred miles east of Tasmania? In fact they could be wearing nothing, it might be an improvement. I mean, it's got to come down to how people make use of the rules. They have to believe in them.

—Geoff Ross, skipper, Yendys

Geoff Ross is fanatical about safety. As a university student, he put seat belts in his car long before they were compulsory. Ross has never been interested in rules made by other people, unless they are as good as the rules he sets for himself. He wore a seat belt because, to him, it seemed like a sensible idea. Not because someone told him to.

A couple of decades later, Ross still approaches life in much the same way. Energetic, thorough and a high achiever, one of his passions is yacht racing. He owns and skippers a top of the line, 15-metre cruiser-cum-racing yacht called *Yendys*. He and *Yendys* have already done four Sydney to Hobarts. He's come third, second and, in the last race, first in his division. This time *Yendys* is well in the running for another placing. Ross runs a tight ship, with a tight crew that sails together regularly and trains like professionals. Between them, the crew of eleven has raced to Hobart more than fifty times. As he says, 'We've sailed together basically for the last five years and every year done the Hobart together. We've probably done thousands of ocean miles together. The people on the boat are a mixture of people who are very skilled, who have sailed together for a long time. Without exception, they're people who have strong backbones. When things get difficult, they look to do more work, rather than less.'

Ross runs *Yendys* with a management plan in the same way he runs his global high-tech business. The crew has clear objectives and a clear organisational structure. 'We always say being the winning team is our key competitive edge. We work very hard on preparing the boat and preparing ourselves, and sort of document it like a quality-control manual for business. That's our secret. We have a clear view of what we are doing. The boat's very good, but not particularly competitive. But we prepare it together, do all the maintenance ourselves, work on the boat-handling manoeuvres. By the time we get to the start line, we believe two-thirds of our long ocean race is over. By the start line there's only one-third of the race left. So we have a program to win the first part, the first two-thirds of the race.' Geoff Ross is still fanatical about safety. These days it's far more complex for him than just wearing a seat belt. Part of his crew organisation includes a safety sub-committee.

This year, the *Yendys* crew's objective is to win its division. Geoff Ross has been to the weather briefing and spoken to Ken Batt from the Sydney bureau. He knows a southerly front will hit the race, he expects it will be heavy and he thinks he knows roughly when it will come. 'In my experience, the weather bureau has usually been fairly accurate in the timing of the southerly. If we've got a rough idea of when it's going to hit—within, say, plus or minus two hours—then we're mentally prepared for what's going to happen. I mean, we were hoping we would get it, to be honest, before the race. We were hoping we would get a southerly because we know we can handle that well, and we think some boats in our division might find it a bit harder. So we would see that as a plus for our ability to compete.'

Geoff Ross is more honest than many yachtsmen about what he loves about yacht racing, and what he loves about the Sydney to Hobart in particular. Some of his reasons are the usual ones given by most sailors. He originally comes from Melbourne, but he loves Sydney Harbour. He also loves Hobart. 'Hobart is the best place in the world to finish a race. Unquestionably. It's the most knowledgeable group of people. They know the boats, they're attuned to the race. And the Sydney to Hobart is probably the world's greatest ocean race. It's like Wimbledon. Wimbledon's got very little to do with tennis, it's just one of the peak events. Well, the Sydney to Hobart is exactly the same, it's an institution. It's much more than an ocean race. It's something that transcends a sporting activity, it's an event.'

But Ross has no illusions about what really drives him. It's the same urge that pushes every cold, wet and exhausted sailor in a long ocean race. It drove the first yachtsmen who raced to Hobart more than fifty years ago and it still drives them today. The whole point of the race is that it's sometimes risky and always difficult. 'If you read the world cruising books,' he says, 'they basically say: "Don't sail through Bass Strait in December and January. Go around the south of Tasmania." So it's a difficult race. You encounter all sorts of conditions. So it's a big challenge. As we sail into Hobart, we feel we've achieved something quite significant. We take great pride in the fact that we've dealt with a difficult and complex situation. So we feel great when we finish. At first, when you finally get to Hobart, you think: "Thank goodness we're here." That's the first thing. That rapidly translates into: "How clever we are to get here." By the time we've relaxed a bit, we become the world's greatest sailors. So there's a steady climb to self-importance. But the overwhelming feeling is that you've achieved something that's authentic. It's liberating. Of course it's also completely irrational. If you were rational, you'd never go. Because it's difficult, it's potentially dangerous. And you can get to Hobart lots of easier ways and certainly lots of cheaper ways. And have more fun on the way. And have a decent meal.' He's right. Trying to be rational is irrelevant—racing across the ocean has nothing to do with reason. Like many other adventures, it's all about facing challenges, taking risks and coming out ahead. 'You know, for those of us who like ocean racing, being on the ocean is just a wonderful experience. I love being on the water. Particularly at night, when things are settled and the boat's moving well and we're doing well in the race. It's the most exhilarating feeling.'

This year, with two-thirds of the hard work already tucked under its belt, *Yendys* has a great start in the Sydney to Hobart. The boat flies out of the Harbour and races down the coast. Ross stays west of the fleet, and for some time *Yendys* is the closest boat to the shore. The afternoon wears on and the breeze strengthens. Then all of a sudden it jumps to about 38 knots. Down below, having a rest, Ross feels the change. 'We had a one and a half ounce spinnaker up and the boat was starting to hump. I was thinking to myself: "Is this a good thing or a bad thing?" You have this strange feeling of speed, which you like, but also a slight feeling of instability.' The call comes from up on the deck that it's time to get the spinnaker down. 'I'd never taken a kite down in 38 knots of breeze. It's a big boat with big sails, so it's a lot of pressure on the boat. In the process we made an avoidable mistake.' The crew is a whisker too slow and *Yendys* broaches, turning up into the wind and rolling over on its side. Two men are up on the rail to pull the kite in. Suddenly, to Ross's horror, the bowman, Peter Seary—the toughest guy on the boat—is sucked overboard. Seary isn't hooked on because everything—the stronger winds and the decision to take down the kite—has happened so quickly. Ross is in the cockpit, up to his knees in water and wearing only thermals. He thinks Seary is lost. 'The other guy next to him, he's lying on his back, hanging onto the stanchion and under water. I'm in the cockpit looking down on these guys and thinking, "This is not what I had in mind at all". This is only the first night. *Yendys* is heeled over because the spinnaker's out on the side and Pete is gone.' Suddenly a big wave picks up Peter Seary, lifts him over the lifelines and throws him back on board. A few moments later, Seary climbs up the mast to rescue the spinnaker. It is completely shattered and half of it is still flying from the masthead. When Seary gets down, Geoff Ross jokes, 'Pete, I just can't get rid of you.'

'The fact of the matter was,' Ross says later, 'it was early in the race. It happened quickly. We should have had our harnesses on and we didn't. We made a mistake. Basically, in sailing, like most things, a little thing leads to another thing, leads to another thing and all of a sudden you have something quite major happening. And it all stems back to some trivial thing. That is what happened. That's what we try to avoid. It was a pretty good lesson.'

Soon, *Yendys* settles back into racing. Ross makes a mental note to talk to the safety sub-committee. The internal rules about putting on harnesses need to be tightened.

ELEVEN

◄ ►

*Yachtsmen are used to forecasts being wrong, or
partially wrong, all the time. So they look at it but they
take it with a grain of salt. If it's a forecast for quite
severe conditions, they look at it and think: 'It probably
won't be quite that bad.' If it's a forecast for conditions
that they'll probably only experience once or twice in a
lifetime, they think: 'Well, it can't be that bad, we'll
keep going.' It's the eternal optimism of the human
being.*

—Roger 'Clouds' Badham, yachting meteorologist

*We can only make decisions based on the information
we receive. It's the GIGO principle—Garbage In,
Garbage Out. If I get good information, I believe I can
make a good decision. I would have loved to have
known that the start of the Melbourne to Hobart yacht
race was delayed because of conditions in Bass Strait.
We don't live near Bass Strait and I pay tribute to
their knowledge of local conditions. If I was given that
information, I am sure I would have made a different
decision.*

—Iain Moray, skipper, Siena

When the explorer George Bass first saw Wilsons Promontory it
impressed him so much that he immediately assumed it had to be

geographically significant. He described it in his journal as 'worthy' of being 'the boundary point of a large strait, and corner-stone to the new continent'. He was right. The headland of Wilsons Promontory, which juts south into Bass Strait, is the southern-most point of mainland Australia. Its granite cape rises 800 metres but seems higher, looming over Bass Strait on three sides and towering over the low bushland behind it to the north. Bass surmised the head of the Promontory had once been an island. He had plenty of time to ponder his theory. For six days, he was trapped there by a gale. His whaleboat was forced to take shelter behind the headland in a cove on the east side of the Promontory—not far from the place where a furious storm would be born 200 years later.

The germ of the storm that hit the Sydney to Hobart first showed up on satellite images during the week before Christmas. Its initial appearance was as nothing more spectacular than a band of cold air blowing along in the westerly winds of the upper atmosphere. Satellite images showed it crossing the Great Australian Bight and from there the various computer models plotted its probable development. At first, two computer programs suggested the wind would carry the cold air south-east, past Tasmania, before the trough deepened into a low-pressure system. A third, the American model, predicted it would deepen more quickly and turn into a low-pressure system over Bass Strait. But the American model is known for crying wolf too often. Yachting forecaster Roger 'Clouds' Badham describes it as 'bullish': 'That model has a slight tendency to want to "spin up" perhaps too many systems like this.'

But this time the American model gets it right, soonest. Soon after the race begins, other computer models agree with it. About twelve hours later, in the early hours of Sunday, 27 December, the cold pool of air rapidly deepens into a low-pressure system, slows down and gets cut off from the high winds that might have carried it further out to sea. Sometime between midnight and 3.00 a.m. the mass of cold air begins spinning around like a ballerina with her arms out. It pirouettes out of the sky and drops down over south-eastern Australia. As it deepens and falls, the cold air turns a summer heatwave to a mid-winter chill.

By 4.00 a.m., midsummer snow is falling on the ski fields in Victoria.

By daybreak, children on summer holidays at Mount Buller are throwing snowballs and racing down snowdrifts on toboggans. Melbourne had melted in a Christmas Day heatwave; two days later it is freezing. Newspapers call it a 'late white Christmas'.

Low-pressure systems are so called because they bring low air-pressure with them. As cold air moves, being heavy, it forces the warmer air ahead of it upward. Where the air is forced upward, the atmosphere is lighter, and air pressure is lower. The rising air expands, cools and turns into clouds and rain. Air rushes in to take its place at the bottom of the system and turns into wind. As the low-pressure system descends over Victoria, winds whip up wild dust storms in some parts of the state and fan bushfires in others. By early Sunday, airport flight forecasters measure winds of 200 kilometres an hour at a height of about 10,000 metres. It isn't much calmer on the ground.

On the morning of Sunday, 27 December, very few, if any, yachtsmen in the race hear about the snowballs and toboggans. The next radio sked and the official race weather forecast from *Young Endeavour* isn't due until two in the afternoon. The last sked and race forecast was at three in the morning. Both skeds, says Clouds, are at bad times for weather forecasts. A forecast heard at 2.00 p.m. or 3.00 a.m. might be compiled two or three hours earlier, often missing out on the latest runs from computer models. Few weather stations give new observations at midnight. So a report relayed to boats at 3.00 a.m. may have no data more recent than about 9.00 p.m. the night before, and no computer analysis less than twelve hours old. Even more significantly, the sked times are out of step with the usual patterns of weather itself. Low-pressure systems tend to intensify in the early hours of the morning, usually too late to be included in a 3.00 a.m. weather forecast. After this Sydney to Hobart, sailors and race organisers will talk about changing the forecast times for future races.

Early Sunday, the first forecast issued by the Bureau of Meteorology's Sydney office is in fact issued after 2.00 a.m., quite close to the sked time. But it's still drawn up before many of the bureau's first daily observations from weather stations are taken at 3.00 a.m. The forecast repeats the storm warning and predicts 40- to 50-knot winds. But the

Sydney forecast is only intended to cover an area that ends at Gabo Island, and the yachts are moving faster than expected. A forecast from Melbourne predicting slightly stronger winds, 45 to 55 knots, is slightly more accurate. But at this early stage of the race, the official race forecast is still the one issued in Sydney.

But at 6.00 a.m. the bureau's station at Wilsons Promontory records winds of 71 knots (more than 130 kilometres an hour). Three hours later, at 9.00 a.m., it records 79 knots (146 kilometres an hour). The readings are an average of wind speeds over a 10-minute period. The weather station actually records wind gusts of 92 knots (about 170 kilometres an hour). A weather bureau pamphlet advising on survival in emergencies says winds of that speed will wipe out crops and trees, destroy caravans and damage houses. The pamphlet doesn't say what a 90-knot wind might do to an 11-metre sailboat.

That morning the Wilsons Promontory wind readings are broadcast on radio by at least three specialist shipping weather services: Penta Comstat, Tasmar and Melbourne Radio. The coastguard at Eden knows about them. So does John Wittingham, the coastguard on Bass Strait's Lochsport oil rig, who broadcasts weather for oil rigs and shipping. So do fishermen, like Locky Marshall in Eden. But most of the yachtsmen don't hear them. Some are too busy sailing. Some are asleep. Others don't know about the radio services or don't use them. Some can't hear the broadcasts because the storm is already interfering with radio reception. The vast majority don't even try. Knowing the weather bureau prepares specialised race reports, they assume they can rely on the forecasts read out at the fixed times from *Young Endeavour*. Only a few yachts listen in to the radio-relay boat in between briefings. Lew Carter says his team does pass on wind readings if they are useful. But when asked after the race, Carter says he can't remember hearing anything that morning about Wilsons Promontory. He certainly doesn't remember anything about 70-knot winds—the radio team is there to read out weather reports, not to compile them. And Carter, as he readily admits, is no more of an expert weather forecaster than most of the yachtsmen he's talking to.

In Sydney, one expert forecaster does hear the wind readings at

Wilsons Promontory and they worry him. Clouds Badham knows Wilsons Promontory is notoriously windy and its anemometer is high up in a lighthouse. Clouds says Wilsons Promontory readings can often be discounted by ten or fifteen per cent. On that basis, a 79-knot wind reading at Wilsons Promontory would still mean an average wind speed of about 67 knots on the water. (After the race, the Sydney weather bureau claims the Prom readings should be discounted by as much as 25 knots, which would mean a speed of 54 knots on the water, putting the speed within the bureau's maximum forecast.) But Wilsons Promontory lies dead to windward of the yacht race. Some very experienced yachtsmen say wind gusts around 90 knots in a lighthouse are likely to be even stronger on the water. Clouds takes the readings seriously. 'Around 9.00 a.m. it was 79 knots gusting to 92. Now that is a very significant reading from that station. I can only recall one or two times—and that was in winter, not in summer—when winds of that speed flow across that station. So it's a very significant observation and certainly in the top one per cent of observations.'

That morning, Clouds sits down and draws a detailed weather chart. What he produces reminds him of the storm that devastated the Fastnet race in 1979. Nearly two decades later re-analysis of the Fastnet storm led forecasters to develop new theories about airflow in intense low-pressure systems. Clouds digs through his journals till he finds the articles on Fastnet. The new theory helps explain why the high winds at Wilsons Promontory aren't easily spotted by computer models. Says Clouds: 'Models forecast by averages. And so, if they're showing an average of 40 or 50 knots, then it's likely that you're going to have winds far in excess of this in a small banded area. That's what the theory is coming up with now. I thought I must be seeing what I'd been reading in the journals. I re-read that article then and there, on the spot, and I thought, "There's probably a banding of winds, or a zone, a banana-shaped cone of winds around this low that's probably stronger than what the numerical models can possibly pick up."' As he explains, the models aren't good at predicting the unusual. 'Reality shows that the computer models are generally bland, that they can't forecast extreme events.' By now, it is beginning to be clear to Clouds that this is an extreme event.

It might occur once in twenty-five years. The problem is, it coincides with a yacht race held only once a year. As the storm moves east across Bass Strait, more than eleven hundred yachtsmen are racing towards it.

When he finishes reading the journal article, Clouds is worried. But he doesn't know what to do. Since he stopped giving the official race forecast he has no formal link with the race organisers, the Cruising Yacht Club of Australia. But it occurs to him that he does know someone who is, at least, very close to the action—Rob Mundle, a journalist, yachting promoter and sailor, who has been reporting on the Sydney to Hobart for thirty years. Since the early 1980s, Clouds has given Mundle briefings on weather before and during the Sydney to Hobart. 'This is generally,' says Clouds, 'a one-sided relationship. That is, he calls when he wants something.' Now, Clouds calls Mundle. Mundle doesn't answer his phone because he's flying to Hobart, but Clouds leaves a detailed message. He says the situation looks very grim for boats that will enter Bass Strait later that afternoon and night. He explains the Wilsons Promontory readings and says he's certain of wind speeds of 50 to 60 knots.

By now, having read the journal articles on the Fastnet race, it occurs to Clouds that the nastiest winds will probably lie in a thin, elongated band on the western flank of the low-pressure system. He has another look at the weather chart he's been drawing, and concentrates on what might happen on that western flank. Once again, he picks up the phone and calls Mundle. This time Mundle has arrived in Tasmania. Clouds tells him about the second, higher, wind report from Wilsons Promontory and his concern that the boats will be hit by excessively strong winds and large nasty seas right off the south-east tip of Gabo Island. He expects it will happen right where the currents converge. Clouds says later: 'I believe I told Mundle that the worst conditions would be between 3.00 p.m. and 3.00 a.m. the following morning, and I estimated that half the fleet would be knocked out.' After the race, Clouds says it wasn't his 'role to be giving advice'. He didn't really imagine his phone calls would make any difference. But he phoned up anyway. 'In future,' he says, 'I guess they'll think differently.'

By midday, officials of the Ocean Racing Club of Victoria abandon plans to start yacht races across Bass Strait from Melbourne to Hobart and Devonport, on the north coast of Tasmania. Conditions are so bad at the entrance to Melbourne's Port Phillip Bay that it's difficult for yachts to get out. The club officials announce that the forecast of 50-knot winds and the already dangerous conditions in Bass Strait have convinced them to postpone the races till the next day. It's only the second time they've made such a decision. The Victorian club's commodore says, 'Given the conditions today and the obvious risks to crews and boats, it would have been irresponsible for us to put pressure on crews who didn't want to go out there, by attempting to start the races.' But the Sydney to Hobart race is already underway. Delaying it isn't an issue. In the race's whole history it has been postponed only once and that was in 1948, when the start of the race was due to fall on a Sunday. In those days even yacht racing was judged to be sacrilege if done on a Sunday.

This time, Sunday is the second day of the Sydney to Hobart. It will be the blackest day in its 53-year history. During the night, the yachts have raced down the coast in double-quick time, surfing south in winds that are mostly nor'easterly. By dawn, boats at the front of the fleet are picking up winds from the west-south-west, the direction of Wilsons Promontory. Early Sunday afternoon very few, if any, sailors in the Sydney to Hobart have heard about the postponement of the other Bass Strait races. Some say later that if they had heard they would have pulled into shelter. By morning the Bass Strait storm is no longer a statistical outcome showing up on a computer model. The storm is a reality. The last scheduled race weather forecast is hours past, the next still hours away. Sitting at his computer, Roger Badham thinks that 2.00 p.m. forecast 'should be a humdinger'.

TWELVE

*We see ourselves as tackling difficult tasks and finishing
them competently. There's the feeling that we're here to
conquer this mountain and one way or another we
will. So it would be a pretty hard decision to stop.*

—Geoff Ross, skipper, Yendys

Sunday, 27 December 1998
Morning

The two huge yachts leading the race, *Sayonara* and *Brindabella*, hit Bass
Strait far ahead of most of the fleet. There's no light, the clouds are low
and heavy and it's pouring rain. By now the wind is coming from the
south-west, the direction of Wilsons Promontory. On *Sayonara*, the
massive mainsail starts tearing. At 3.00 a.m. Larry Ellison comes off the
helm and goes below deck to find his navigator, Mark Rudiger, looking
at a satellite photo on one of *Sayonara*'s computer screens. It shows a
menacing ring of white clouds blotting out Wilsons Promontory. Ellison
asks Rudiger if he's ever seen anything like it before. Rudiger tells him
he has: 'It was on the Weather Channel. And it was called a hurricane.
What the fuck is that thing doing out here?'

But until later that day, most of the fleet, still in the lee of the mainland, has no idea of the storm that is waiting round the corner. On
board *Young Endeavour*, Lew Carter remembers Sunday morning as
lovely and sunny: 'There was quite a buzz in the air. Our young trainees
were all as happy as Larry. Some were up on deck doing an Irish jig. I
can always tell the condition of the sea by what is going on in the mess

room when you go down for lunch or breakfast. That day I remember going in to get some lunch and it was pretty hard to find a seat.' Even *Young Endeavour* has made the trip south in record time. According to Carter, by midday the radio-relay boat would normally be just south of Jervis Bay, about 160 kilometres from the start. Instead, it's already south of Montague Island, nearly 300 kilometres south of Sydney.

Another boat making record time and now right near the front of the fleet is Gary Shanks's 17-metre *DocTel Rager*, from South Australia. *Rager* leaves Sydney Heads in about twentieth place and sails straight down the rhumb line. Shanks doesn't go out to sea to chase the warm current, but he picks up three knots of current anyway and *Rager* does better than he expects. Gary Shanks is a doctor in general practice in Adelaide and this is his, and *Rager*'s, second Sydney to Hobart. The '*DocTel*' part of *Rager*'s name comes from a business he has set up to deliver remote-control medicine to far-flung Aboriginal communities. Either because of his work, or in spite of it, Shanks is endlessly cheerful, energetic and patient. He's sailed since he was seven years old, and now *Rager*'s regular crew includes his two children, fifteen-year-old David and sixteen-year-old Catherine. Last year, the three of them sailed their first Hobart along with a crew with little ocean racing experience. This year some more experienced sailors, including the chief South Australian yachting safety officer, David Woods, and 'Chook' Smith, a fifteen-race veteran, have joined them. Before coming on board, Chook tells Shanks he wants *Rager* to be able to handle 80-knot winds. So Shanks takes the bottom out of the boat, reinforces the hull, puts in a longer keel and adds a fourth reef point to the mainsail. (Reef points are used to fold up the mainsail near the boom, so that its wind face is smaller. Most yachts don't have more than three reef points, some have only two.) Everyone tells him he's crazy.

Now prepared for anything (so Gary Shanks hopes), *Rager* has a great run down the coast. 'We had spinnakers up and the wind built steadily from 20 knots through 30 and then 40 knots. We blew out another spinnaker as we went through each wind range! First our pink hounds kite exploded, so we put on our indestructible "shock" kite, which is 2.4 ounces and has double cloth on the luffs. [The luff is the leading edge of a sail.] I got the boat surfing at 26 knots boat speed, 29 knots over the ground, with the three-knot current. An absolutely awesome ride that we will never forget, the sort of boat speeds we all live for. We gobbled up the nautical miles and we were up in the top five boats for several skeds. At that stage many of the fleet were well in front of record time. At one point the GPS said we would take thirty-three hours to complete the course! The "shock" kite blew out in a 40-plus-knot gust and we pulled it down.' By sunrise on Sunday, about eighteen hours into the race, *Rager* has sailed as far as it did in thirty-six hours the previous year.

But this year, as *Rager* and the fastest of the small- and medium-sized boats are turning the corner of the mainland and heading into Bass Strait, the Wilsons Promontory storm is moving east to catch them. As the storm approaches, the air-pressure in front of it falls. For more than three hundred years, since the invention of the barometer, sailors have known no surer sign of trouble than falling air-pressure. And the faster and further the fall, the worse the trouble in store. On *Rager*, one crewman, an aviator, wears a barometer on a wristband. He watches the readout plummet. Shanks is at the helm. 'We saw a large, black, horizontal sausage and lightning arcing down, up ahead. The barometer dropped 100 points in forty minutes, which is unheard of, and we knew we'd be in for a belting.' Suddenly the wind around *Rager* drops off completely. The crew gets ready. They put on a smaller headsail and go down to the third reef in the mainsail. Then they wait.

About twenty minutes later, it starts. The first gust is 35 knots; three or four minutes later, it's 55. At each gust it builds. Soon the wind base is 60 or 65 knots with frequent higher gusts. The crew drops the mainsail and lashes it to the boom. They run *Rager* away from the wind and change to the storm jib. The wind stays solid at about 65 knots and Gary Shanks thinks that might be the worst of it. 'We thought, OK, this is the 65 we were expecting. We could live with it. We thought it would hang in for maybe an hour and then tail out. But then it built. It built to 70, 71 and then it was gusting up to 78 and then one of the guys saw 80 on the clock and we're going, "Ah—this is more, far more than we ever anticipated."' It is a phenomenal increase. In simple terms, this is because the force of a wind is roughly proportional to the square of its speed. That means that if the wind speed doubles, its force increases four times; if it trebles, its force increases ninefold, and so on. So, because wind speed is squared, a 70-knot wind has about double the force of a 50-knot wind.

On *Rager*, sixteen-year-old Catherine Shanks has the nickname 'Someone' because whenever anyone asks for someone to do something, she always volunteers. The worse the weather gets, the more Catherine enjoys it. Younger brother David is less impressed. The wind howls and the spray blows in horizontally, blasting cheeks as if it were gusts of broken glass. Visibility drops to about 200 metres. Waves, their tops blown off by the wind, start standing up from the swell and come at *Rager* from every direction. Gary Shanks tries to keep them at 45 degrees and slide *Rager* down their backs. But he can't always manage it. 'They were breaking in both directions. So you'd fly over the top and try to angle the boat down the back and then find yourself slamming straight into a wave coming head-on. The boat was doing about 12 knots and slamming really badly. I thought if I couldn't slow it down it would break in half.'

Sometime around 10.00 a.m., dead ahead of him and on the same course he's sailing, Shanks sees another yacht. It's a Sydney boat, slightly bigger than his own, called *Team Jaguar*. Every few seconds *Team Jaguar* disappears into the trough of a wave so that even the top of its 26-metre mast vanishes. *Team Jaguar* is about fifteen minutes ahead of *Rager*. Shanks uses it to steer by. Then, suddenly, *Team Jaguar* disappears completely. 'I thought, "Hmm—where have they gone?" Then I heard on the radio they'd lost their mast and I thought, "Well, we're sailing on the same line, we'll probably be able to see them." But we sailed to the position they were at and never saw them. They must have been in a trough when we were on a peak, or on a peak when we were in a trough.' *Rager* gives *Team Jaguar*'s position to *Young Endeavour*. A little later Shanks hears that *Team Jaguar* has turned on its motor and is heading back to Eden.

Rager's own 25-metre mast is being dwarfed by waves. The yacht slides sideways down a few of the big ones. Three times, with the wind blasting 75 knots, *Rager* is rolled on its side and puts the top of its mast in the water. Shanks can feel the whole boat shudder and groan under the strain. Below deck, it is chaos. The boat's navigator is thrown from the navigation desk and lands on the oven, smashing it off its gimbles and wrecking it. Shanks starts to realise things are getting serious. It occurs to him that smaller boats than his could easily be swamped. 'We decided that it would probably be sensible to make a radio call and let them know that the wind speed was building beyond 65 knots and it was a helluva lot more than anyone really anticipated. Mike Sabey made the call to Telstra Control [the radio operation on *Young Endeavour*]. He said "We've got a solid 50- to 60-knot range over the deck with gusts up to 72." I felt we had a responsibility to do it. We were probably up in the first half-dozen yachts. Having sailed into something like that, I thought we were sort of duty-bound to let the guys behind know that it was building beyond 65. They might want to get their sails down and change things.'

In ocean racing, *Rager*'s call is highly unusual. Official Race Radio Instructions say that, in general, yachts shouldn't ask for or broadcast information about weather. The only exception is when the weather is 'severe'. As Lew Carter explains it, 'The reason yachtsmen don't do it normally is that if they're getting a lovely nor'easter, for argument's sake, and they give their position, a competitor might be nearby with no breeze and it gives that yacht an advantage because he thinks, "Gee whiz, we only have to get over there a bit and we're in a lovely breeze, as opposed to what we're getting now." It's the competitive edge, it's practised in all of yachting. All over the world, chaps don't divulge what sort of wind strengths they're getting, because the other yachts will certainly make towards that area.'

When *Rager* decides conditions *are* severe, and radios its position and wind speed, the radio operators on *Young Endeavour* confirm the call and say they will record it. But almost immediately Shanks hears another boat call in and question the report. 'Inside the boat, our watch, who were supposedly resting when we heard it, were all pretty annoyed that someone would question it. I would have thought there'd be very few boats that take the Sydney to Hobart seriously who would put in a false report. So we were terribly annoyed to hear this call to Telstra Control and someone say, "Is that a legit call on the wind?" It put our noses out of joint.' *Rager*'s crew is shocked that someone might think they would be deliberately misleading.

Gary Shanks remembers *Rager* calling in sometime around 12.30 p.m. About five minutes after the report is queried, Lew Carter asks if anyone else can confirm it. One boat radios back to say it's getting winds in the high seventies, backing up *Rager*. A few minutes later, two others do the same. Though the reports are recorded on *Young Endeavour*'s log, they don't strike Carter as particularly significant. After the race, he can't remember the calls clearly: 'I think, from memory, a yacht came in, and I don't know whether he identified himself, maybe he did. But the weather bureau had said there'd be 45 or 50 [knots]. At that stage *Young Endeavour* wasn't getting that, we were probably getting thirty-fives. But of course we were a fair bit in the lee of the land. Anyway, he came in and said he was experiencing more than we were getting—that he was already in it, I think those were the words. So we knew there was more breeze and I expected it as soon as we put our heads round the corner, so to speak.' Whatever reports Carter or the rest of his team do hear, they don't take further action. 'No, no. I was waiting for the sked. I mean, you don't relay everything. I mean, these yachties are aware of it, they can tell by the sea conditions. They know, if they're getting 30 knots five miles off the coast, that once they get down to open waters, they'll get more. They're all pretty seasoned sailors. They're all quite aware of all that.'

Most boats don't hear *Rager*'s call because it's outside the sked time. Everyone is supposed to keep a listening watch on the radio, but most don't bother. 'The problem with having the radio on "monitor" the whole time in the boat', says Shanks, 'is that it makes a dreadful noise for the guys who are downstairs trying to sleep. The requirement to have the radio on the whole time is a pain, so we actually turn the volume fairly well down. You really only listen, or turn the volume up to listen, when you know you have to. So, if there'd been any major changes in terms of weather reports, we would have missed them anyway. I guess a lot of other boats didn't hear our call. These radios suck a lot of power; some boats just turn them off.'

Gary Shanks gives his report because he thinks it might help other yachtsmen prepare themselves. His own boat has gone too far to turn back but even if it hadn't, pulling out of the race is never an issue. 'We don't do that, we continue regardless. We stopped racing though, as soon as it got really dirty. We stopped racing and basically went into survival mode. We knew, by a process of elimination, we'd get nine or twelve hours of really dirty stuff. Provided you survive that, you know you can start racing again.' Shanks doesn't believe in turning around. 'If the boat sank, we'd have to go home, but we'd never turn around and go back. You never run with the storm. Always fight into it. It's just the way we do it.'

Not far away another yacht hits Bass Strait and the 70-knot winds at about the same time as *Rager*. It's Geoff Ross's *Yendys*. Ross's navigator has been monitoring the radio and the wind readings at Wilsons Promontory all morning. Like Gary Shanks, Geoff Ross never considers turning back. 'I mean, what happens in one place doesn't necessarily happen in another place. Also, things change. So you're never quite certain that what might happen *will* happen. And we were already in pretty heavy conditions, and it was getting heavier and the waves were getting bigger.'

Turning around in a storm is one thing; pulling out before it hits is another. Geoff Ross says it probably wouldn't make a difference to him. 'If I was going to leave Sydney and someone guaranteed that in twenty-four hours I'd be in really bad conditions like those in Bass Strait, would I leave or not? It's a good question. I've wondered about it myself and discussed it with some of the crew. If we *knew* this was going to happen, would we have gone into Eden or kept going? Our conclusion is, we would have kept going. I know it's irrational. But in the boat I have and with the crew I have, and now that we've done it once, we'd certainly do it now. I don't know what most yachtsmen would do. I know some who would go anyway. It's a difficult decision, because, rationally, why take the risk? There is no up-side, other than you've done it. So it's a personal challenge, which is basically what the whole race is anyway. It's an adventure, because why else do it in the first place? It's a pretty stupid race anyway, from the point of view of rationality. It's just a challenge. We think we're good ocean-racing sailors and we've put thousands of hours of preparation into the boat and ourselves, so, yes, we'd go.'

Like many yachtsmen, neither Gary Shanks nor Geoff Ross ever considers pulling out of the race. They both make it to Hobart. After the race, some sailors say they used to think the same way. But now, they say, they think differently.

THIRTEEN

➤

We were in a cyclone. It was a cyclone in Bass Strait.
    —John Stanley, helmsman, Winston Churchill

*I don't think the yachts were damaged by the winds, as
much as by the seas. They were damaged by rogue
waves, as the sailors call them; superimposing wave
trains that cross or whatever, and suddenly produce a
wave that's out of the norm with waves on either side.
And the boats can't survive. It's like putting a very
small boat in the surf. A wave can just crash onto it.
Or the boat can get to the top of the wave, have
trouble riding down the back of it and fall off. That's
where the damage occurs.*
    —Roger 'Clouds' Badham, yachting meteorologist

When Cyclone Tracy struck Darwin on Christmas Day in 1974, fifty
people were killed in town and sixteen more were lost at sea. The first
warnings of a possible cyclone came four days earlier, when satellite
photos picked up a large cloud mass about 500 kilometres north-east of
Darwin, in the Arafura Sea. Soon, infra-red pictures showed spiral bands
forming in the clouds and the storm was reclassified as a cyclone and
named Tracy. Satellites and radar tracked Tracy's every move. To begin
with, it moved south-west. But early on Christmas Eve, it changed
course. At first Tracy went south, then it turned to the east-south-east
and headed directly for Darwin.

A weather station about 15 kilometres from Tracy's centre picked up average wind speeds of 120 kilometres an hour. But then satellites tracked Tracy as it passed over a narrow belt of very warm water and intensified. Warm water puts cyclone development on fast forward.

When Tracy first hit Darwin shortly after midnight, the airport anemometer recorded winds of 110 kilometres an hour, with gusts to 195 (over 90 knots). The strongest winds were in a narrow band, less than 40 kilometres wide. But they followed the worst possible path. Tracy swept through the centre of town like a tourist following a roadmap. The 'eye' (the calm centre) of the cyclone came in through the suburbs, went straight over the airport and then left Darwin along the main highway. The winds behind the eye were even stronger than those in front of it. Cyclone Tracy moved fairly slowly, at about eight kilometres an hour. It took just five hours to wipe out most of Darwin. There's no record of Tracy's highest wind speeds. The airport anemometer was knocked out soon after it measured a gust of 217 kilometres an hour—only about 30 kilometres faster than the gusts at Wilsons Promontory.

In Australia, cyclones are generally tropical. They come in five grades. The strongest cyclone ever measured in Australia, Orson, which passed over the North West Shelf of the continent in 1989, was classed as top of the range in Category Five. Winds from Orson, measured from an oil platform, averaged 224 kilometres an hour. Short gusts are thought to have topped 280 kilometres an hour. Tracy was a Category Four cyclone. If the Sydney to Hobart storm had been classed as a cyclone, the wind speeds reported by a number of sailors would have nudged it into a rank just below Tracy, in Category Three.

In northern Australia, the Bureau of Meteorology's Severe Weather Unit sets up a watch if it expects gale-force winds to hit the coast within forty-eight hours. The first warning comes when the winds are twenty-four hours away; then warnings come every three hours until the cyclone gets close enough to be tracked on radar every ten minutes. The bureau's advice is to stay inside, in the strongest part of the house, generally the bathroom or the basement. The bureau's radar tracking focuses on tropical cyclones. It doesn't operate radar tracking south of the tropics because tropical cyclones don't usually form there. But cyclonic storms can form in southern latitudes. The difference is, that when they do, they are often simply called low-pressure systems. And they usually appear not as one single low but as a cluster of lows or, as meteorologists call it, a 'family'.

Fourteen hours after the start of the Sydney to Hobart, weather maps show five low-pressure systems scattered over Tasmania and Bass Strait. One, near Wilsons Promontory, is very intense. For much of Sunday, this 'family' of smaller lows is embedded within a main 'parent' low-pressure system. Meteorologists describe intense systems like this, when they occur in south-eastern Australia, as 'lows'. If they develop very fast, or explosively, they're sometimes termed 'bombs'. All but the most violent are simply called 'storms'. To most laymen, 'storm' is an everyday word. But to meteorologists it isn't. And in the Sydney to Hobart, that difference proves to be a problem.

To meteorologists, a 'storm' means anything with winds over 48 knots. But 48 knots is only a minimum. 'I'm not sure all yachtsmen are actually aware of what a storm warning is,' says Roger 'Clouds' Badham. 'I think there's a couple of problems buried in there. There's some confusion about the word "storm". On the first night of the race and until morning there were severe electrical storms right across the fleet. Some people confuse the word "storm" with "storm warning", and "storm" with electrical storms, but they're totally different things. A storm warning is an open-ended warning. It says that the winds are going to average more than 48 knots, and that can be 60, 70, 80, 90 knots, whatever. I think that the average yachtie doesn't appreciate that it's open-ended. The bureau's storm warning is correct. But the winds referenced in their forecasts—at most 45 to 55 knots—were substantially down on what was observed.' According to Clouds, the bureau's forecast for the Sydney to Hobart is to some extent misleading. Though the bureau does issue a storm warning, the strongest wind forecast is for 45 to 55 knots. More often the forecast is for 40 to 50 knots, wind speeds at the lowest end of a storm warning. So, in fact, though the bureau warns of a storm, the winds it predicts don't truly reflect one. 'It seems,' says Clouds, 'a very thin connection to forecast 40- to 50-knot winds with a warning that references winds of 48 knots or more.'

Clouds says communication is the most difficult part of a forecaster's job. Nearly 200 years ago, a British Rear Admiral by the name of Sir Francis Beaufort came to the same conclusion. Training the Royal Navy to fight sea battles against the French and the Spanish, Beaufort realised he needed to be able to describe wind speeds and sea states in a way sailors would understand them. He came up with a scale of thirteen categories of wind and sea waves. The higher the number, the stronger the wind and the wilder the sea. Force Zero is calm ('sea mirror smooth'), Force Twelve is a hurricane. Over the years, most of the poetry of Beaufort's original scale has been lost—phrases such as 'Men o'war reduced to reefed topsails' and 'Fishing smacks seek shelter' have disappeared from modern reprints—but seamen still use the Beaufort Scale, even though the weather bureau doesn't generally use it in forecasts. If the bureau had, its maximum forecast of winds up to 55 knots would have put the Sydney to Hobart storm at the upper end of what the Beaufort Scale lists as Force Ten (Force Ten was the estimated strength of the storm that devastated the Fastnet race in 1979). Beaufort describes Force Ten as 'High waves with long overhanging crests; great foam patches.'

Like fishermen reminiscing about their biggest catches, sailors' stories of bad storms often expand in the telling. Nevertheless, a number of yachtsmen in this year's Sydney to Hobart say they experienced wind speeds over 70 knots. Those speeds are right at the end of the Beaufort Scale, well into Force Twelve—what Sir Francis Beaufort referred to as a 'Hurricane'. Older versions of his scale describe those conditions as 'that which no canvas could withstand'.

But even with the Beaufort Scale, the trouble with a storm is that the only way to really know how bad it is, is to be caught in it. Early this century, Joseph Conrad grappled with the problem in his story 'Typhoon'. Conrad's Captain MacWhirr is on board the steamer *Nan-Shan*, watching the barometer plummet. Soon after, he steams headlong into a typhoon. As MacWhirr explains to his chief mate, Jukes, there is so much foul weather in the world, that it is pointless trying to avoid all of it:

'But suppose I went swinging off my course and came in two days late and they asked me: "Where have you been all that time, Captain?" What could I say to that? "Went around to dodge the bad weather," I would say. "It must've been dam' bad," they would say. "Don't know," I would have to say; "I've dodged clear of it." See that Jukes? I've been thinking about that all this afternoon.'

A few hours after this conversation, MacWhirr's ship is all but destroyed.

Meteorologists define storms by wind speed. But for sailors, storms hold two dangers—wind speed and sea state. And in the Sydney to Hobart the biggest problem for sailors isn't the wind; it's what the wind does to the sea. During the race, the bureau's highest prediction, from its Victorian office, is for waves of five to seven metres. But according to the Beaufort Scale, a violent storm can build waves up to 16 metres high. In a Force Twelve hurricane, Beaufort lists *average* wave height as around 14 metres. There is no listing for maximum wave height in a hurricane. It's either too difficult to estimate or too awful to contemplate.

Even today, forecasters have difficulty predicting severe sea conditions and most yachtsmen have difficulty contemplating them. 'The yachtsmen,' says Clouds, 'don't foresee the fact that some wave is going to loom up in front of them that could engulf the boat. Or that the boat could be tipped over completely and have trouble getting upright. That sort of thing, while it can be forecast, you have to be virtually on the spot to be aware of the confluence of the currents and the history of the event itself and the way the wave trains have developed. Models are being developed now that in ten years or so will get the numerical guidance much closer to reality.'

Oceanographers don't pretend to fully understand waves so they have to generalise. They know that the faster and longer the wind blows and the further it moves over water, the higher the waves will be. They know that the higher waves are, the steeper their sides. They know that once the height of one wave is more than about seven times the distance between it and the next one, the top of the wave will break off into white water and spray. But beyond those rules, waves start acting much more unpredictably. They can double up. Whole trains of waves can cross, merge, overtake and jump on top of each other. In any sea, about one in every thousand waves will be almost twice as high as the others around it. It might be higher. Such giant waves are called 'kings', 'phantoms', 'freaks' or 'rogues'. Exactly how they happen is unclear, and when they might happen can only be guessed as a statistical average. What's certain is that sooner or later they *will* happen. Ships have reported rogue waves up to 40 metres high appearing out of nowhere. A steep chaotic sea can produce more than its share of monsters. In Bass Strait the shallowness of the sea turns some waves into backless, breaking crests much like sheer cliffs of water. By mid-afternoon on Sunday, yachtsmen in the Sydney to Hobart will report enormous waves coming so thick and fast they can barely be called rogues. Some sailors will estimate that as many as one wave in every fifteen is a giant.

But until mid Sunday morning the main intense low-pressure system stays to the west of the rhumb line that most yachts are following. Then, in the early afternoon, it passes directly over the race track. As Clouds has predicted, the worst of the winds and the worst seas they generate hit the shallows of Bass Strait. A swirling cold-water eddy has formed near the tail end of the warm East Coast current. The wind and the waves crash into the confluence of currents. They whip up Bass Strait like an egg beater.

FOURTEEN

◄ ➤

*When there's a storm warning it isn't a time to be at
sea and it isn't a time to be fishing. But we have a
professional crew and a very big steel vessel that's
designed to navigate through the sort of weather boats
wouldn't normally attempt to work in.*
— Joe Pirello, Ulladulla fisherman

*In hindsight I realise the police sergeant anticipated this
wasn't going to be a normal Sydney to Hobart yacht
race because he made the comment that his officers were
all on stand-by and he'd already brought some of them
into the station. Looking back, I believe he felt we were
going to have a lot of problems.*
— Locky Marshall, Eden fisherman

As Gary Shanks slams through Bass Strait on *Rager*, setting his course
by *Team Jaguar*'s bobbing mast ahead, the youngest crewmember on
Team Jaguar is below deck, asleep on a bunk. Eighteen-year-old Melissa
McCabe has sailed for a few years with the CYCA's youth program. A
student at Eden's Marine Technology High School, she scored her place
on the *Team Jaguar* crew by winning an essay competition. After spending Christmas with her family in Eden she arrived in Sydney just before
the start of the race. Eighteen hours into it she's mostly enjoying herself,
despite, as she writes later, almost being washed overboard and the fact
that her pasta and vegetables made a reappearance soon after dinner. By

morning she's playing it safe, sticking to small packets of nuts and sultanas, and hanging on tighter during her two-hour shift on the rails. At about 10.30 a.m., when her watch finishes, Melissa goes below and falls fast asleep. About an hour later she hears someone shout, 'all hands on deck'. Melissa McCabe doesn't need to be an experienced sailor to know it means something bad.

Melissa gets as far as the hatch. Outside, she can see *Team Jaguar*'s mast flapping and twisting in the wind. The boat's sail is half in the water. After the race, she tells a journalist, 'I remember thinking "This can't be good". The crew was pretty calm but one of the other girls started getting a bit hysterical. I stayed below so as not to get in the way. I also got sick.' Eleven other people on board *Team Jaguar* keep below, out of the way, too. On deck, the remaining six slash at the rigging, cutting it away with whatever they can find. Those in the cabin hand up hacksaws, pliers and hammers. The shattered mast crashes over the stern of the yacht, taking the main radio aerial with it. The crew tries to get communications going, then turns on the motor and heads for Eden, about 60 kilometres north.

Team Jaguar is out of the race. It isn't the first time. The previous year, the yacht broke its mast in much the same area. This time, the boat's skipper and owner, Sydney solicitor Martin James, isn't too worried. James is a well-known director of the CYCA and *Team Jaguar* is carrying a large crew and a camera team but his boat couldn't have struck trouble at a worse time—it is almost at the front of the fleet, with a good chance of missing the middle of the storm. When its mast breaks, *Team Jaguar* becomes trapped in some of the worst conditions.

At first, the waves make hard work of motoring and for a while the trip north just looks like being a slow one. But the sea hasn't finished with *Team Jaguar*. A wave breaks over the deck, picks up a rope that hasn't been stowed and washes it overboard. The rope wraps itself around the propeller. The motor stops. Melissa McCabe recalls, 'That's when we really had trouble. We were desperate for communications as we needed someone to know what was happening to us. At one stage we were even getting mobile phones out and seeing if we could contact anyone—ringing up home numbers to see if they could get in touch with the Waterways but nothing worked.'

Eventually someone coaxes the radio back into life and some other boats pick up the signal. One is *Sword of Orion*. Rob Kothe knows Martin James and some of the crew. He's heard they're in trouble and out of radio contact, so he's relieved to hear from them. He radios the control boat: *Team Jaguar*, with no motor and a broken mast, needs help to get into Eden. On *Young Endeavour* Lew Carter swings into action and helps arrange a rescue. It doesn't take long. That morning, *Team Jaguar* is the first yacht to get into difficulty and Lew Carter can give it plenty of attention.

By 2.10 p.m. Eden's local police sergeant Keith Tillman has heard the message, driven across town and is knocking on Locky Marshall's front door. If anyone can help with a tow it's Marshall, who runs two trawlers and knows just about every boat in town. Over the years Marshall has helped rescue dozens of craft, including his fair share of Sydney to Hobart casualties. In 1992 he steamed more than 300 kilometres and spent fifty-four hours towing back one of them, *Hummingbird*, that had broken its rudder. These days he won't go out to sea himself if he can avoid it but he will send his fishing boats. Locky Marshall isn't surprised to find Keith Tillman at his door. He tells Tillman that one trawler he part owns, the *Moira Elizabeth*, is sheltering from the storm behind Gabo Island. It's probably the closest boat to *Team Jaguar*. Marshall calls his co-owner in Ulladulla, Joe Pirello; Pirello checks with the insurance company, then calls the trawler's skipper, Tom Bibby, and Bibby and his crew agree to head out. Bibby figures he can get to *Team Jaguar* in about three hours.

It isn't the last time that day Sergeant Tillman will be arranging a rescue. By evening, as yacht after yacht radios that it's heading for Eden, Tillman is running a personal relay service between Marshall's house, the police station and the Eden Coastal Patrol. It isn't all altruism for the fishermen. Many of the tows, like *Team Jaguar*'s, are commercial. Even so, Locky Marshall says profit doesn't usually play a part: 'Mostly, the cost isn't recoverable. You're risking damage to your own vessel and risking lives. Quite often a lot of yachtsmen don't seem to appreciate the effort and costs outlaid to rescue them or tow them in. And that eventually wears a bit thin. These days there are a lot of fishermen who disappear or aren't available when these calls come out.' But at the time, Marshall and Pirello judge *Team Jaguar* is really in trouble. Later that day they are less certain about some of the numerous other requests for a tow into Eden harbour.

≺ ≻

While Keith Tillman is knocking on Locky Marshall's front door, about 60 kilometres out to sea Melissa McCabe is deciding she definitely wants *out*—out of Bass Strait and out of *Team Jaguar*. The storm's 70- to 80-knot winds have caught up with the disabled yacht. The sea builds. At about 2.00 p.m., a 25-metre wave appears out of nowhere, heads for *Team Jaguar*, and buries three-quarters of the 21-metre-long yacht in water. The helmsman, Tim Messenger, doesn't think *Team Jaguar* will come out the other side. It does, but two men are washed overboard in their harnesses and have to be hauled back on deck.

Melissa McCabe thinks the deck is cracking. 'It was like a waterfall in the middle of the boat. People were being sick. One of the guys told me to get up on deck but the guys on deck sent us straight back below. It was too dangerous. Fortunately the water didn't keep pouring into the cabin. It was just the huge pressure of the wave that forced it in. It was probably the scariest moment for us. I didn't think I was going to die, but I definitely wanted to be out of there.' Amid the panic someone sets off a distress beacon. Some of the *Team Jaguar* crew think it's an overreaction. As Melissa says, 'They're pretty tough guys.' She's right. After the race, skipper Martin James says he never believed the crew was in danger or the boat needed urgent assistance; the distress beacon was only set off because it was close to the sked time and the yacht's radio wasn't working. When the radio started working again, James says he realised other yachts were in worse trouble than *Team Jaguar*. He planned to rig up a sail on a spinnaker pole and limp into Eden.

But *Team Jaguar*'s rescuers don't know any of that.

In Ulladulla, Joe Pirello is soon phoning the *Moira Elizabeth* for a progress report. The skipper, Tom Bibby, hasn't gone far, but he says the weather is about as bad as it was a few hours ago when he gave up fishing. Joe Pirello is worried about his crew and his trawler and worried about the yachtsmen. His wife makes him a fresh pot of overproof Italian coffee. It won't be the last that night. Pirello goes downstairs to his office, sits down with his coffee and waits by the phone.

FIFTEEN

*The top wind speed we recorded was 92 knots, which is
about 170 kilometres an hour. That sort of wind speed
blows dogs off chains.*

—*Rob Kothe, skipper,* Sword of Orion

Sword of Orion hits the first southerly change some time around
2.00 a.m. Sunday. The wind reaches about 35 knots and holds there till
dawn. At first light there's a dirty yellow-grey haze. Soon the sun disappears into a ceiling of low, heavy cloud. Steve Kulmar notices the
wind increase to 40 knots, back down a little, build to 50 knots and
back down again. Then it starts nudging 60 knots: 'The seas were building the whole time. We were in Bass Strait by this stage and the seas
were getting bigger and bigger. The tops were blowing off the waves
and conditions were becoming treacherous. Around 11.00 a.m. the wind
was consistently over 65 knots, occasionally gusting to 80 knots.'

By mid-morning, says skipper Rob Kothe, *Sword of Orion* stops
racing: 'Racing means you've got people up on the rail and you're really
pushing the boat as hard as you can. We were conserving the crew,
trying to slow the boat down. We had our storm sail up, rather than a
trisail which you'd do if you were still racing. We only had two people
on the deck. Normally you might have eight or nine.'

Rob Kothe spends most of the morning below deck on the radio
trying to work out what's going on with the weather. 'I think the
maximum wind forecast was 45 to 55 knots. There was a midday report
of that. The morning reports tended to be lower wind speeds. They're

averages. I expected gusts, say, ten per cent higher than that, so I thought we could have winds of 60 knots. But it got up there very fast.' Before the race, Kothe has tried to find out about the different computer models and he says he knew one of them was looking ominous. 'We were suspicious because we knew there was a possibility we might get an east-coast low—the estimation was something like a ten or twenty per cent possibility. But the words that rang in my ears from our private briefing were, "Don't believe the weather forecasts." So I was trying to drag information from anywhere I could, oil rigs, ground stations, whatever. I wanted some forward notice of things rather than just waiting for the weather forecast.'

Finding out what's ahead isn't as simple as it sounds. As Steve Kulmar describes it, 'On a yacht in an 80-knot wind, the noise levels below deck are extraordinary. There's so much crackling going on through the radio even when you can hear it. Then, you might be getting a weather forecast from somewhere but you go up a wave, the sea crashes over the top of you and you bounce down the other side and you don't hear anything for five seconds. You just don't hear anything. No matter how loud the radio is, you just won't hear it.'

Kothe manages to pick up the 70-knot-plus wind reading from Wilsons Promontory, but doesn't really know what to make of it. He thinks he remembers that oil rig forecasters discount Wilsons Promontory by about 25 knots. And the weather bureau is still predicting only 45 to 55. In his heart Kothe wants to continue to Hobart. The trouble is that, by now, the weather around *Sword of Orion* is nothing like the forecast. Just helming the boat is a battle. 'It required a great deal of physical effort,' says Kothe. 'It was very nasty and very, very scary. For much of that period we had a guy who weighs about 110 kilos on the helm with the second guy basically holding him so they wouldn't get knocked over by the force.'

On deck the screech of the wind makes conversation impossible. The only sound louder than the wind is the thunder of oncoming waves. The big ones start roaring and rising up more than a kilometre away. After a while it gets so hard to see that the only warning of a wave is the increasing growl as it gets closer. *Sword of Orion*'s mast is just under

23 metres. Measured against it, Kothe estimates some of the waves are about 20 metres high: 'When you're at the bottom of a wave you can't see anything more than the one that's about to fall on you. And when you're at the top of the wave you can't see much beyond the next crest. The helmsman's just dealing with each wave and surviving it and surviving the next. He's pretty busy. If a wave comes over the boat, anyone who's about to clip on or hasn't clipped on is in jeopardy. Guys were clipping on while standing on the cockpit floor or reaching up and clipping on from below deck. A lot of the time you'd have two tethers on to move around the boat.'

Between them the *Sword of Orion* crew has notched up about a hundred Sydney to Hobarts. But none of them has experienced conditions like this. They start having regular discussions about turning back. Some, including Kulmar, are keen to retire. But the yacht is doing well in the race—coming about seventh. It's almost halfway across Bass Strait, about 150 kilometres south of Eden and about 180 kilometres north of landfall at Eddystone Point in Tasmania. Either way, the seas are mostly coming at an angle. Heading one way seems no easier than the other.

But Steve Kulmar, the most experienced yachtsman on board, is growing increasingly concerned that it's getting later in the day and the weather is worsening. Kulmar runs a successful ad agency in Sydney. Information is his business and now he wants more of it. In particular, he wants to know precisely where the storm is and which way it is moving: 'We didn't know exactly where the centre of the low-pressure system was, or if there was more than one low-pressure system affecting us. All we knew was that we were sailing into a 70- to 80-knot breeze coming from the direction of about 250 or 260 on the compass. That basically says you are on top of the low-pressure system and you're sailing towards it. What normally happens is that as you get closer and closer to the low-pressure system, depending on what forces are around it, the isobars close up and it gets windier. Now we didn't know whether we were within two kilometres of the centre or eighty kilometres away from it. That's what we didn't know. We just didn't have the information.'

Kulmar, Glyn Charles and Rob Kothe figure the only way to decide what to do is to see if they can find out what's happening to the yachts in front of them. It seems clear to them that conditions are extreme—that the weather is no longer a question of competitive edge, but a matter of survival. It's almost time for the 2.00 p.m. fleet weather forecast and sked. If they don't get anything more from the forecast, *Sword of Orion* will report her conditions and see what advice they can get from yachts ahead of them.

As they are talking about what to do, a mountain of green water flings *Sword of Orion* sideways. Kothe, heading down the companionway to get back on the radio, hurtles into the console. The forecast flashes on—still 45 to 55 knots and no more information. On *Young Endeavour* Lew Carter starts checking off the yachts in alphabetical order. Kothe waits till the letter 'S'. He gives his latitude and longitude. Then he says, 'I don't know where that weather forecast comes from, but it isn't what we're getting here. We're getting 70 and 80 knots.'

Sword of Orion's weather report reverberates through most of the fleet. Its two sentences are a turning point in the Sydney to Hobart. In the space of a few seconds dozens of yachtsmen decide finishing the race is no longer as important as surviving it. There's no doubt *Sword of Orion*'s message saves lives. But, cruelly, one life it won't save that day will be one of its own.

SIXTEEN

It's like most sports—there are grades from the very
experienced to the less experienced. The Sydney to
Hobart encourages a lot of people. It might be the
major race that a lot of people do in that year. So you
get the very experienced who want to do it again and
again and the ones who are less regular and having a
go once or twice.

     —*Steve Kulmar, helmsman,* Sword of Orion

*An ill wind was blowing nobody any good in the 54th
Sydney to Hobart.*

     —*Brian Emerson, skipper,* Miintinta

As a yachtsman, Brian Emerson is a self-confessed 'weekend warrior'.
He's sailed for more than thirty years, done two Hobarts and has raced
to Lord Howe Island. An industrial safety inspector, he's a careful man
who has sailed across a fair bit of ocean but doesn't call himself an
experienced off-shore racer. His yacht *Miintinta*, just under 13 metres
long, is a heavy boat built for cruising the world. More than twenty
years old, *Miintinta* is no cutting edge competitor but, under various
owners, she's made it to Hobart twice and done a round trip to America.
Miintinta is the kind of yacht that doesn't have a computer or weather
fax but does boast a settee, two fridges and a sturdy navigation desk.
Before the Sydney to Hobart, Emerson's comment on the race entry list
notes he and his crew are 'looking forward to a comfortable ride to

Hobart with plenty of baked dinners and chilled wine'. Emerson only hopes to float over the finish line as 'duck' in the cruising division. The *Miintinta* crew will be happy enough to just get to Hobart in time for the New Year's Eve party.

By lunchtime on Sunday it seems likely they will. There's a 35-knot breeze and *Miintinta*'s doing 12 knots on the clock and, with the current, another three or four 'over the ground'. The yacht is about 30 kilometres past Eden and about 60 kilometres out to sea. Emerson's positioning it to make a good Bass Strait crossing. All *Miintinta*'s sails are up and the boat is flying. Then, at about a quarter to three, Emerson hears *Sword of Orion* on the radio.

Emerson doesn't need to think twice about sailing through high seas and 70-knot winds. Within minutes, he takes down *Miintinta*'s mainsail, lashes it as tight as he can, swaps his number two genoa for a storm jib, battens down and turns the yacht on a tack for Eden. He is more than grateful to *Sword of Orion* for the warning. 'My God,' he says later, 'if that had hit us without warning, we would have been in all sorts of strife.' In the light of what happens next, Brian Emerson must put a very high measure on the word 'strife'.

For about forty minutes *Miintinta* makes reasonable progress. Then the sea around it gets heavier. Before long, *Miintinta* is hit by a barrage of backless waves. Emerson sees them towering over him by six, eight, sometimes ten metres. *Miintinta*'s too big to slide down all of them. The boat starts being flung off crests. It feels as if all its 20-tonne weight is being slammed down onto a concrete floor. The waves that don't throw the yacht break over it. But Emerson knows when he's beaten. He has a 72-horsepower diesel engine and plenty of fuel. He doesn't need to be persuaded it's time to use it. 'We withdrew from the race in the interest of crew safety. The waves were coming from all angles and the whole thing was a mass of froth and surf. I just tried to keep the boat on course. Even with the motor on, we were going round in circles. You're just at the mercy of the weather.' Twice, *Miintinta*'s hull hits something so hard Emerson thinks it must be thudding into something more solid than just water. He wonders if he's hit a small whale.

With some relief, after thrashing through the seas for four hours at full speed, Emerson gets *Miintinta* in sight of the shore. He thinks his ordeal is almost over. But his glimpse of the coast is the last land *Miintinta* will see.

Almost as soon as Emerson spots land, *Miintinta*'s powerful motor overheats and dies. The yacht's cabin fills with steam. Emerson pulls open the engine-room doors and checks the water and hoses. He can't see anything wrong. He guesses that, jumping out of the waves so much, the motor has sucked in air which has wrecked its cooling system. There's nothing he can do but let the motor cool down and rely on the storm jib. But just then, the crew notices *Miintinta* is taking on water. The water has come in so fast that there's already too much of it in the cabin, and too much furniture, for them to find the leak. The water starts lifting the floorboards. Emerson and his crew pull the boards out and check the fittings underneath. The water seems to be coming in from the middle of the hull but they can't work out where.

Emerson still isn't too worried. What *Miintinta* lacks in electronics, she makes up for in an impressive array of pumping equipment. Emerson has spent thousands of dollars on some of the best pumps he could buy. He has three pumps altogether. The first is a brand new large-volume electrical bilge pump he's recently had fitted by a licensed marine electrician. It has automatic and manual switching and is connected to two large batteries and a back-up bank of starting batteries. Sailing down the coast, he has heard it switching itself on and off automatically. Now, when he needs it, he puts it on manual. But nothing happens. He lifts the flap over the switching device and checks it. He can't see what's wrong. Suddenly a wave flings *Miintinta* sideways. He flies across the cabin and crashes into the stove. The force of his body breaks the stove apart and smashes one of the galley lockers. It's no time to be fixing electricals.

Emerson turns his attention to a second pump, installed two weeks before the race. This one's manual but should be powerful enough on its own. The pump's already had one problem, just before the race, when its handle broke off. But he had the handle remoulded by a shipwright. Now the handle works fine but another fitting, between the handle and the diaphragm, falls apart after only a few minutes. That leaves pump number three, the last resort, a big double-action bilge pump in *Miintinta*'s rear cabin. The crew take turns working it. But the yacht's still being pounded by waves and each big one is pouring more and more water into the hull. The pump can't keep up. After a few hours, clogged up by debris, it gives up too.

It's old seagoing wisdom that the best pump is a frightened man with a bucket. *Miintinta*'s crew of five has been bailing all along. With the second pump gone, they bail faster. The yacht has two buckets Emerson bought specifically for bailing. If the pumps won't work, at least the buckets should. But soon, adding insult to injury, the bottom of one of the buckets falls out. 'It wasn't going all that well,' muses the luckless Emerson later. 'I thought, somebody up there really doesn't like me.'

To keep bailing, the crew has to resort to two-litre plastic milk containers. Someone cuts the tops off a few of them with a knife. The five crew stand in a line and pass the milk containers and the remaining bucket through the hatchway to be emptied over the side. After a while someone realises they don't need to bother. The boat's flying around so furiously, they just scoop up the water and lob it into the galley sink.

After about four hours, the water level is still rising and everyone is worn out. With only the storm jib to keep it on course, *Miintinta* is being blown further and further out to sea. Brian Emerson decides he has to face the fact that his boat is sinking. But he thinks it will take a few hours to happen. It doesn't seem desperate enough to put out a mayday. So he gets on the HF radio and contacts the Coastal Patrol in Eden. 'We're sinking,' he says. 'We've got time. I don't think there's any drama immediately, but can you get something out here that might tow us in?' After a while, Coastal Patrol calls back to say a trawler has been diverted and should reach *Miintinta* in about three hours. Emerson's message is also picked up by a container ship, *Union Roetigen*. It changes course and in less than an hour the relieved *Miintinta* crew see it standing by a few kilometres away from them.

Emerson helps the others keep up with the bailing. Then, listening to the radio, he hears other boats that sound like they're in more trouble than his own. He's worried that one of them may need *Union Roetigen* more urgently than he does. So he contacts the ship to thank its captain and say he thinks *Miintinta* is OK for now. The crew keeps emptying the milk containers and the bucket. But the water is still rising. Half an hour later, Emerson reluctantly gets back on the radio to *Union Roetigen*. 'Look,' he says, 'are you still there?'

SEVENTEEN

Six lives were lost and fifty-five people were rescued. It could easily have been the other way around.
—*David Gray, spokesman, Australian Maritime Safety Authority*

Just before three o'clock that afternoon, and more than 300 kilometres from the entrance to Bass Strait, Rupert Lamming crosses a deserted, windswept courtyard in Canberra, the national capital. He walks between the glass walls of two identical office buildings, enters one of them, presses the lift button and heads up to the third floor, to the headquarters of the Australian Maritime Safety Authority (AMSA). So far this year, AMSA's Search and Rescue division, where Lamming works, has directed 338 rescue operations. This afternoon, when he turns up for duty, Lamming has no idea that in the next forty hours Search and Rescue will do the equivalent of about six months work. It will have to coordinate seven ships and forty-five aircraft on more than 250 rescue missions.

Even before Rupert Lamming reaches his desk, a red target on his computer screen is blipping a distress signal. The target is in Bass Strait. A Thai freighter, *Thor Sky*, radios in that it has accidentally set off its Emergency Position Indicating Radio Beacon (EPIRB). So the red target appears to be a false alarm. But Lamming, a veteran of fifteen years merchant marine work, isn't satisfied. He decides to check it out.

Emergency beacons, like the global positioning system (GPS) now used by most sailors, work on the same principle used by the military to bomb enemy targets with so-called pinpoint accuracy. GPS works by bouncing a signal off a satellite, converting it to a latitude and longitude reading, and sending it back to the navigator. In the case of a distress beacon, the satellite relays the signal to a ground station. Once an emergency beacon is triggered, it should transmit for at least forty-eight hours. If a beacon is in Bass Strait, its signal should be picked up within an hour by one of the seven polar-orbiting satellites that will regularly pass over it. About once an hour there's a fifteen-minute window in which the satellite can relay the signal to rescuers, through ground stations in Queensland, Western Australia and New Zealand.

Emergency beacons are listed as compulsory equipment for each yacht in the Sydney to Hobart. Some boats carry more than one and some sailors carry their own personal beacons. Two kinds of beacon are in regular use. The older, smaller and cheaper ones transmit on 121.5 MHz and are accurate to about 20 kilometres. The newer, bigger and more expensive beacons transmit on 406 MHz and give a location within five kilometres, as well as a digital readout that includes details of the beacon's owner. Some advanced models can give a position accurate to 100 metres within five minutes. Most yachts in the 1998 Sydney to Hobart rely on the older style of EPIRB. Until this race there has been no reason not to.

But for some time, aviation authorities have been reporting problems with the older beacons. Although the International Civil Aviation Organisation (ICAO) only requires most small aircraft to carry the older beacons, it recommends pilots use the newer ones if they can. The ICAO has found that the older beacons are notoriously unreliable. It has estimated that more than nine calls out of ten are in fact false alarms. There have been reports of searches being instigated in response after stray signals have been picked up from discos and vending machines. The ICAO has also found that search target areas can be skewed if more than one of the older-style beacons are triggered simultaneously.

In Canberra, Rupert Lamming looks again at the target on his computer. He already knows there's bad weather in Bass Strait. He also knows the Sydney to Hobart yacht race is sailing right into it. He checks the report from the Thai freighter. The freighter's beacon is the new style with a signal on 406 MHz. But the target showing up in Bass Strait is transmitting on 121.5 MHz. Lamming asks another Search and Rescue officer to check it out by calling an air charter service in Mallacoota, the town closest to the target. Half an hour later, the charter service phones back. It has picked up a mayday from Bass Strait. It's coming from a yacht. And it doesn't sound like a false alarm.

EIGHTEEN

> *I've never known such a discrepancy. I've never seen such a discrepancy. I wasn't prepared to count on such a discrepancy. I must say that in this day and age when we can put a man on the moon, we should be able to get a closer weather forecast than that.*
>
> —*Iain Moray, skipper,* Siena

Severe storms play havoc with yacht races all over the world. Depending on where they occur, the storms go by various names. In the China Sea they are called typhoons. There, they sometimes coincide with the China Sea Race, a yacht race from Hong Kong to Manila. Iain Moray has done three China Sea races and struck one typhoon. But even the typhoon was more manageable than what he is now experiencing in Bass Strait. Moray, a merchant banker, is a prudent sailor. After the race, he says that if someone had told him about the delayed start of the Melbourne to Hobart yacht race, he would have pulled in to shelter in Eden. But no-one did tell him. At least, not when the delay was first announced, when he could easily have changed course. Now it's too late. It's early afternoon and Moray and six friends, several of them bankers and lawyers, are on his small yacht *Siena*, deep into Bass Strait and heading for the worst of the storm.

Iain Moray is a Scotsman, and comes from a family of sailors. His grandfather was born on board a ship as the family migrated to Australia. His father raced in the Sydney to Hobart, and Moray, who started sailing when he was five, did his first Hobart twenty years ago. This is his sixth

race. Moray wasn't put out by 70-knot winds in the China Sea typhoon.
But he's never seen conditions like he's seeing now. And he never wants
to see them again. *Siena*'s brand-new wind gauge is reading 86 knots,
nearly 160 kilometres an hour. There's so much spume in the air, Moray
can barely see. 'You experience something called "white out", which
means that the sky goes white and the tops are blowing off the waves.
Everything's coming in at you horizontally, like bullets. You can't look at
it, it's so painful. The risk is that if a really big wave comes along and
you're finding it too painful to look into the conditions, then it can catch
you unawares. During the daytime, if you can see a rogue wave, well and
good.' Moray knows that if conditions don't improve before nightfall,
keeping a lookout for rogues will be close to impossible.

Moray often races in Sydney Harbour, but doesn't belong to the
Cruising Yacht Club. This year, his yacht is one of only a few in the
race from the club on the other side of the harbour, the Royal Sydney
Yacht Squadron. The two clubs are separated by a few kilometres of
water and nearly eighty years of tradition. Since early colonial days the
Squadron's roll-call of commodores has included lords, viscounts, gov-
ernors-general and the Duke of Gloucester. Squadron ladies have been
taking tea on the club's lawn and playing bridge in its waterfront rooms
for more than 130 years. In 1962, the club's centenary year, it was Royal
Sydney Yacht Squadron's blue ensign that flew on Australia's first America's Cup challenger, Sir Frank Packer's yacht, *Gretel*. Compared with
the Squadron, the CYCA and its high-profile flagship race, the Sydney
to Hobart, are relative newcomers.

By now, Moray's *Siena* is about 50 kilometres past Gabo Island. In
the twenty-four hours since it left Sydney, *Siena* has sailed more than
400 kilometres. It's an incredible run for an 11-metre yacht, one of the
smaller boats in the race. But the weather has been steadily worsening
since midday. Iain Moray can hear the storm starting to howl. It's a
chilling, almost malevolent, sound.

Iain Moray and his crew talk about turning back, but he is worried
about the seas: 'The problem with turning back was that then you'd
have these very big waves behind you. The trouble with that is you can't
see them till it's too late. So my preference was to sail in and across

them with some sail up, provided it didn't blow out, and to try and keep some steerage and good vision for the waves that were coming.'

There isn't much of a choice, so they keep going. Turning back might put most of the waves behind, but not all. The problem is, they aren't all coming from one direction. And Moray knows that's the danger. 'Bass Strait is different from a place like the China Sea where the water's much deeper and the waves are longer, and they don't do nearly as much damage. In Bass Strait, they come from here one minute and over there the next minute and you have to be able to react to them. If you go to the top of one and launch off, the boat can free-fall. Free-falling does the most damage.' He knows about free-falling. In the 1986 Sydney to Hobart a maxi-yacht he helmed cracked a dozen ribs in its hull coming off the top of waves and had to pump out water all the way to the finish. Now at the beginning of the afternoon, Moray is sailing with two reefs in the mainsail. By the time the wind hits 80 knots *Siena* has only a storm jib.

At 2.00 p.m. *Siena*'s navigator, Tim Evans, tunes into the radio-relay boat *Young Endeavour* for the forecast and the sked. Evans, a solicitor and long-time friend of Moray's, notes down the positions of a few other boats, including a handful within five or six kilometres. He also notes down the forecast: 'A low centred east of Flinders Island will move to the east-south-east. Winds, west to south-west 25 to 35 knots (greater in gusts) increasing to 30 to 40 knots offshore and 40 to 50 knots near the Victorian coast. Swells 1 to 2 metres increasing to 3 metres. Waves 2 to 3 metres increasing to 4 to 5 metres.' But *Siena*'s already getting a consistent 70-knots-plus over the deck and the wind, if anything, seems to be building. Moray can't believe that the forecast can be so out of kilter with what he is seeing.

When Lew Carter reaches the letter 'S', Evans checks in and gives *Siena*'s position. A little later, he writes in the log, 'Note: *Sword of Orion* reports it's recording gusts of 70 to 80 knots.' By the time Carter runs through all 115 yachts, it's around 3.30 p.m. Then Evans, monitoring the emergency frequency, channel 16, hears a TV helicopter trying to reach a yacht called *Wild Thing*. There's no response. A little later, at 3.42 p.m., Tim Evans hears another call. The TV helicopter hears it too: 'Mayday. Mayday. Mayday.'

NINETEEN

There are risks in all sports and there's only been one or two people lost in the history of the race. It's like, why do people live in San Francisco when there's a chance they'll be dead next year because they live on a faultline. It's the same sort of thing.
— *Mike Marshman, crew member,* VC Offshore
Standaside

You're underneath the water, ropes all over you, all tangled up. Your first thought is: I've just got to get to the surface, I'm losing air.
— *Charles Alsop, crewmember,* Standaside

I love the sport dearly, but not enough to die for it.
— *Iain Moray, skipper,* Siena

It's hard to earn a living sailing boats. It's a lot easier to survive selling things to their owners. Sydney to Hobart crews are studded with boat designers, boat insurers and dealers in boating equipment. Andy Marriette is one of them. He sells things yachtsmen will never stop needing—life rafts and safety gear. Marriette is solid, cheerful and doesn't seem easily astonished. It's just as well.

Andy Marriette is doing his third Hobart on a 12.5-metre South Australian yacht, *VC Offshore Standaside*. The skipper, James Hallion, is a senior state public servant. Most of the crew has been put together just for the race. Marriette is one of the more experienced. Among the twelve are Simon Clark, who's sailed since he was a boy, and Mike Marshman, who, like James Hallion, has done one previous Sydney to Hobart. Another, John Culley, is doing the race for the first time. *Standaside* is a fast boat, but Hallion's never raced it to Hobart. Before the race, it's one of the boats randomly checked for safety by race organisers. It passes with flying colours.

The first night out, *Standaside*'s doing well. Later, Simon Clark tells a journalist he thought Hallion drove her 'a bit conservatively'. But Clark obviously has high expectations. The boat, like many others that night, breaks its own speed record. By early Sunday, conditions start getting more difficult. When the wind swings to the south-west and hits 35 knots, the boat's watch system breaks down. A number of the crew are too seasick to keep to their shifts.

By midday Sunday, *Standaside* is getting the 50 knots forecast and the weather isn't improving. Andy Marriette is at the navigation desk, listening to the radio. He hears *Rager* report stronger winds ahead. Soon *Standaside* is surrounded by dark-green waves. They seem to come from the depths of the ocean. Sometime in the afternoon the crew meets to talk about the weather. But by then, *Standaside* is well into Bass Strait, about eight hours from the first landfall to the south and at least six hours from Eden to the north. In the end, they decide to continue south and keep racing, heading a little to the east on a slightly more comfortable course. But at about a quarter past one, the wind speed leapfrogs from 50 knots to 80. Until now, *Standaside* has sailed over the waves. Suddenly they're breaking over the deck. The crew decides to take down all the sails and run east under bare poles. It makes the yacht difficult to manoeuvre, so they try to hoist the storm jib. But the jib blows out of its fittings.

Half an hour later, at 2.15 p.m., Marriette is still below on the radio, waiting to check in for the sked. He has to wait a while. *Standaside*'s full name is *VC Offshore Standaside*, and the sked is in alphabetical order. He hears Carter going down the letters and everyone replying with positions. Marriette keeps waiting for his turn. But he never reaches it. Carter is only about halfway through the alphabet when Marriette hears someone above shout: 'Watch out, there's a big wave coming.' On deck, Simon Clark sees a wall of green water that he thinks looks like a tennis court standing on end. Clark yells, 'Bear away!' But Hallion can't steer down it.

Standaside rides to the top of the wave and sheers to the left. The wave breaks, crashes onto the deck and rolls the boat onto its left side. *Standaside* rolls with the wave. The boat goes down and around, spirals inside the wave, lands upside down and then bounces back upright. It's a 360-degree roll. Below deck, at the navigation desk, Marriette is on the right-hand side of the boat and the top outside edge of the spiral. There's so much centrifugal force that, after the roll, he ends up still sitting in the same place. He doesn't feel a thing. It's like being on a sideshow ride.

Mike Marshman does feel it. Like Clark, he's up on deck and sees the wave just before it hits. Marshman thinks it looks 30 metres high, a green wall towering over *Standaside*'s mast like a ten-storey building. Where the top floors would be, there are two metres of white breaking water. Marshman feels *Standaside* being sucked into the bottom of the wave and flying up to the top of it. When the boat gets near the crest, a blast of wind knocks him over. Next he feels the hull crash into breaking water. Then he doesn't know what happens. He can't tell whether *Standaside* is tipping, rolling or being dumped. All he knows is the boat's upside down and he's in the water, in the middle of Bass Strait, still hooked on by his lifeline. He doesn't have a lot of time to think. 'I was trying to work out what had happened and what I was going to do. Then the boat does its righting motion.'

As the boat spins upright, Marshman is on one end of his lifeline and the whole weight of the yacht is pulling on the other. He feels as if he's being shot out of a cannon. Only he isn't shot out anywhere. He's still under water. 'Amazingly it wasn't all that dark, probably because there was so much air in the water. I remember seeing bubbles. I should have come up the other side. But I didn't.' Marshman thinks he's dead. He isn't scared; he says he's gone too far past it. Like many others that day, he's already been pounded by towering seas, whipped in the face by a jet-stream and thrown across the deck and from one end of his harness to the other. Now he is overboard, under water and trapped like a netted fish in the rigging.

'When I was under water it was amazing what went through my mind,' he says later. 'I saw my family. I thought I would be scared when I was confronted with death, but this wasn't fear for me; it was fear for them without me. It shocked me that I thought like that.' He goes to unhook but something in his brain tells him the last thing to do is let go of the boat. So he tries to untangle himself. Somehow he wriggles free. Before he can work out what's happened, he pops up to the surface and starts breathing.

Marshman grabs the side of the boat, gulps in mouthfuls of air and looks around. The yacht's mast has broken off at deck level and the boom has snapped in half and is folded almost double. On board, everyone is calling out names to see if anyone's missing. Eight of the crew have gone overboard, none of them wearing life jackets. Seven of them were tethered to the yacht but one, John Culley, isn't wearing a harness.

'I was sitting on the rail,' Culley tells a reporter. 'I think I was the furthest forward, and I just heard somebody say "Wave" and somebody say "Oh shit". I had this sensation of a slow-motion roll into the sea. I opened my eyes and I could see the deck underneath the water and a few bodies floating around. When I surfaced, the boat seemed like it was a mile away but it was probably only about 40 metres. I had my waterproof boots on which were filling up with water. I thought, "I'm not going to make it."' The waves and the wind push Culley back to the boat and he and the seven others are dragged back on board by the four crew who were below deck during the rollover. It takes about fifteen minutes to recover them. Mike Marshman has lost a piece of his finger, Simon Clark has snapped a ligament, someone has broken ribs, someone else a gash on the forehead.

The inside of the boat is knee-deep in water. The top of the cabin has been broken off and forced into the main hatchway. Andy Marriette has to push part of the cabin roof out of the navigation station to get out of his seat. A winch handle's gone through the radio control panel. Someone gets out the two life rafts, but one of them doesn't inflate. Then it gets lost overboard. Now there are twelve men on a sinking boat with only one six-man life raft. They set off every emergency beacon they can find, two personal beacons and one for the yacht, and fire a red parachute flare and two orange smoke flares. Fortunately, the boat has a large set of bolt cutters. They cut away the rigging and the broken mast to stop it banging against the boat and holing the hull. Then they ditch the remains of the cabin top and bail till the water only reaches their ankles. 'While we were bailing we could actually see that the bulkheads had moved slightly. One was flapping in the breeze. It was like we were sitting in an egg shell,' says Marriette. The winch handle has destroyed the radio but *VC Offshore Standaside* still has a handheld VHF radio. Someone quickly connects it to the emergency antenna.

TWENTY

◄ ►

*A mayday call denotes an emergency involving
imminent danger to a vessel. If you hear a mayday call
you should not transmit, but continue to monitor the
radio. If a shore station such as the local Coastguard or
Coastal Patrol fails to respond to the call, you should
attempt to relay the message and render any assistance.*
> —*New South Wales Government,* Safe Boating
> Handbook

*A boat or competitor shall give all possible help to any
person or vessel in danger.*
> —*Australian Yachting Federation,* Racing Rules of
> Sailing, *Fundamental Rules, rule 1.1*

*I suppose it really depends on where you draw the line
between safety at sea and success in the race. I feel an
obligation when there are people in distress. Perhaps
other people don't feel it as keenly as I do. But safety is
the number-one issue. I won't compromise the crew and
I won't compromise the boat.*
> —*Iain Moray, skipper,* Siena

VHF radio doesn't travel much further than line of sight. But by a stroke
of luck *Standaside*'s mayday is picked up by the helicopter covering the
race for ABC-TV. On *Siena*, monitoring the emergency channel, Tim

Evans hears the helicopter relaying the mayday and *Standaside*'s position to Canberra. Evans and Iain Moray wait to hear whether any other boats respond. In these conditions, Moray isn't surprised that someone's in trouble. But he's never done a rescue at sea, and he doesn't relish the idea of trying one in this weather. When no-one other than the helicopter responds to the mayday, Evans and Moray check *Siena*'s position. *Standaside* isn't far away. Evans radios the ABC pilot, Gary Ticehurst. Fifteen minutes after the mayday, Ticehurst is hovering over the dismasted yacht. Soon, Iain Moray, having changed course, is heading towards them.

Siena is about a metre smaller than *Standaside* and, even before the mayday, Moray has been struggling to keep the boat upright. He can barely steer down the biggest waves, let alone keep an eye out for the ones that are coming. But until *Siena* picks up the mayday, Moray is still racing south and doing well, coming about second in his division. The last thing he wants to do is turn around. But he does it, without hesitation. 'I have a legal obligation to render assistance,' he says, 'I also have a moral obligation. I'd hope that if I were in distress, somebody would come and rescue me. We only had two excuses for not going to the rescue of another yacht, two questions to ask. One, was our boat in mortal danger? And two, were any of our crew in mortal danger? My answer was no to both questions. So, given they'd issued a mayday call, we had no excuse not to go. You don't issue a mayday lightly.'

Until that afternoon, not too many yachts have had to answer a mayday in a Sydney to Hobart race. The most dramatic rescue occurred in 1993, in Bass Strait, not far from where *Siena* and *Standaside* are now. Back then, the yacht *MEM* lost its skipper, John Quinn, overboard. It was the middle of the night, and there was a 50-knot wind and wild seas. *MEM* sent out a mayday, threw a life ring to Quinn in the vain hope he'd find it, and fired off distress flares. One yacht that saw the flares, *Mark Twain*, called in to say that the conditions were so bad it couldn't do anything to help. The radio-relay boat—back then, also *Young Endeavour*—heard the mayday and *Mark Twain*'s response, and directed the next three closest yachts, *Bacardi*, *Atara* and *Elusive*, to head for Quinn, even though they all estimated it would take them more than three hours to reach him. In Canberra, rescuers also diverted an oil tanker, the *Ampol Sarel*. For four hours, as the three yachts and the tanker headed for the search area, *Young Endeavour* and *Mark Twain* stayed in contact with *MEM*. Finally the diverted boats reached the stricken yacht. By then, Quinn was presumed lost. But half an hour later, a crewman on the tanker heard shouts and spotted him in the water. Quinn was alive. The tanker kept him in sight for another fifteen minutes, until a crewman from *Atara*, Tom Braidwood, could jump overboard in a safety harness and help pull him onto the yacht. By that time, *Atara* had its own problems and was dismasted. Later, it was reported that when Quinn was finally dragged on board, Braidwood said to him, 'You think you're a lucky bastard. You've got onto an ambulance that's about to sink.' *Atara* didn't sink. But two other yachts in the 1993 race did. Fellow yachtsmen rescued the fifteen crewmembers from life rafts.

The story of John Quinn's rescue is legendary, but another incident three years later is less well known. This one involved Ray 'Hollywood' Roberts. Famous for showing businessmen and corporate sponsors a good time on the Harbour, Roberts is just as famous for taking the Sydney to Hobart extremely seriously. One night in the 1996 race, Ray Roberts and his crew on *BZW Challenge* were charging across Bass Strait when they thought they saw a white flare fired ahead of them, to starboard. They reported it to *Young Endeavour* and were directed to investigate. *BZW Challenge* had been flying south with her spinnaker up but Roberts changed course and headed west. He searched the area but couldn't find anything. Forty minutes later, he contacted the control boat—once again, *Young Endeavour*—and reported he was giving up the search and heading back on course for Hobart. Later Roberts argued that the diversion and delay cost him honours on handicap. He asked the race protest committee for a two-hour time allowance, which would have put *BZW Challenge* at the top of the handicap list. But the committee only granted thirty-three minutes. The chairman of the committee, Ken Morrison, said that once Roberts had been directed to investigate, he had no choice but to turn back. But Morrison was skeptical about the basis of Roberts's appeal. Asked why he thought Roberts had asked for a two-hour time allowance, Morrison answered, 'In the minds of the individual requesting redress, they're always going to ask for anything they can get.' In the end, despite Ray Roberts's protest, *BZW Challenge* was placed fourth on handicap.

In the 1998 Sydney to Hobart, there is no record of the radio-relay boat directing any yacht to assist another, though *Young Endeavour* itself does join the search for at least one missing boat. It's likely that, in the conditions, most boats wouldn't have been able to do much to help anyway. But no-one is even asked to try. In theory, race officials shouldn't need to direct boats to assist others—the race rules and the law of the sea already do it. Assisting others where possible is the most fundamental principle of seamanship. It is why rescuers travel far into the Southern Ocean searching for lone sailors. It is why helicopters will fly into the Bass Strait storm, and why rescuers will risk their lives dropping into the water on winches. But the law of the sea is one thing; an individual's decision to follow it is another. For all its comradeship, yacht racing is a costly, competitive and often ego-driven pastime. It can be dangerous and, even for the toughest sailors, frightening. Maybe, in a race, only one person on a yacht sees a distress flare being fired nearby. Maybe they aren't certain what they see. Maybe only one person on a yacht hears a mayday call. Maybe they can't hear the radio clearly enough to be sure. They might turn around to help. Or they might not. They might decide they are in too much danger themselves. Or they might decide there isn't anything they can do, and keep going. In John Quinn's case, turning around saved a life. In the case of Ray Roberts, it may have cost a race victory.

In another incident, not long before the 1998 Sydney to Hobart, a yachtsman almost drowned during a short ocean race off Sydney. That time, a yacht called *Quest* was rounding a mark when it got into trouble and lost a crewman overboard. A number of other boats in the race were nearby. The crew of at least one other boat saw the man in the water, but didn't stop. When he was eventually picked up after twenty-five minutes in the water, the man was close to exhaustion. He said he could only have survived a few minutes longer.

After that Sydney race, the CYCA's commodore, Hugo van Kretschmar, was sufficiently concerned to publish a warning in the club's magazine:

> Losing a crewman overboard at any time is a serious matter. What is of particular concern about this incident is that at least one boat, which may have been able to recover the man sooner than anyone else, elected not to. I cannot imagine and certainly do not suggest, that their decision not to render assistance was based on any disregard of human life. The skipper of that yacht has said that they did not know that *Quest* was unable to turn around and pick him up, they were monitoring the radio and heard no call for assistance from *Quest*. They saw that the man in the water was unhurt and not distressed and they were experiencing considerable problems keeping their own boat under control. They also saw a number of other boats in the vicinity which would have seen the incident, and so they reasonably assumed he would be quickly rescued.

But van Kretschmar points out that these assumptions might be wrong. He adds that, from personal experience, a fully-clothed man in the water without a life jacket can get in trouble very quickly. A few years earlier, the same thing had happened to him.

That time, it was van Kretschmar's then nine-year-old son, Matt, who went overboard (without a life jacket) during a race. Realising that it was going to take some time to sort out the problems and get back to pick him up, van Kretschmar dived overboard (also without a life jacket) to stay with him. Father and son spent nearly twenty-five minutes in the water before the rest of the crew could pick them up. Hugo van Kretschmar continues:

> When we were eventually picked up, Matt and I were close to drowning. I was numb from the exhaustion of keeping both our heads above the breaking two-foot chop in the harbour and could not have kept us afloat for much longer. During that time at least a dozen boats passed within 25 metres of us, saw us and sailed on. Each of them (I spoke to many of them afterwards), said the same thing—'we had our hands full; we

could see you were alright and we thought the next boat/the fishing boat/ your yacht would pick you up'.

The incident happened in broad daylight in Sydney Harbour.

After the *Quest* incident in Sydney Harbour, the CYCA spoke to a number of skippers whose boats passed by the man overboard. The club came close to taking further action but decided against it. It wasn't the only time the issue arose that year. Earlier in the season, another yachtsman faced a criminal charge of failing to render assistance. He was competing in a CYCA harbour race when his boat caused a small skiff sailed by two teenagers to capsize. The court convicted him.

The club's commodore, Hugo van Kretschmar, emphasises that yacht racing is based on honour. 'Sailing isn't a professional sport,' he says. 'There's no money at stake here. It's not people competing for prize money, trying to get an unfair advantage, it's a sport where you get a valueless silver trophy. You're out there to achieve your own personal goals, to compete with your peer groups. If you're going to cheat or play outside the rules, where's the enjoyment for you?' Soon after the 1998 race van Kretschmar says he'd be horrified to think one boat wouldn't help another. But he already knows it can happen.

When *Standaside* maydays, Iain Moray doesn't hear race organisers direct anyone to help it. They certainly don't direct him to do so. Like most in the Sydney to Hobart he has spent thousands of dollars preparing for the race. He knows he's throwing in the chance of a place in his division. But he has no doubt about what to do. Six months earlier, in the winter race season, he saw a man and his son in trouble in a small boat in Sydney Harbour. 'I saw a number of people sail past them. They weren't in our race but I took down my spinnaker and went back to pull them out of the water.' Now Moray does the same for *Standaside*. 'Obviously,' he says, 'there were people in distress and we got to them as quickly as we could.'

Shortly after hearing the mayday, Moray turns downwind. His first vision of *Standaside* is of a yacht with no mast, floating low in the water. It looks as if the top of its cabin has been torn off with a can opener.

TWENTY-ONE

*These are the worst conditions I've seen. I'm starting to
ask questions like, 'Why am I here?' and, 'How come I
didn't know about this?'*
                                        —Iain Moray, skipper, Siena

'Can you believe this fucking weather, mate?'
'I really thought you'd seen all this before.'
*'Not as bad as this, mate. Does what I'm saying make
sense?'*
'About what?'
'Advice to these guys.'
*'Oh sure. But Siena's crazy to come in close. One boat
on top of the other. That would be ugly.'*
    —ABC helicopter pilot Gary Ticehurst to cameraman
        Peter Sinclair, as they hover above Standaside

Australia's national broadcaster, the ABC, has been covering Sydney to
Hobart yacht races for as long as most people can remember. Even now
that a rival commercial network owns the broadcast rights, most of the
televised pictures are still shot by the ABC. That's because few people
know how to cover the race better than the ABC's chief helicopter pilot,
Gary Ticehurst.

In TV news, Ticehurst is one of the best in the business. He's nursed
generations of raw cadet journalists through their first stories. He's found
fishermen washed off rocks and children missing in bushland. Reporters

know they couldn't be in better hands. If they need to fly somewhere, he will usually be the first pilot to get there and the first to find the story. He'll probably know more about it than the journalists do.

After Ticehurst hears *Standaside*'s mayday and relays it to Search and Rescue, he heads for the yacht, and reaches it shortly before *Siena* does. *Standaside* tells him three of its crew are quite badly hurt. Canberra calls Ticehurst back: a rescue helicopter should be on the spot within the hour.

About 400 kilometres away, paramedic Peter Davidson is sitting in his office in Victoria's Latrobe Valley. It's almost the end of his shift and he's trying to wind down. Davidson's forty years old and has been with the Victorian Ambulance Service for thirteen years. For the last eight years he's worked with the air ambulance rescue wing, Heli-Med. As he puts it, he's 'the guy who goes down a wire'. Helicopter rescuers are paramedics' elite troops, selected from among the most experienced ambulance workers by exams, interviews and more exams. If they pass all of that, they are put through a year's training in surgery and winching. Several times a year Peter Davidson practises being lobbed down into lakes, bushland and mountains. At least once a year, he's dropped into Bass Strait. Davidson, who used to be a welder, stumbled into the job by accident. 'I remember driving past the ambulance bay one day and thinking, "I wonder what it would be like to be an ambulance officer."' He went for an interview and found out.

Now Davidson's feeling warm and comfortable behind his desk. In two hours time he's heading off on his annual holiday. But the holiday is about to be delayed. A call comes in. Search and Rescue in Canberra is reporting an emergency beacon in Bass Strait. Davidson, pilot Peter Lee, and winch operator David Sullivan head out to the chopper. Two hours later, Davidson will be in the ocean, struggling to keep air in his lungs and his head above water.

Davidson and the crew have worked together for years. Soon after take-off, they pick up details of the emergency. Over the helicopter's radio they hear *Standaside* telling the ABC helicopter the yacht has rolled over and several people on it are injured. They check with Search and Rescue, and are directed to rescue the yacht's crew. But first they have to refuel at Mallacoota, on the Victorian coast just near the New South Wales border.

At around the same time, about 60 kilometres out to sea, Gary Ticehurst is struggling to hold his position. He's got 60 knots on the dial, just trying to hover. The cloud base is low and, even up at this level, the air's filled with spume from the breaking waves. He spots *Siena* coming to stand by, and keeps up communications with its navigator Tim Evans, as well as with *Standaside*. *Standaside* has sent its one remaining life raft overboard. On *Siena* Iain Moray is doing his best to circle the disabled yacht. He has his engine on, but the 20-horsepower motor isn't much help in these conditions. Huge, steep waves are standing up and breaking in every direction. Moray is close enough to see that the crew on *Standaside* looks worried. That's close enough. Moray's not quite sure how he'd rescue them if they end up in the water. Below deck, Evans is being thrown around the cabin while trying to stay on the radio.

'*Siena*, *Siena*, this is search aircraft. Over.'

'This is *Siena*.'

'Will you be able to hold your position there OK?'

'I'll inquire and get back to you.'

'Have you still got the boat in sight?'

Shortly, Evans calls back: 'Search aircraft, this is *Siena*. We're trying to hold position. It is very difficult. Over.'

'I know. We understand that. No problem.'

But now, the calls from *Standaside* are sounding more urgent. Ticehurst radios Search and Rescue: 'There's 30-foot waves hitting this boat and the skipper's justifiably getting anxious. You can tell that. I'm not quite sure how long he can hold this out. What's the latest estimate for the rescue heli?'

The message comes back: two helicopters are on their way, the first one, coming from Latrobe Valley, will be followed by another from Canberra; but both need to refuel, and they'll take about another half-hour. Gary Ticehurst reports that *Siena* is still standing by. From where Ticehurst's trying to hover, *Siena* looks small and vulnerable. He starts to worry there could soon be two yachts in trouble. Ticehurst radios

Search and Rescue: 'I do have a smaller yacht, *Siena*, close by but I believe in these conditions it would be more hazardous to put another yacht next to this one than the worth of what *Siena* could do for this yacht. Over.'

'Roger. Copy that. The thing that he may be able to assist with, though, is that if they have to get into the water, either individually or in life rafts, he may be able to help them.'

Search and Rescue wants *Siena* to stay nearby.

Ticehurst calls *Siena* back: 'Message from Maritime Safety.'

'Roger.'

'AMSA wondering if you feel able to hold in the area of *Standaside* here in case persons have to take to a life raft or abandon ship prior to rescue.'

Evans answers: 'This is *Siena*. I will inquire. However we are not that manoeuvrable. We are under very small sail. The sea is very rough down here though we do have our engine on.'

It's about 4.30 p.m. when Evans stands up to go and talk to his skipper. By now everyone on *Siena* is exhausted and Moray is having a break from the helm. Suddenly the other helmsman calls 'Wave!' Moray grabs onto a winch. Tonnes of water dump over him and almost throw him out of the boat. Down below Evans is pitched clean across the cabin. From the chopper, Ticehurst sees the top of *Siena*'s mast hit the water.

When Evans tries to pick himself up, he's in so much pain he can hardly breathe. He has broken three ribs and punctured his lung. Another crewman's hand is badly hurt. Moray is worried: 'I felt very responsible for everyone on board. We had a young guy of twenty and the oldest fellow was fifty-five. I was worried about him in particular. I had wanted him to come to Hobart with me for many years and he'd always said "no". But this year he said, "Yes, I'll come", and I felt a particular responsibility to Steve.' It was more than just a personal responsibility. Moray's friend Steve, who has sailed for most of his life, is better known as deputy governor of the Reserve Bank of Australia, Dr Stephen Grenville. Moray says later, 'I couldn't help thinking: the economy is going pretty well. I'd better not lose him.'

After the knockdown Moray decides that *Siena*'s own safety has to be his first priority. He has to abandon the rescue. Moray contacts Ticehurst, reports that *Siena*'s crew is injured and asks permission to leave. Ticehurst tells him the rescue helicopter is less than five minutes away. *Standaside*'s ordeal is almost over.

But for Iain Moray and his exhausted crew, the ordeal is only beginning. Tim Evans is in agony, but even a rescue helicopter can't help him. The only way to lift him off *Siena* would be to have him winched up, but putting a sling round his broken ribs would probably be too dangerous. Moray thinks *Siena* would be safest sailing south to Tasmania, but he worries Evans is in too much pain to last the distance. Evans needs a hospital as soon as possible, so Moray decides to head back to Eden, about 110 kilometres to the north. Soon after he sets a course, *Siena*'s motor packs up. Moray guesses it has taken in water. He continues heading north, but without the motor the yacht can't make it into Eden. It's blown in front of the gale till Moray finally lands it north of Eden, in the small fishing port of Bermagui. But that's not until midday the next day. The trip takes nearly twenty-four hours. By then, Evans is coming down with pneumonia. As soon as Moray gets ashore, he calls an ambulance. Evans is rushed to Moruya Hospital. By 4.00 p.m. that afternoon, he's undergoing surgery. He's lost sixty per cent of the use of his lung. It will take him months to recover.

Watching the doctors operating on his friend, Iain Moray decides that unless something changes in the future, he won't be racing in another Sydney to Hobart—he'll only race again if the weather forecasts are improved and if they are more frequent.

Moray isn't the only skipper who helps other sailors during the Sydney to Hobart storm. But some others, in much bigger and heavier boats, say the conditions are too bad for them to even try. Moray and his crew pay a high price for trying to help. But Moray says they would do the same thing again. 'Safety,' he adds, 'has to be the number-one issue. When do you stop racing? When you get to the finish, or when everyone's dead?'

TWENTY-TWO

*We picked a wave, picked the conditions and turned
back to Eden. It turned out it was the wrong decision
because the weather moderated much more quickly
going south than it did going back up north. But that's
the information we didn't have and couldn't analyse.
We were without information. It would have been
lovely to have had it and we might have gone in a
different direction. We certainly wouldn't have turned
back if we'd known how the weather was actually going
to go. What actually happened is that we turned back
into the worst of it.*

—*Rob Kothe, skipper,* Sword of Orion

Sunday, 27 December 1998
Mid-Afternoon

Sailors can't change the weather. All they can do is chase after the best of
it and, if they are racing, hope to find it sooner, and more often, than
their opponents. Usually, apart from the various radio forecasts, boats
aren't supposed to get outside assistance with weather. Generally, it's not
the done thing to give away information and it's not the done thing to
ask for it.

As a result, although *Sword of Orion*'s weather report sounds an alarm
through most of the fleet, only one yacht decides to add to it. That
boat, Geoff Ross's *Yendys*, calls in to say that it too is getting winds over
70 knots. But *Yendys* is quite close to *Sword of Orion*. Its confirmation

disappoints Steve Kulmar because it doesn't throw any light on the conditions ahead. 'We didn't hear from anybody. We heard from one other boat who was within two miles of us and he just confirmed he was in the same conditions. It was of no assistance. I think he felt that he had an obligation, because we had said something, to confirm it, which was good of him. We just would have liked more detail: which way the storm was moving, where we were in respect of it and the conditions that the yachts in front of us may have been encountering.'

Other yachts could give more useful information, but they don't. 'I think,' says Kulmar, 'we purposely informed the fleet, hopeful that some-body in front of us might have said something. We were about seventh, eighth or ninth in the fleet at that stage. So there were six or seven boats in front of us and also the two maxi-boats, both of which had radios, and one of which came up in the sked at a pretty similar time to us. I think it would have been nice to have known what they were experi-encing because they were about 60 miles in front of us. There was another group of yachts about 20 miles in front of us, which would have been where we'd be at about dusk. It doesn't mean conditions would be exactly the same when we got there because things alter too much. But at least we would have had an indication of what maybe our next twelve to eighteen hours of sailing were going to be like.

'I mean, some may classify it as outside assistance and outside the rules,' Kulmar adds. 'That may be so. But I think, when you're sailing in survival conditions, you should help each other. We were all in essentially the same conditions. I don't think anyone had the weather information that gave them everything they needed. We could have all used the information, even the guys in front of us. They may have been sailing in 50 knots, so if we're back behind them in 70, they'd know that maybe conditions are altering. So it may have helped them, too.'

On the radio-relay boat, *Young Endeavour*, Carter realises *Sword of Orion*'s report is out of the ordinary. But he sees no need to break the taboo and ask others for more information. Carter interprets *Sword of Orion*'s call as simply a personal warning: 'It's unusual, most yachts don't do that, but he's an experienced yachtie, the owner. He realised where the smaller yachts probably would have been, so he was probably trying to forewarn me to forewarn other yachts as to the weather he was getting.'

Carter adds that the last thing that's needed is everyone else chipping in and clogging up the radio. 'You only really need the one yacht to warn you. Everything's honesty in yachting, so whatever information they passed on would certainly be accurate, within maybe two or three knots, or whatever their instruments are showing. In this case it was reinforced by another yacht. It's important to keep the airwaves open, so we really only need one or two to suggest what the weather is. We don't want all the yachts to come in and start telling me what the weather is, otherwise you block the airwaves and the safety factor goes out the window.'

That afternoon in Bass Strait it's probably impossible to guarantee *anyone's* safety. But some places are more perilous than others. By early morning Clouds Badham has already worked out that the storm's worst winds will lie behind it and that the most dangerous seas will build up around Gabo Island, near the confluence of warm and cold currents. His analysis is far more detailed than any of the forecasts provided by the Bureau of Meteorology. Though the bureau's forecasts are said to be specially tailored to the Sydney to Hobart, the only real difference between the race forecast and the general shipping forecast is that it is recast to cover the race area.

After the race it is clear that many of the yachts that decide to change course and head for shelter strike trouble. But they aren't the only ones. And turning around isn't the problem. The problem, as predicted by Clouds but unknown to the yachts at the time, is that the worst seas build up where the storm hits the confluence of currents. And that is near Gabo Island, on the way back to Eden.

On Sunday afternoon, as the sked ends, the wind around *Sword of Orion* drops off almost completely. For about fifteen minutes, it hovers around 15 knots, like a light habour breeze. There's some talk about putting up more sail. Rob Kothe wonders if *Sword of Orion* is in the eye of the storm. But how to tell? 'We didn't know if this thing had five eyes, whether it was a local squall or how big its diameter was. So we just waited. And breathed deeply.' Then, at about 3.15 p.m., the wind comes back. It's worse than before. The *Sword of Orion* crew has another discussion. As Steve Kulmar recalls it, 'Rob Kothe left the decision for retirement ultimately between three helmsmen, myself, Glyn Charles and Brownie. Our decision to retire was unanimous. Rob would have dearly loved to continue, but at the time we made it, given the information we had, I'm sure the decision to retire was the right one. We were left with no other option.'

Kothe backs up the decision, 'I had said to the guys, "If it gets beyond 70 knots I'll seriously look at pulling the pin." Now, no-one wants to do that. But the problem was, it was getting late in the afternoon. We were going to run out of daylight. So the plan was to go back, and sanity was very much prevailing. People have got families. The aim is to survive and do it again, not be gung-ho. Many of the boats had turned back at that stage.'

So, at 3.35 p.m., *Sword of Orion* re-organises its crew, picks a wave and turns around. It is a fateful decision.

TWENTY-THREE

I don't think you can go out expecting to know what the conditions are like. It was a once in a lifetime experience. If I had to do it again, I'd be prepared because I know how horrible and dangerous it can be. At least I've seen the worst.

—Kristy McAlister, paramedic, SouthCare

Looking out of the chopper, Heli-Med paramedic Peter Davidson, can see waves crashing around the floundering yacht below him. He guesses some of the walls of deep-green water are rising up more than 18 metres. The wind's blowing so hard, pilot Peter Lee is having trouble holding a hover; the chopper is tossing around in the air almost as wildly as the yacht is pitching in the water.

Below them, Mike Marshman is sitting on *Standaside*'s deck. He has turned his back to the waves so he doesn't have to watch them. It's bad enough feeling the boat being lifted up and flung down with each one. Sometimes a burst of spray flies over him. But none of the waves matches the size of the giant that rolled them earlier. Marshman has seen so many rescues on television that he never had the slightest doubt someone will rescue him. When the helicopter arrives, he isn't surprised. He watches it trying to hover nearby, figuring that the rescuers are trying to work out what to do. He's right.

Davidson is thinking through the options. He realises he can't drop down onto the boat to lift anyone off it directly—he'd probably be killed just trying to land on its lurching deck. The Heli-Med crew, Peter

Davidson, Peter Lee and David Sullivan, have worked together for a long time and have developed a system. Before every rescue, the three of them talk through the risks and alternatives. They make a joint decision whether or not to go ahead. But the final call is Davidson's. He's the one who has to go down on the wire. The cable he'll go down on is between 100 and 200 metres long and rated to carry about 270 kilos, easily enough for two people. It's Sullivan's job to drop him in the right place, leaving some slack on the cable. Lee has to maintain a steady hover above while Davidson puts a strop on the survivor. Then Davidson signals he's ready by sticking his arms out, both thumbs up, and Sullivan hauls in the cable. But hauling in the cable isn't as easy as it sounds. In the water, if the line catches, it can pull the chopper and the whole team down with it. On the way up, the cable can easily start twisting or catch on the skids of the helicopter.

Unsure how badly the yachtsmen are injured and how they would manage in the water, the Heli-Med crew decides to get them into the life raft two at a time and pull them up from there. The first two into the raft are Simon Clark and Mike Marshman. In the raft, Marshman can no longer avoid looking at the waves. They're coming right at him. Any minute, he thinks, the life raft will flip over. Marshman sees Davidson drop down on the wire and swing close to the life raft. Then a wall of water breaks on top of him and sweeps him away. Seven or eight times, David Sullivan tries to winch Davidson into the raft. But it's impossible. Each time Davidson is blown or washed away from it. Finally, looking up from the end of the line, Davidson sees Sullivan throw both hands in the air and shrug his shoulders. The plan isn't working. Sullivan winches Davidson back to the chopper. Yelling at each other over the wind and engine noise, they decide to give up on the raft and instead put Davidson straight into the water.

Though Marshman can see they're in trouble, he isn't too worried. The rescues he's seen on television are always successful and he can't imagine this one will be any different. It only occurs to him later that television doesn't usually show the disasters. This time Davidson comes down on the wire and lands in the water. He swims to the life raft and throws his arm over the side. Just then a wave hits him. Davidson is tumbled under the raft. When he comes up, he's been dragged about 25 metres away from it.

Finally Davidson swims back to the raft and climbs in. He shouts instructions. Until now, Marshman hasn't realised that all there is on the end of the line is a sling. He has to put his arms up while Davidson puts it over him. Then, if he doesn't keep his arms pinned to his sides he'll fall out. But Davidson isn't planning to let him go. He locks Marshman in a bearhug. Suddenly, a wave launches both of them out of the raft. They surf about 20 metres sideways through the water. Then Sullivan tightens the wire and the two fly upward. Marshman doesn't look down. All he can see is Peter Davidson's face. Davidson breaks into a smile. Later, Davidson tells Marshman he felt like he'd just caught his first big fish.

That day, Davidson almost loses count of the fish he catches. He just keeps going. The whole time Peter Lee has to struggle to hold the helicopter steady. He aims to keep it about 25 metres above the boat. But the boat's rising and falling wildly. Sometimes it tumbles metres into wave troughs. Several times it's only a few metres below the chopper. At one point a wave throws Davidson out of the life raft so violently, he thinks he's broken his back. 'There was so much force it was like being in an explosion. I remember being under water and I didn't know whether the guy was still in the chest harness. I was surprised to see he was still there.' Above Davidson, Lee feels the force of the wave tug on the helicopter. It's so strong he thinks the winch cable has broken.

Davidson has practised martial arts for eighteen years. He's extraordinarily fit. Barely pausing, he does eight rescues in a row. During the eighth one, just before he's pulled up, the winch cable loops around his leg. 'The cable is very taut and can cut you in half. One of the things you learn early on is never to get the cable caught.' He has to summon his last drop of energy to kick his leg free. After that, he's too tired to signal Sullivan that he's ready to be lifted, 'I couldn't lift my arm. I tried to lift it but it fell down. I tried to lift it again. I think the crew got the gist of it.' When he lands in the helicopter, he's so exhausted he can't move. He can't get up to close the door. He lies on his back dry retching.

With the crew, there are eleven people crammed into the helicopter. It's too noisy to talk and the yachtsmen seem too stunned to try. Peter Davidson sees Sullivan grinning broadly. Davidson feels lucky to be alive. Over the last eight years on the helicopter, he's done about eight ocean rescues. Now, he's just done another eight in one afternoon. He thinks, 'Thank Christ it's over.' But he knows it isn't. As he puts it, 'You don't really rescue anyone till you get back to dry land.'

Peter Lee has been thinking much the same thing. He's running low on fuel. And he knows that the trip back to Mallacoota, against the wind, will take a lot longer than the trip out to sea. (He's right. The chopper takes thirteen minutes on the way out and fifty-five minutes on the way back.) As Davidson hauls up the eighth man, Lee is relieved to see another chopper has arrived to take over. It's the SouthCare helicopter, based in Canberra. On board is thirty-year-old paramedic Kristy McAlister.

McAlister has never been winched down into the sea, much less into a full throttle storm. Only two months ago she was working with the ambulance service, mainly doing road accidents. Then she decided she wanted something different. Over the last two months she's abseiled from buildings, done swimming tests, running tests, more medical training and a psychological assessment. She's even practised winching people out of the calm, waist-deep waters of Canberra's Lake Burley Griffin. But she's never winched anyone out of the ocean.

That day McAlister is working with pilot Ray Stone, crewman Mark Delf and another new recruit, Michelle Blewitt. Earlier in the day they picked up a man who had fallen off a balcony in Jervis Bay and flew him a couple of hundred kilometres north to a Sydney hospital. On their way back to Canberra someone joked about being called out to the Sydney to Hobart yacht race. Twenty minutes later, they are. At first they assume they'll only be needed as back-up. It's only when they land in Merimbula to refuel that they see the extent of the problem. 'We realised,' says McAlister, 'shit, this is a big job.'

Until the helicopter is over the sea, Kristy McAlister has no idea how bad the conditions are. By the time they reach *Standaside*, she and Michelle Blewitt are airsick. 'Our crewman, Delfy, said "Are you alright to go?" I was quite sick,' says McAlister, 'but once he said that, I had something else to focus on. All I could think of was how I was going to do the job. Before I went down, I was absolutely petrified.'

Below, one of the four remaining *Standaside* crew is equally anxious. Having watched eight rescues, Andy Marriette is starting to think he'd be happier staying where he is. He has survived the roll with only a cut to his thumb. The sea is still frightening. But Andy Marriette has one greater fear. It's heights. He looks at McAlister sitting in the doorway of the helicopter. She's wearing a wetsuit, life jacket, flippers and a lightweight helmet. It doesn't occur to Marriette that McAlister might be a woman. He doesn't care. He just wants to get the whole thing over with as quickly as possible.

Sitting on the edge of the helicopter, McAlister feels the wind hit her face. It feels as if she's stuck her head out the window of a speeding car. She looks down. For some reason, the next crewman isn't in the life raft. He's in the water. And he's already drifting away from the boat. She has to go. She holds her breath and jumps. Slamming into the water she is driven under by a wave. As she splutters back to the surface she sees the man a few metres away from her, shows him the strop and screams that she's putting it over him and he'll have to keep his arms down. Everything goes according to plan. Minutes later she is going down to do a second rescue. It goes routinely, too. But after it, and at the end of a sixteen-hour workday, McAlister is exhausted. She lies in the helicopter, vomiting up seawater.

There are two men still left on the boat. One of them is Andy Marriette. Reluctantly, he gets into the life raft. But at that moment, it flips over. 'It catapulted me out. We'd squashed the roof down so we could be lifted out. I had to swim back.' He struggles back and climbs in. 'Then it rolled again and I was trapped underneath. I was drinking water for a while, then the wind lifted the side of the raft and I popped back out, coughing up water.' For a while, Marriette thinks he's finished. 'I'd already said my goodbyes. I was sure I'd gone. It was just a surprise that I actually came back.'

In the helicopter it's Michelle Blewitt's turn to go down the wire. Like McAlister, Blewitt has never done a winch from the ocean. 'I didn't want to watch what Kristy was doing,' she says, 'I didn't want any preconceived ideas. I wanted to think about my training.' Blewitt is already throwing up from the air turbulence. She's so sick that crewman Mark Delf is surprised she takes the leap. During his years in the Navy he knew experienced frogmen who would have refused.

'I couldn't just sit there and say I can't go down because I'm frightened,' says Blewitt. 'It isn't an option because I'm here; I'm trained to do it and it's my job to do it. It wasn't till I was on the way down—it was like—*whoa!*' She goes into what rescuers call 'ambo mode'—total focus on the job at hand. She drops down near Marriette and tells him to put the strop over his shoulders. It's too small for him and he has to put it around his legs. He slides in, she grabs him and they fly out of the water. Marriette finds it far more terrifying than anything he's been through on the boat. 'I *hate* heights,' he screams. 'Will you hurry up and get them to pull this thing up, I'm scared stiff.' But Andy Marriette isn't destined to get out in a hurry. He and Blewitt are about eight metres above the water when the winchman notices the life raft is tangled in the cable. He lets out the wire, and Marriette and Blewitt plunge back into the water. Blewitt knows that if she can't cut the raft away, the helicopter crew might have to cut the cable loose. She only has a small knife in her harness. 'I thought I was going to die. I have a husband and two children. I thought, what am I doing this for?' But she manages to cut away the raft and she and Marriette fly up again.

Marriette doesn't even feel the down-draught from the helicopter. The wind's too ferocious. Propelled skyward, he looks down to see the contents of his pockets falling into the ocean. He watches his new strobe light, the skipper's cheque book and $400 in cash float off into Bass Strait. He wonders if someone will find them in New Zealand.

'It takes a little bit of convincing to get me to go down again,' says Blewitt. She needs a few minutes to recover, but there's no time. The last man, skipper James Hallion, is already in the water. The winch goes relatively easily. After his rescue, the chopper turns and heads back into the wind. McAlister and Blewitt are violently ill. But the two chopper crews have pulled it off. By 6.30 that evening, a little more than four hours after they were rolled, the twelve *Standaside* crew are heading back to dry clothes and warm food in Merimbula. It's only then that they and their rescuers realise how many other distress calls are coming through.

'I don't think until then anyone understood how horrendous the conditions were,' says Kristy McAlister. By the time they land, she has already made up her mind that she'll go back if she has to. 'When you save lives, you save lives. It's my job and I love it.'

Michelle Blewitt needs more time to decide. Lying in bed that night, she knows she has to make up her mind before morning. She feels that she needs, 'to get back on this horse.' She decides she will.

Later that day James Hallion's wife hears the race is in trouble and phones the organisers in Hobart. Just as she's being reassured that *Standaside* is safe, she glances at the television. She sees the yacht's crew being winched up into a helicopter. Within hours, pictures of the rescue are being shown all over the world. On television, it all looks deceptively easy.

After the race, Mike Marshman can't help wondering what might have happened if *Standaside* had not been one of the first yachts to mayday. The first time he sees the rescue on TV, he can't bear to watch it. After the race, his yacht club holds a gathering in Adelaide. Marshman meets his rescuer, Peter Davidson: 'I didn't know how I'd feel. It was great to meet Peter. But that night, when I drove away from it all, I felt very funny. I can't help but think: if our mayday was received after *Winston Churchill*'s, we might have lost lives on our boat. I feel sick about those deaths and think we may have been saved because we were going so well in the race, and hit the storm first, and therefore managed to get our mayday in first.'

Above: The fleet on its way out of Sydney Harbour at the start of the 1998 Sydney to Hobart race, with maxi-yacht *Sayonara* in the lead. (Gregg Porteous/News Limited)

Below: The route of the race, which covers 630 nautical miles (1000 kilometres). (James Mills-Hicks)

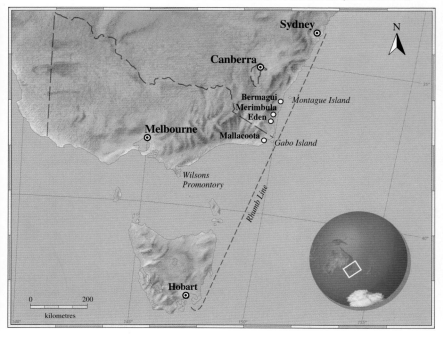

Above: A gleaming *Winston Churchill* and her crisply attired crew at the start of the race. (Roy Haverkamp/News Limited)

Left: The next day: *VC Offshore Standaside* wallows with a broken mast and snapped boom after being rolled by a massive wave. (Peter Sinclair/ABC-TV)

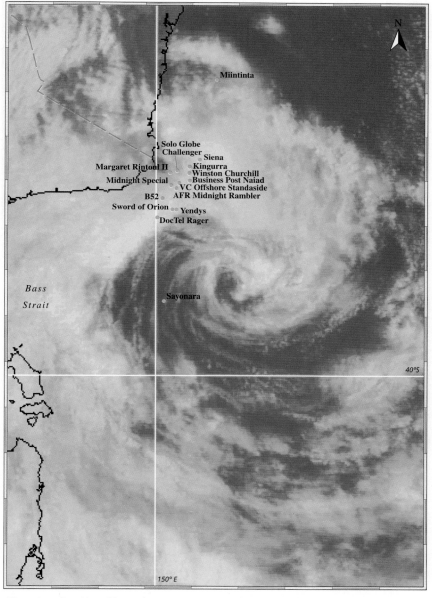

The estimated position of key yachts at 2.00 p.m. on Sunday 27 December, superimposed on a satellite image of the ferocious storm—an extreme event, in meteorological terms.

(Positional map by James Mills-Hicks, superimposed on a satellite image processed by the Bureau of Meteorology, originally from the Geostationary Meteorological Satellite of the Japan Meteorological Agency)

Above: A *Standaside* crew-member is winched from the wild seas by the SouthCare chopper team.
(Peter Sinclair/ABC-TV)

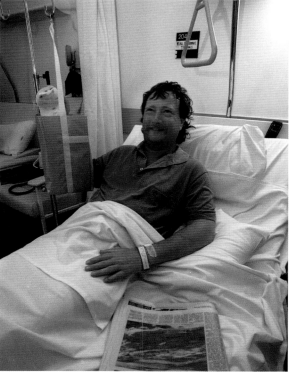

Left: *Standaside*'s Mike Marshman recovering in Latrobe Regional Hospital after the dramatic rescue.
(Peter Smith/News Limited)

Above: *Business Post Naiad*, with the bodies of Bruce Guy and Phil Skeggs still aboard, after the helicopter rescue of its seven surviving crew. Sails were streamed from the bow in an attempt to steady the yacht. (Jay Towne/News Limited)

Below: *Business Post Naiad* crewmember Jim Rogers, splattered with engine oil from the boat's roll, back on dry land, shocked and grief-stricken. (Ray Strange/News Limited)

Above: Police examine *Business Post Naiad* after it was towed into Eden. The boat was later scrapped on the Eden tip. (Nick Cubbin/News Limited)

Right: The damage inside *Business Post Naiad*, looking aft to the fractured port bulkhead, with the galley to the right. Food, ropes, clothing, sails and personal belongings are strewn around the cabin. (Drew Murray)

Left: *Sword of Orion* floundering. Its crew were forced to abandon it after they were hit by a huge wave that washed British Olympian Glyn Charles overboard to his death. (Andrew Taylor/*Sydney Morning Herald*)

Above: *Kingurra*'s John Campbell, perhaps the luckiest man in the race, with his rescuers, Victoria Police Air Wing's David Key, Barry Barclay and Darryl Jones. Campbell was plucked from the ocean more than half an hour after being washed overboard.
(Peter Meikle)

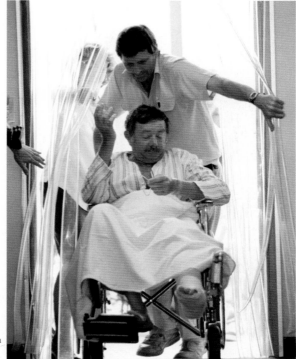

Right: *Winston Churchill*'s helmsman John 'Steamer' Stanley, rescued after seeing three of his teammates swept away from the life raft in which he spent more than 18 hours.
(Nick Cubbin/News Limited)

Above: *Winston Churchill* skipper Richard Winning rescued after surviving a harrowing day in one of the yacht's two life rafts.
(Michael Klein/News Limited)

Left: The six wreaths cast into the water off Hobart's Constitution Dock in the memorial service for the sailors who died in the race.
(Tony Palmer/News Limited)

TWENTY-FOUR

I don't think any sport has the right to endanger someone's life. If you're doing something for a living or with some absolutely hellbent twist to achieve something, well, that's your own course. But if you're participating in a sport like sailing or any other sport, I don't think you should be at the mercy of that kind of extreme fury. I'm still shattered by the experience. I haven't come to grips with what to do from here.
—Steve Kulmar, *chief helmsman,* Sword of Orion

At 3.35 p.m., while the *Standaside* crew is still waiting to be rescued, *Sword of Orion* starts its motor and turns around. It's the beginning of what will be a treacherous journey. A direct course to Eden would put the seas at a bad angle, so *Sword of Orion*'s plan is to sail for two or three hours on a more comfortable course. Only two men are on deck. One, Glyn Charles, is steering. The other, the boat's young, full-time professional crewman, Darren Senogles, is keeping a look-out. Below, everyone except Rob Kothe is lying down, resting. Kothe is strapped in at the navigation station. He's tried to drift away from the radio but *Sword of Orion* has a strong signal, and the *Young Endeavour* team, who are starting to be swamped by calls, need help relaying messages. Kothe is relieved when he picks up a call from his friends on the disabled *Team Jaguar*. He lets Lew Carter know that the *Team Jaguar* crew is okay.

Then, at 3.50 p.m., as he is reaching down to tidy some rope, Darren Senogles hears a roar. Before he knows what's happening, he feels the boat thud onto its side. Senogles, waist-high in foam, sees the yacht's mast hit the water. *Sword of Orion* is sliding mast-first down a huge wave. It seems to slide for about 50 metres. Then, he is under water. The boat rolls through 360 degrees. When it bounces back upright, he is hanging off the side in his harness. He clambers back on board and sees Glyn Charles's harness hanging over the side. The harness is empty. Looking astern, Senogles sees Charles 30 metres away in the water. 'Man overboard!' he screams. The wind is gusting up to 80 knots and the boat is being blown further and further away from Charles. 'Swim!' bellows Senogles. He sees Charles do about six weak strokes, but he seems to be in pain. Senogles throws a life buoy but the wind blows it back in his face. He thinks Charles is trying to tread water. Within moments, Charles is about 50 metres away from the boat.

Below deck, the rest of the crew don't realise what has happened. They see everything go black and hear a horrendous noise. Kothe is pinned under a pile of sailbags with an injured knee. The next thing, Senogles is yelling and they rush up on deck. Screaming for gear, Senogles starts tying a long rope to his harness, planning to jump in the water. Then a wave breaks over the deck. Someone grabs Senogles. By the time the wave clears, Glyn Charles is 100 metres away. Between him and the boat there are, by now, several huge walls of water. Even if someone could swim to him, how would they find him? *Sword of Orion* is littered with ropes, rigging and sails, and its smashed mast is wrapped around the bottom of the boat. So even if the motor would help, they can't turn it on before clearing the mast and ropes away.

It takes Kothe a minute or two to realise who it is in the water. He grabs the radio and tries to get a position fix for a mayday. There is a rush to set off the EPIRB, grab rescue gear and try to start the motor. Four metres of *Sword of Orion*'s deck is cracking away from the hull. The boat seems to be taking on water.

No-one on *Sword of Orion* knows exactly what happened to Glyn Charles. The steering wheel he was holding is partly ripped away. After the race, the stitching on the tether of his harness is found to have failed. He isn't wearing a life jacket. As he drifts away from the yacht, those watching say it doesn't take long for him to weaken. They see him for briefer and briefer periods between the waves. Within about seven minutes they lose sight of him.

Rob Kothe calls mayday after mayday. But his main HF radio is wrecked by water, only the VHF emergency radio is working and the boat is more than 100 kilometres out to sea. Nobody responds. Kothe maydays for two and a half hours continuously, giving new positions, until he loses his voice. A few times, he hears aircraft nearby. But for nearly three hours none of them sees or hears *Sword of Orion*. The boat is breaking up. The life rafts are out and everyone has their life jacket on, expecting they'll have to get into the rafts. Never in his wildest nightmares has Rob Kothe imagined anything like this happening in the Sydney to Hobart, let alone to him as a skipper. Once, in his gliding days, he watched two friends in planes collide in mid-air. As the aircraft plummeted to earth, he remembers waiting to see the parachutes and screaming, 'Jump! Jump! Jump!' That time the parachutes came out. This time it's different. 'It was just such an absolutely shocking thing,' he says. 'And much harder to come to terms with than any of us imagined, because whoever had been driving that boat on that day—and it could have been any one of us—would have had the same fate.'

TWENTY-FIVE

I'll never look at waves the same again. Those waves were out to kill you. That was our attitude. You could see death working in that water.
　　—*Tony Mowbray, skipper,* Solo Globe Challenger

You go out there to beat the elements. This time they beat us.
　　　　　　—*Peter Carter, co-owner,* Midnight Special

Some people say ocean racing is a rich man's sport. But it's more accurate to say it's simply an expensive one. A handful of billionaire adventurers, like Larry Ellison, are at one end of the scale. And a great many ordinary yacht-lovers are at the other. One of them is Tony Mowbray, from the New South Wales town of Newcastle. Six months before the race, Mowbray mortgaged his house and spent his savings on a new boat. He called it *Solo Globe Challenger* and, as the name implies, he planned to sail it around the world, non-stop and single-handed. It was to be a charity trip, to raise money for a specialist children's cancer unit at the local hospital. As part of the lead-up, Mowbray put together eight friends to sail with him in his fourteenth Sydney to Hobart. He hoped the race would test out his new boat and start building up its profile for the fundraiser.

On Sunday morning, as the wind builds, Tony Mowbray takes down more and more sail. By midday, *Solo Globe Challenger* is under bare poles—the wind's so strong that its force on the mast and the rigging alone is enough to push the boat forward. By the time *Sword of Orion* reports it's getting 70-knot winds, Mowbray is getting the same. At that stage, Mowbray thinks he's going okay. But then, at about 4.00 p.m., and with no warning, *Solo Globe Challenger* runs out of luck. A 20-metre wave rears up behind the boat and dumps on top of it.

Mowbray is below deck. He feels the thud. 'The wave tipped the boat back on its bum and pushed it side-on to the waves.' In a more regular sea, there might have been time to recover. But there isn't. Another dumper looms up, smashes the boat over on its side and bulldozes it mast-first through the ocean. For about twenty seconds *Solo Globe Challenger* is almost, but not quite, upside down. A perspex skylight smashes inward. Water pours in, wiping out the radios and flooding the engine.

Mowbray rushes on deck to find the mast has broken off about a metre and a half above its base, and his friend Glen Picasso is trailing behind the back of the boat on his lifeline. Mowbray sees Picasso, blood streaming down his face, struggle to grab onto the stern. The two men's eyes meet. But there's no time for discussion—two more men are lying injured in the cockpit. One of them, Tony Purkiss, has been hit on the head by the mast and is covered in blood. The other, Keir Enderby, is trapped under part of the smashed mast and the rigging. Mowbray and the rest of the crew rush to help him. Before the race, Mowbray had spent a long time stripping back the mast and meticulously rebuilding it. All up, the mast cost him about $50,000. Now, in the space of a few minutes, he and a couple of others dismantle what is left and toss it overboard.

Solo Globe Challenger sets off two EPIRBs. Soon, a small yacht called *Pippin* passes by. *Pippin* stops and reports *Solo Globe Challenger*'s position but after a while, deciding it can't do anything more to help, it sails on. A few hours later, *Pippin*, too, is knocked down. Its radio fails and it heads back to Eden.

On board *Solo Globe Challenger* those crew who aren't too badly injured turn on the pumps and try to make the boat watertight. It's David Cook's first time sailing in the Sydney to Hobart: 'There were bodies and blood everywhere. It really hit home that we could sink. If we didn't fix it up we could lose everyone, especially with the injuries.

We were pretty much too busy to be frightened. Too tired. The skipper was at the helm for fourteen hours straight. We had to talk to him non-stop to keep him awake.' Cook says he wasn't frightened; he was thinking about his kids. 'I had my four-year-old's good luck charm: a plastic dolphin. It kept me going.'

Mowbray thinks about his family, too. Over the next two days, he rethinks his life and reconsiders his plan to sail alone around the world. He says he realised that being with his wife and kids was more important to him.

That Sunday afternoon, when Tony Mowbray and his friends heard *Sword of Orion*'s warning, they decided to try and ride out the storm. On another yacht, a different group of friends do the opposite. They decide to turn around and head north for shelter.

< >

A year before the race, five mates from Queensland pooled their money and bought a racing yacht. It went like a train, so they christened it *Midnight Special*. The regular nine-man crew—made up of a solicitor, a bus driver, a sailmaker, an auto-electrician, an electronics salesman, a flower grower, a bricklayer, an earthmover and a doctor—is out to have fun. Before the Sydney to Hobart *Midnight Special* enters every yacht race in Queensland. 'There's a lot of fellowship in ocean racing,' says Peter Carter, the earthmover. 'That's why you do it. The start is great, the finish is great, but the bit in between can be a bit ordinary. It's an accomplishment. Racing makes a lot of lasting friendships.' On Boxing Day, on the way to the start line, one of the co-owners, Peter Baynes, plays a tape that has on it the Creedence Clearwater Revival song for which the boat is named. Half the crew is singing along with the line about the ever-loving light; the other half is groaning.

Twenty-four hours later, Baynes is sitting on the rail, staring at the mass of foam breaking around him and thinking he shouldn't have put the theme from *Titanic* on the same tape. 'I thought to myself, "We're going to come to grief here",' he says later, 'and in time we did.'

By about 2.00 p.m., *Midnight Special*'s wind instruments are record-ing 80 knots. Then they're simply blown away. Only two or three crewmembers are on deck at a time and they are harnessed on. Ten- to 12-metre waves smash over them every few seconds. A few of the crew are horribly seasick. Two men already suspect they have broken ribs from being smashed around below deck. Then the crew hears the radio start to jam up with the chaos of calls for help and retirements. Neil Dickson, the sailmaker says, 'We thought at that stage it was about as bad as you'd want to see it. The radio [relay] boat said the weather would last eight hours, then updated it to say it would last twenty-four. Then *Sword of Orion* broke in to say it was getting 68 to 78 knots windspeed.' At the time *Sword of Orion* is only about 18 kilometres from *Midnight Special*.

Midnight Special's five owners go below to decide what to do. While they're talking, a particularly big wave slams into the boat and flings one of them, Ian Griffiths, across the cabin. Griffiths breaks most of a locker and, as he finds out later, his leg. It's enough. Everyone agrees to go back to shelter near Gabo Island and wait out the storm. When *Midnight Special* turns around, it's less than four kilometres from another, smaller, yacht with a similar name: *Midnight Rambler*. *Midnight Rambler* eventually wins the Sydney to Hobart on handicap. 'Turning around was the safest decision, so we did it,' Peter Baynes says. 'In hindsight, it was a mistake.'

As *Midnight Special* heads for Eden, the seas around it get steeper and the wind seems to blow harder. Two hours after turning around, another huge wave hits the yacht. Below, Neil Dickson is lying on the cabin floor, trying to get some rest. He's thrown across the cabin and into the roof, smashing into two other people on the way and hitting his head on a window frame. For the next two hours Neil Dickson is unconscious.

TWENTY-SIX

*You could just listen to the radio, there were people
breaking in over the sked; discipline being lost in the
sked. There were boats calling to retire and needing
help and 'Man Overboard' right through a sked. I
mean that sort of stuff doesn't usually happen, so it was
quite clear there was chaos.*

—*Gary Shanks, skipper,* DocTel Rager

After the 1993 race, when two-thirds of the fleet didn't make it to
Hobart, the race organisers, the CYCA, proposed a number of changes
for the future. Like many reforms, some were implemented and others
were forgotten. But one change was to include a Search and Rescue
officer in the race management. For some years, that officer has been
Anthony 'Safety Sam' Hughes. Another change was to move most of
the management from Sydney to Hobart. But everyone wants to be in
Sydney for the start. As a result, on Sunday morning, when some of the
faster boats begin reporting severe conditions, many of the race officials
are in transit from Sydney to Hobart.

Usually, Race Control's main interest is listening to the skeds and
drawing up progress reports. On Sunday afternoon, as the calls for assistance mount, Safety Sam is the liaison between Lew Carter's team on the
radio-relay boat and Search and Rescue in Canberra. Race management
assists him. But what is the club's plan for a crisis? After the race, a number
of outsiders and competitors are astonished to find there isn't one.

'I think it's important to recognise that as soon as a search and rescue situation arises, AMSA takes control completely and entirely,' the club's commodore, Hugo van Kretschmar, explains. 'There are no decisions that are being made by Race Control, other than decisions—well, but there aren't. I mean, the role of Race Control during the course of the race is to provide the best possible information that is helpful and useful to the competitors out in the fleet.'

But despite van Kretschmar's confusing comment, that afternoon some club members and officials do seem to be making decisions. One is Peter Bush, the race spokesman. Because van Kretschmar is sailing in the race, Bush is the club's official spokesman in Sydney. Bush arrives at the club's Sydney headquarters just before 3.00 a.m. on Sunday, to hear the day's first radio sked. Even at that early stage, according to the club's official post-race report, Peter Bush is concerned. The report says that Bush has been

> monitoring weather reports and was concerned that conditions similar to 1984—a low-pressure system called an East Coast Low—might develop. With this, he anticipated winds of 45 knots and a likely high attrition rate. Although these conditions were still some hours away, Bush decided to stay at the CYCA after the [3.00 a.m.] radio sked until he was no longer required, expecting a large number of retirements and the need for media comment.

But strangely, by mid-Sunday afternoon, when the race really is in trouble, it seems Peter Bush is not so worried. At 4.00 p.m. another club member, Greg Halls, the former race director, phones him in Sydney. In 1993, Halls coordinated a number of successful rescues, including the direction of several yachts to rescue John Quinn, who'd spent nearly five hours in the water. In 1998 Halls is following the fleet on his own HF radio. By Sunday afternoon he is concerned that the race is in difficulty. There are different accounts of the conversation between Halls and Bush. After the race, the minutes of a debriefing meeting held in Eden record Halls as saying that he told Bush the race was likely to experience 'severe difficulties' and that Bush replied 'they'll be right'. Peter Bush later denies that. He says the conversation was simply about likely retirements and whether someone from the club should go down to Eden. Bush tells Greg Halls he will 'think about' sending someone down, but at that stage, says Bush, 'There were only about four retirements and all of them were as a result of hard running conditions in the nor'easter.' It is an odd comment. Though the nor'easter did cause a handful of retirements, all of them occurred hours earlier on Saturday evening. By Sunday, most boats are getting winds from the west or south-west. By the time Halls phones Bush, *Sword of Orion* has reported 70- to 80-knot winds, the *Standaside* rescue is underway and Lew Carter and his team on the radio-relay boat are already being flooded with calls from yachts asking for advice and assistance.

In fact, some time around 3.00 p.m., after *Sword of Orion*'s report, Lew Carter realises that conditions are unusually severe and decides to take his own action. Worldwide, ocean racing is bound by a vast number of rules. But five rules, known as the RRS (Racing Rules of Sailing), are fundamental. One of those, Rule Four, states that the sole responsibility for deciding whether to start a race or whether to continue it lies with the skipper of each boat. Now Carter decides to remind skippers of that rule: that the decision whether to pull out of the race or stay in it is theirs and theirs alone.

'It was probably around two o'clock in the afternoon, 2.00 p.m. or 3.00 p.m.,' says Carter. 'Obviously, the weather was worsening and the smaller yachts that were in our vicinity, I realised, within a few hours they would be going into Bass Strait and out of the lee of the land. I really wanted to get the message across at that stage that it was the responsibility of the skipper to make sure that the crew and the skipper were sufficiently capable of continuing the trip in those conditions.' The club doesn't instruct Carter on this. He acts on his own initiative. (In fact, although Carter and his team are the main communication point for 115 boats and more than 1100 sailors, after the race Carter reveals he didn't speak directly to anyone from the club until the early hours of Monday morning. And then, when he did speak to a club member on shore, it was Greg Halls.)

'They [the club] didn't intervene at all,' says Carter proudly. 'They're listening at all times, probably. They've usually got a 24-hour watch. I mean, the CYC trust all that in ourselves. And I wouldn't do anything to misplace that trust.'

But van Kretschmar describes Carter's position somewhat differently. 'Lew's a radio operator,' he says, 'he's not an operative in the scheme of things. His job is to man the radio and communicate messages from one to the other. I mean, he doesn't have an organisational responsibility. Ninety-nine per cent of his role there is to act as a—I don't wish to demean his role in any way, because it is a very important role—is to act as a communication facilitator. Lew is an amiable sort of fellow and knows a lot of the people that are out there on the water, and did, during the course of this race, say some things and issue some personal warnings. That was him, if you like, chatting to his friends that are out there on the water. Saying, "If you want my opinion, just think about this for a bit."'

Ocean racing is an individualistic sport. And the rule about the skipper's responsibility goes right to its heart. No skipper wants to be told what to do on the ocean. Sailors argue, correctly, that it's impossible for anyone at a distance to decide the best course of action for a boat at sea. But immediately after the race, when the club is asked why it didn't have a crisis plan, officials quote the skippers' rule in reply. There is little acknowledgment that responsibility for each boat's actions is quite different from responsibility for a large sporting event involving more than a hundred boats and more than a thousand sailors.

By the time Lew Carter reads the skippers' rule, the club's commodore, Hugo van Kretschmar, has himself already retired from the race. 'We heard that forecast at 7.00 a.m. [Sunday],' he says, 'and we made a decision to retire and head back to Sydney.' Van Kretschmar says *he* realises the seriousness of the whole situation 'at two or three o'clock in the afternoon of the 27th when really disastrous things started to happen'. It seems that some club members in Sydney took longer to realise.

At 5.00 p.m. on Sunday afternoon Search and Rescue declares a general mayday for eastern Bass Strait. Two hours later, at about 7.00 p.m., Peter Bush decides he needs Greg Halls after all and phones him back. At 9.00 p.m., Halls sets off for Eden.

Afterwards, in its own inquiry, the club finds that race management 'did not suffer appreciably' due to the lack of a crisis plan. Despite that finding, one of the report's compulsory recommendations is that the club does develop a crisis plan, and that it does it *before* the next Sydney to Hobart.

TWENTY-SEVEN

We are sinking fast. Position ten miles south of San Remo ...
        —*Mayday from* Winston Churchill, *April 1959*

At around 5.00 p.m. Gary Ticehurst, in the ABC helicopter, is still hovering near *Standaside*, filming the rescues. He knows that cameraman Peter Sinclair is picking up great vision for the evening news but he also knows he should already be heading back to the mainland—he's running low on fuel. But Sinclair is still filming and Ticehurst is reluctant to leave. Then, at 5.15 p.m., Ticehurst hears a desperate voice breaking through on the VHF emergency frequency:

'Mayday. Mayday. Mayday. Here is *Winston Churchill, Winston Churchill.*'

Ticehurst: '*Winston Churchill. Winston Churchill. Winston Churchill.* [This is] ABC chopper. Go ahead with your position. Over.'

Winston Churchill (shouting): 'Twenty miles south-east of Twofold Bay. Over.'

Ticehurst: '*Winston Churchill.* Two Zero miles south-east of Twofold Bay. Nature of your mayday? Over.'

Winston Churchill (more urgently): 'Affirmative. We are getting life rafts on deck, ABC chopper. We are holed. We are taking water rapidly. We can't get the motor started to start the pumps.'

Ticehurst: 'Roger. How many on board?'

Winston Churchill: 'Niner. Niner.'

Ticehurst: '*Winston Churchill*, ABC chopper. Do you respond? Over.'

Winston Churchill: 'Read you, ABC chopper.'

Ticehurst: 'Roger. We will relay your mayday call. Over.'

Winston Churchill: 'Roger.'

Ticehurst (to Sinclair): 'Okay, Peter, we've got to leave. I'm running out of fuel.'

Ticehurst relays the mayday to Canberra. Then he tries to raise *Winston Churchill* again, but the radio is silent. The mayday came through so clearly that Ticehurst can't help thinking *Winston Churchill* must be quite close to him. But he doesn't have enough fuel to look for it. Upset and frustrated, he has no choice but to head back to Mallacoota. On the way back he thinks he may have already left the decision too late. The headwind's much stronger than he expected. Thinking that a forced landing would be better than ditching in the water, he tracks over Gabo Island. Finally, he makes it to Mallacoota with a only few minutes to spare.

Just as Gary Ticehurst is heading for the shore, *Winston Churchill*'s skipper, Richard Winning, hears the airwaves go silent. That lone mayday will be *Winston Churchill*'s last call. The yacht's batteries are already submerged.

Until now, *Winston Churchill* has been sailing relatively comfortably. For most of the afternoon, the boat manages with a storm jib and three reefs in the main. When a reef line breaks, the crew takes down the main and continues with only the storm jib. As Winning says later, 'We were in good shape: the boat was going well, it was snugged down and we didn't have a problem.'

But as the sea begins building, helmsman John Stanley starts to be concerned. 'You get to the stage where the wind has reached its predicted 50 knots, but then it's starting to get to 60 and 70 and you think, "Hang on, what have we got here?"' He thinks about turning back to Eden but decides it won't be any better. Double-size waves, rogues, loom up around the yacht. Stanley starts trying to count them. One in fifty. Then, one in fifteen. He is worried about the night ahead. Maybe they should heave to: head into the wind, stop sailing, maybe turn on the motor if they have to. They'd be out of the race, but so what? 'Obviously,' says Stanley, 'this weather was completely out of hand. There's no way we were getting what was forecast.'

At about 5.00 p.m. Stanley is below deck, getting up from a bunk. Suddenly he's jolted three metres across the cabin. 'I think Richard was steering at the time. This wave must have come out of nowhere, one of those big waves, a rogue wave. It felt like he tried to ride up the side and put the bow just over the top of it, but as he got to the top I could feel the wave just pick the boat up and throw it sideways at a 45-degree angle into the trough of the wave in front. So the wave's just picking up 25 tonne of boat and just hurling it sideways. I was in the aft coach-house when the boat hit the brick wall on the other side. The water pressure came across the deck, smashed three windows in front of me. Then the water came across and pinned me inside the coach-house.' For a minute or so, Stanley can't move. Then he hears shouts for help. Heaving himself free, he rushes on deck. Richard Winning and John Dean are trapped in mid-air, hanging from their safety harnesses.

'They'd been thrown around the backstay—we have what they call a split backstay on the boat—so the force of that water had thrown them both out, out overboard, around the backstay and suspended them in the air,' Stanley recalls. 'Their feet were about two foot off the deck. So that was a big wave. A big wave. When I looked down to leeward, there was about six foot of the bulwark—which is a little fence piece above the deck—completely gone, just smashed completely out of the boat. Now that's a lot of pressure.'

Stanley knows they have to get the pumps going fast. He untangles Winning and Dean. 'I said, "C'mon Richard, you start the motor. I've got to go down and change the valves over to get the pump working." By the time I got down there, the water was probably up 14 inches. I don't know how much water went down that hatch—the awning came out of the centre hatch—but there was about 10 inches of water over the floorboards, which was a lot of water. I don't know how much water came through those back windows as well—there was a hell of a lot.' But the broken windows and the hatch aren't the only problems. Water is flooding in from below. About four minutes after the wave, the water is rising up more than half a metre over the floorboards.

'We started taking water very rapidly,' says Richard Winning. 'We couldn't work out why we were sinking so fast.' From the position of the damage he can see on deck, Winning thinks the water must be coming in amidships. Much later, when he is told about the gap that was seen near his yacht's bow before the race started, he is convinced that the gap, if it existed, had nothing to do with the damage caused by the wave. John Stanley, too, thought *Winston Churchill* took on water through the middle section of the hull rather than the front: 'I'm sure it sprung a plank somewhere on the side of the boat. I couldn't tell where it was.' At the time, as Winning goes to start the motor, Stanley yells out to him, 'Must have sprung a plank!'

'By now,' says Stanley, 'the water was up to the top of the batteries, so when he turned the motor on, we only got about five seconds till it stopped. Then I knew we had a problem, a big problem. Richard got a mayday out. Fortunately the radio worked but he only got one call out. Then the batteries went dead. They'd just been completely drowned.'

The crew tries hand-pumping for a few minutes but they can see it's hopeless. Up until now, Stanley has only ever taken a casual interest in life rafts. He's seen them demonstrated, but he's never had to get into one. Richard Winning, John Stanley and Bruce Gould, the three most experienced sailors on board, decide not to inflate the rafts until the yacht's deck is completely submerged. They want to wait till the very last minute, when the boat's moving as slowly as possible.

≺ ≻

It isn't *Winston Churchill*'s first mayday. Forty years earlier, one of the boat's previous owners, the renowned yachtsman (and Victoria's then Minister of Transport) Sir Arthur Warner, had better luck than Richard Winning and his crew. Back then, sailing through Bass Strait, not far from Wilsons Promontory, Warner felt the boat hit something in the water. He recalled the incident for Murray Davis's *Australian Ocean Racing*:

> The yacht hit something hard—it could have been a whale—and she concertina'd. The door flew off a heavy refrigerator and a radio receiver was hurled from its mounting onto the cabin floor. The bulkheads

fractured and the galley was turned into a shambles. The fellows down below, some of whom were sleeping, or trying to in the gale we were having, rushed on deck. The caulking was sprung in many places and no amount of bailing would stop her from filling. To make matters worse there were storm conditions. When it became evident that we couldn't keep her afloat, I ordered everything up and drove her for the beach.

In 1959, the message that *Winston Churchill* was sinking fast went out four times before water flooded the batteries. But then the yacht was close inshore and as she slid lower and lower into the water Warner looked for somewhere to beach her. He headed for a strip of sand that lay inside a bar near Wreck Beach in Victoria. He surfed the boat over the bar and beached it. When the storm calmed, *Winston Churchill* was left high and dry. Eventually a bulldozer came in to flatten the sand and the yacht was towed away on a trailer. In what would be one of its many refits, it was repaired and strengthened. Later Sir Arthur Warner sold *Winston Churchill* to his son Graham, who raced it, with the same crew who had survived the beaching, in four Sydney to Hobarts.

Forty years later there are no handy beaches. *Winston Churchill* is the Sydney to Hobart's oldest surviving veteran and one of Sydney Harbour's best known and best loved yachts. Richard Winning once proudly said that his yacht would 'be here long after we have all gone'. Now it is sinking beneath him, into Bass Strait. It takes about twenty minutes to go down. At the last minute the crew set off the nitrogen cannisters to inflate their two life rafts.

'There was no panic, no arguments or conflicts of opinion on how to get things done: we just knew what we had to do and we did it,' Winning says later. 'I thought we were in pretty good shape—as good a shape as it was possible to be in.'

'It was very sad,' says Bruce Gould, 'I can tell you that.' It's nineteen-year-old Michael Rynan's first time in the ocean. As he climbs into the life raft, he looks back and sees *Winston Churchill*'s mast disappear under the water.

Richard Winning, Bruce Gould, Paul Lumtin and Michael 'Beaver' Rynan take the round life raft; it's four years old and the smaller of the two. John Stanley, John Gibson, John Dean, Mike Bannister and Jim Lawler take the bigger, and brand new, square raft. *Winston Churchill*'s one emergency beacon, now triggered, goes in the four-man raft with skipper Richard Winning. As his yacht sinks, Winning manages to tie the two rafts together. Stanley swims over to the smaller life raft, before going back to the bigger one: 'They had the EPIRB and young Beaver was in it, and I was quite happy with that because it was my responsibility to look after the young kid, having invited him.' About ten minutes after the rafts hit the water, a wave tears away the line between them. They drift apart. Winning remembers last seeing the bigger raft drifting about 100 metres away. Soon, rising and falling over 15-metre waves, the two groups lose sight of each other.

Cocooned under their raft's bright-orange roof, Stanley, Lawler, Bannister, Dean and Gibson start going through the raft's emergency gear. They find a container of food and a drogue (a type of sea anchor designed to keep the raft stable). They put the drogue out but it soon breaks off. 'We lost a lot of stability then,' says Stanley. 'We were like a beach ball in the surf, just being thrown around at will.' It starts pouring sheet rain. Stanley hopes the rain will calm the sea down, but it doesn't seem to. To keep dry and keep the water out, they close the raft's doorway as best they can. Now, isolated inside, all they can do is listen to the sea and wait for the waves to pick up the raft and throw it. In the cramped space, the five men sit facing one another. To hold on, they interlock their legs. Stanley's legs are on the bottom. 'Then this big wave hit us. It lifted my body but my feet were trapped.' A bone snaps in his leg. 'When we came down, I said, "Boys, we've got this wrong—I think we'd better sit parallel so we're not interfering with each other's bodies." Which we did.'

Forty years ago, *Winston Churchill*'s mayday touched off an intense search. But it wasn't needed. Back then, the crew made it ashore and one man walked five kilometres to a phone to call off the rescue. This time, Stanley feels sure the rescuers will find them. 'The mayday's been sent, the EPIRB's activated and my experience was there'd be some help around. But at the same time, I knew this was a big storm and there were going to be a lot of people needing assistance.'

John Stanley is right about the storm and other boats needing assistance. But none of the men in the life rafts could know that their mayday couldn't have come at an unluckier time. They also don't know that the last position they have given is wrong. When Richard Winning maydays, the GPS is no longer working. He has to estimate his position from memory. He puts the yacht about 20 nautical miles (37 kilometres) south-east of Eden. But it isn't there. It's further out. More like 90 kilometres from Eden.

TWENTY-EIGHT

> *We had a steady 75 to 80 knots on the indicator. The weather bureau says those speeds were only wind gusts. My reaction to that is that we had a 75- to 80-knot gust that lasted twelve hours.*
> —Rob Matthews, *helmsman,* Business Post Naiad

On *Business Post Naiad*, Steve Walker's been watching the dark bank of clouds ahead since early afternoon. The yacht's crew has downloaded a pre-midday weather fax, but all it shows is a U-shaped cold front near Victoria. The information in the fax is probably about six hours old, too early to pick up the tightly knotted low-pressure system that's now sitting in Bass Strait. Walker reckons the 45- to 55-knot forecast might bring a few gusts up to 65 knots. No-one expects more. But by 4.30 p.m. *Business Post Naiad*'s getting a constant 75 to 80 knots. When the wind instruments stop working, Walker, the sailmaker, estimates the wind at 80 to 90 knots.

But measuring the elements and dealing with them is getting harder and harder. It's so surreal, Steve Walker feels as if he's in a movie. The only way he can look out to windward is to put his hand to his face and peer through the slits between his fingers. When he does, there's nothing to see but dark walls of raging water. To leeward, when *Business Post Naiad* rides up a wave, all he can see is wave tops. Most of the time the view is more limited—the boat is buried deep in the wave troughs, hemmed in by mountains of seawater.

Visibility gets down to about 20 metres. 'It was virtually a whiteout,' says navigator Peter Keats. 'Huge, grey, moving walls of water with spume coming off like little needles, going into your eyes.' The wind flattens the waves into giant aerated rollers. Wild gusts eddy and swirl off the sea, driving sheets of spume, spindrift and pelting rain into the boat, like sprays of bullets from an automatic rifle.

'It was very, very noisy,' says Walker. 'The spume and rain were hitting the side of the boat so hard that it sounded like a massive hail storm. The wind was shrieking through the rigging. To speak to someone, you had to get right up to their ear and yell. By about 4.00 p.m. the wind was so strong that if you just sat on the deck and didn't hang on, you'd get blown away. You actually had to hang on to stay there, because the force of the wind was blowing you off. We've got waterproof hoods that come down over your face, but if you looked into the wind, they'd just blow open and you couldn't do a thing. The only way for the helmsman to steer was for one of the crew members to actually sit in front of him with his back to the sea and make a little eddy, so the helmsman could look forward to actually see where he was going.'

Until mid-afternoon *Business Post Naiad* is sailing with three reefs in its main. When a batten pops out of the main, Bruce Guy calls all hands on deck to take down the mainsail and put up the storm jib. Resting below, Rob Matthews comes up for what he expects to be only a few minutes. A couple of hours later, Matthews, as the boat's most experienced helmsman, is still at the tiller. He hasn't had time to put on his thermals and he's getting cold. 'I was starting to think that perhaps we shouldn't be here,' he says. 'We just hoped it was a temporary aberration and would blow itself out. But it didn't.'

While the wind stays under about 75 knots, Steve Walker feels the boat is still relatively controllable with the storm jib. The boat's doing about six to eight knots and Matthews has enough steerage to manoeuvre it up the breaking waves. It doesn't seem too unsafe. In the cockpit, Tony Guy screams into Rob Matthews's ear, 'I'm dying for a fag!' Matthews looks around. Guy has managed to light a cigarette in a 70-knot gale. 'Bloody smokers!' thinks Matthews.

But the wind keeps building—to 80 knots, then 90 knots. Steve

Walker is worried. Eden's at least twelve hours away, not much closer than the next chance of shelter, near Flinders Island. The wind and waves are just as bad either way. Heading to Eden, slightly more into the wind, might be more difficult than continuing.

Rob Matthews has sailed in stronger winds before. In 1972, the first time he crossed Bass Strait, the wind hit 98 knots. 'When I got to Melbourne that time, I phoned my wife, Carmel, and said there's no way I'm getting back on that boat,' he recalls. 'But the storm that year was so bad, it was in the newspaper. People kept coming up to us and asking if we were the ones who sailed through it. After about two days it didn't seem so bad. I got back on the boat and I've never looked back!'

But Matthews doesn't ever remember the sea being this wild. Soon *Business Post Naiad* is surfing so fast down the wave faces that it can no longer take even the storm jib. The yacht's bouncing in every direction, being pushed sideways and constantly laying over to 45 or 50 degrees. Any minute the rigging will start breaking. 'The boat was accelerating down the face of the waves,' says Matthews. 'It was doing huge speeds. I knew we couldn't keep doing that all night and get away with it.'

The crew is reluctant to take down the storm jib. But sometime after 5.00 p.m. they agree to try it. 'We decided to see what it felt like with no sails,' says Matthews.

At first, it doesn't seem too bad. The boat slows down. Walker knows the storm jib has to come down, but he doesn't like doing it. Now, he thinks, *Business Post Naiad* is in the lap of the gods. 'At that point, in 80- to 90-knot winds, we felt quite vulnerable,' he says. 'We were under bare poles which means the boat's only moving at three to four knots and you've got limited steerage. You can't point the boat up into the waves, which is its best angle of attack, to avoid them. All you can do is just be broadside to the waves, and if we got a breaking wave sideways we were in danger of rolling. The sea was so big. The rollers were about 15 to 25 metres high and occasionally there were breakers where the top five or six metres would just break and dump, and a wall of breaking water would come at you.'

Twenty minutes later, at about 5.30 p.m., the crew is still considering their options. At first Rob Matthews doesn't see the wave coming. It doesn't seem to be much bigger than any of the others. But suddenly, looking up from a trough, Matthews realises that this one is beginning to break just as it reaches the boat. He just has time to yell, 'Hang on!'

'It was like a wave on a beach with a high curling face. It dumped on us like we were a surfboard. We rolled so fast you didn't have time to take a breath. I could just feel myself being pulled to the end of my harness.'

Below deck Peter Keats sees everything go from daylight to pitch black, in an instant. Steve Walker is thrown from one side of the boat to the other. 'It was pandemonium,' he says. 'Things were flung everywhere.'

Within a few seconds *Business Post Naiad* spins upright. Rob Matthews, Tony Guy, Phil Skeggs, Jim Rogers and Bruce Guy are all in the water. Rushing on deck, Walker sees their five bedraggled heads hanging off the side. From the water, Matthews can see that only three metres of the mast is left standing—it's broken in two places. Tony Guy clambers back on board and pulls Matthews up. They and Walker help the others. Amazingly no-one seems badly injured.

Afraid the smashed mast will hole the side of the boat, the crew grab a runner rope, winch the mast back on deck and secure it. 'The wind was still screaming,' says Matthews. 'In fact, the wind and the sea were getting worse. At first all I thought was that we weren't going to finish the race. But then I saw how much damage there was. There was a crack across the top of the cabin that flexed every time the boat went over a wave. Water was pouring in through it. There was a crack on the deck two to three feet long either side of the compass. The whole cabin top and deck had delaminated; it felt like spongy cardboard to walk on.'

'The companionway bulkheads were sprung,' says Walker, 'the couple of knees near the pilot berths were sprung, the windows were broken on the port side, the deck was split—delaminated on the underside, actually split around the windows and above the cabin top. There was a lot of water coming in through the windows, so we stuffed pillows in them to try and stop it.'

Below, the freezer has spilt open, and food and gear are sloshing around in the water. There's a smell of diesel fuel; Bruce Guy thinks the fuel tank might be damaged.

'At that point the race was well and truly gone,' says Walker, 'I suppose you could say we had retired. Our main thought was to motor back safely and survive. We thought the safest thing to do was to get back into the lee of the mainland.' Someone turns on the EPIRB. *Business Post Naiad* seems to be taking on water and Walker is sure one more big wave will sink it. Without the stability of its mast the yacht is rocking more wildly than ever. It seems likely to roll over again.

Like most yachts, *Business Post Naiad*'s main HF aerial is on its mast. Because the mast is broken, Matthews and Keats start trying to hook up the emergency VHF aerial. But while they are trying the VHF, the HF radio springs into life. They realise that, in hauling the mast back on deck, they must have retrieved the aerial. The HF signal reaches *Business Post Naiad* clearly. The trouble is that calling out on the radio is more difficult. The storm is playing havoc with the airwaves, and *Business Post Naiad*'s aerial is down low.

Peter Keats sends out a mayday. Though Keats can hear Lew Carter talking on the radio-relay boat, Carter can't hear him. But HF signals can bounce erratically off the atmosphere and sometimes travel long distances. That night, *Business Post Naiad*'s call is heard by radios on boats as far away as Hobart and Eden. It's also picked up by at least one boat in the Sydney to Hobart.

TWENTY-NINE

◄ ►

When you're doing a rescue, you have to be totally
focused or the person will die. It's a personal mountain
that you have to climb. You get out of a warm
helicopter and go into the same situation as the poor
bugger you're rescuing. Drills and procedures can only
prepare you for how you're going to do it. After that,
you have to fight the elements.

—Senior Constable David Key, Victoria Police
Air Wing

On what seems to be a cool but pleasant enough Sunday afternoon in Essendon, a suburb of Melbourne, Senior Constable David Key is on duty at the Police Air Wing. At forty-four, David Key claims he's too old to still be jumping out of helicopters. But he does. After ten years in the army, six with Victoria Police and another nine as a rescuer in the Police Air Wing, Key is an accredited winch assessor and instructor, a position normally held only by chief pilots. He's a modest man. After 800 winch rescues, David Key still insists he 'isn't an expert'. In a few hours he will apply his skill and experience to pull off one of the country's most extraordinary rescues.

The Air Wing gets a call from Search and Rescue in Canberra at 3.50 p.m. To begin with, it concerns the one distress signal Rupert Lamming registered on his computer when he first arrived on duty. Thirty minutes after the call, Senior Constables David Key, Barry Barclay and Darryl Jones take off in a helicopter. While they are in the air, Search and Rescue issues a blanket request for all available resources. By now three fixed-wing search aircraft and the Heli-Med air ambulance helicopter from Latrobe Valley are also on their way to the search area, about 100 kilometres off the coast from the seaside town of Mallacoota.

The police rescuers start to get their first taste of the storm when a furious 160-kilometre an hour tailwind hits the chopper, shooting it north to Mallacoota. In twelve years with the Air Wing, Pilot Darryl Jones has never seen a wind like it. The helicopter, a Dauphin SA 365, cruises at about 230 kilometres an hour. With the tailwind, its ground-speed hits 390 kilometres an hour. Jones finds it hard to believe his instruments. It takes only about ninety minutes to reach Mallacoota. Circling to land, Jones looks down—the sea is totally white, a mass of spray and breaking water.

At Mallacoota the weather is appalling. Low dark clouds are dumping rain, and gale-force winds tear across the muddy landing ground. At 6.11 p.m. the police helicopter lands, refuels, and unloads unneeded gear. Usually deserted, the small airfield already looks something like a war zone. The Heli-Med chopper lands, bringing in the first eight survivors from *Standaside*. Gary Ticehurst comes down on his last drops of fuel. Everywhere radios crackle in a crossfire of distress calls, maydays and messages about EPIRBs. The Victoria Police crew has a telephone briefing from Search and Rescue; it is given the task of backing up the Heli-Med crew rescuing the last four men from *Standaside*.

The police chopper takes off at about 6.30 p.m., heading for *Standaside*. But the SouthCare rescuers, already diverted to the same job, beat them to it. New orders come through. David Key remembers being diverted to three boats, one after another: '*Sea Anna*' (this might have been a misunderstood call from *Siena*), *Business Post Naiad* and *Winston Churchill*. Finally the chopper heads for the position given for *Winston Churchill*, 20 miles south-east of Eden. But it never gets there. It's soon diverted to yet another emergency.

In Canberra, Rupert Lamming, the man in charge of maritime rescues, and his colleague Dick Jamieson, in charge of aviation, are struggling to keep track of the chaos on a whiteboard. By late afternoon, messages are pouring in second- and third-hand, through radios and mobile phones. Some of them are garbled. One call, first interpreted as coming from a yacht named *Cam Cam* is later translated as 'pan pan' (a maritime distress call, less urgent than mayday).

The distress beacons, nearly all of them the smaller and older variety, can't give details of yacht names or the nature of their emergencies. Each signal only gives the beacon's position within a radius of about 20 kilometres. Some beacons may already be adrift in the water. If there's no radio contact, the only way to prioritise the calls is to physically locate the beacons. In ordinary circumstances, it isn't a problem. Normally the search and rescue computers only have to deal with one target at a time. But that afternoon, the computer-screen maps show the sea, south-east of Eden, ablaze with a cluster of more than a dozen red signals. It's a far worse disaster than anyone has anticipated.

Journalists start arriving at Search and Rescue (SAR) headquarters. The SAR coordinators call on every aircraft they can muster. With daylight running out, they alert the Navy, which has the only helicopters equipped for night rescues. In Sydney, the Navy frigate HMAS *Newcastle* starts recalling its crew.

At SAR the big priority is *Winston Churchill*'s chilling mayday. But the only position given for the yacht is vague and SAR doesn't know whether the men on board are already in life rafts or still on the yacht. Suddenly another mayday confronts Rupert Lamming with an unbearable dilemma. A yacht, *Kingurra*, has lost one of its crew overboard. *Kingurra*'s GPS is working and can give the boat's position to within about 20 metres. The police chopper, on its way to find *Winston Churchill*, is nearby. Lamming has to make an instant decision. He does. He diverts the chopper to the man overboard and sends a fixed-wing aircraft, flown by Neil Boag, to find *Winston Churchill*. Later Lamming tells a journalist that if the helicopter had continued looking for *Winston Churchill*, and found its crew to be safe, he could never have forgiven himself.

THIRTY

> *I think this whole drama has a lesson, and the lesson applies equally to the people running the race as it does to those participating. That lesson is that there are conditions on the sea which are beyond the capability of man to withstand.*
>
> —Peter Joubert, skipper, Kingurra

> *The sea has not changed, maybe our assessment of our ability to handle it has.*
> —Charles Maclurcan, crewmember, Polaris, *in Sydney Amateur Sailing Club News, February 1999*

Australia has produced several world-class yacht designers. These days the best of them conjure up their new designs in 3-D plans on computer screens. But it isn't so long since designers first realised their designs in pen and ink. Some of those drawings are almost works of art in themselves. Among the most admired are the drawings of designer Peter Joubert.

Peter Joubert is a 73-year-old university professor with a crusty sense of humour. Frequently called on to give expert design evidence in court cases, he doesn't mince words, doesn't waste them and is prepared to state his mind. In his younger days, Joubert was as driven by competition as any other yachtsman; but by this race, his twenty-seventh, he's looking for a quiet sail to Hobart with his friends. His 13-metre yacht, *Kingurra*, is one of his own designs. Built in 1972, it is a solid, wooden, heavy-displacement boat. In the past, *Kingurra* has had respectable results in a fair few of its fourteen Sydney to Hobarts.

In the 1998 Sydney to Hobart, none of *Kingurra*'s crew is hellbent on hard racing. The first night out they sit down to a roast dinner. But, like the rest of the fleet, the wind and the current push *Kingurra* south faster than expected. Then, on Sunday afternoon, conditions deteriorate. Not one of the crew, despite their combined tally of eighty-plus Hobarts, can recall sailing in anything worse.

Joubert's friend Peter Meikle is on his eighth Sydney to Hobart. Meikle, who has a PhD in aerodynamics, watches *Kingurra*'s wind instruments hit 68 knots and peg out. The reading range just doesn't go any further. The wind howls; a horrible unearthly wail that isn't coming from the rigging but from the core of the air itself. Seamen who've survived the worst storms nature can dish out talk about that howl. Some say it's like no other sound on earth. Now Meikle knows what they mean. On deck, the spray hits his face like pellets from a shotgun. *Kingurra*'s helmsman, Anthony Schniders, has put on his ski goggles.

During the 2.00 p.m. sked, Joubert hears *Sword of Orion*'s weather warning. He swallows hard. Joubert sailed in one of the Sydney to Hobart's worst races, in 1993. That year *Kingurra* rescued the crew of the yacht *Adjuster*. The entire crew had been thrown into Bass Strait after their boat sank and their life raft overturned. Seeing what happened to them left Joubert with little faith in life rafts. In 1993 the wind never topped 70 knots. Peter Joubert knows physics and he knows the Beaufort Scale. As he puts it, 'The main thing about wind is that the force on the sails is proportional to the square of the velocity. The forecast was for about 50 knots. Fifty squared is 2500. But 70 squared is 4900. That's a 100 per cent error in wind-force.' Joubert considers weather reporting a mediocre science. 'Forty-five to 55 knots is a storm. Over 70 knots is a hurricane. And that's what we had—a hurricane.'

By now Joubert is feeling decidedly nervous. He feels worse when he hears on the radio that a yacht called *Polaris* has pulled into shelter. *Polaris* is skippered by John Quinn, the man who was lost overboard in 1993 and rescued after nearly five hours in the water. 'I'm a great admirer of John Quinn,' Joubert says later, 'I thought, "Oh my God, if he's pulling in, this must be serious."' Joubert doesn't know it then, but Quinn's yacht never experiences winds much over 35 knots. At about 1.30 p.m. *Polaris*, better equipped with electronics than *Kingurra*, picks up the latest weather fax from the Bureau of Meteorology. The fax image of the storm is all they need to see.

'Quinn, ever mindful of his extraordinary experience a few years earlier in the same area, put great store in the weather fax,' *Polaris* crewman Charles Maclurcan explains later. 'The picture clearly showed an intensification of the low-pressure system with the isobars close and concentrated, dead ahead. He handed it to me and others and I believe we were all of one mind.'

Weather maps show the intensity of low-pressure systems in the same way atlases show height. Lines on weather maps join points of equal air pressure, just as lines on land maps join points of equal height. The closer they are, the steeper the air-pressure gradient and the more intense the low-pressure system. On the map the *Polaris* crew sees the concentric circles in Bass Strait are clustered so tightly it's impossible to read the letter 'L' for 'Low' at their centre. It looks as if an ink blot has been dropped on the map between Tasmania and the mainland.

Polaris starts tacking back to Eden. At 10.00 p.m. that night, the crew anchors, cooks dinner and goes to bed. At midday the next day *Polaris* re-enters the race and continues safely to Hobart.

< >

But Peter Joubert, like many others in the race, doesn't have a fax machine. By the time he hears *Sword of Orion*'s warning, *Kingurra* is already south of Gabo Island, well through the gateway to Bass Strait. Joubert sees waves starting to tower over *Kingurra*'s masthead. Their tops are foaming and breaking. The harder the winds blow, the steeper the waves loom. They come at *Kingurra* from every angle and begin to cross over and pile up on top of one another. He isn't sure that turning back will be any better than continuing. The gateway has closed. Joubert feels that there's no escape for *Kingurra*.

Around this time he hears Lew Carter mention the rule about a skipper's responsibility. Joubert is unimpressed: 'To let the race go on is a head-in-the-sand attitude. They get out of it by saying the responsibility is the skipper's.' The organisers do have the power to abandon or suspend the race. But they don't use it. There's no suggestion they even consider it. 'I think that they [race organisers] are driven to a certain extent by sponsorship issues; they've got to turn on a show for their sponsors,' says Joubert.

Unlike Joubert, most yachtsmen scoff at the idea of abandoning or suspending the competition. Stopping a race, they say, won't turn off the weather and won't bring the boats home. 'The reason why we never have [stopped it],' says club commodore Hugo van Kretschmar, 'is because at what point do you decide to stop it? At what point do you decide that it's no longer safe for everybody to continue?'

Peter Joubert says he used to hold the same opinion. But this race changed him. 'It's a psychological thing. They have to press on through gales to prove that they are tough men. I suffer from this myself to some extent. But we were tipped over. You feel differently after you've been tipped over. It taught me a lesson. In future, when there's a storm warning, I'll draw the line. It's not a death race, it's a yacht race. I'm not interested in death races.'

Annoyed at the time by the radio reminder, Joubert goes to his bunk to lie down. By 6.00 p.m. he is asleep.

Up on Kingurra's deck, four soaking-wet crewmen are battling through the waves. Suddenly one of them, Anthony Schniders, yells out a warning. The other three hang on. Two waves seem to collide and join to loom up in what looks close to 30 metres of water. Kingurra rides up it at an angle, hits the crest and slams into four or five metres of broiling surf. The boat tips on its side. Peter Meikle is under water. He feels as if he's trapped in a brutal spa bath. Four or five seconds later, Kingurra bounces back upright.

Below, Joubert is catapulted from his bunk. A crewmember who'd been lying on a windward bunk shoots across the roof of the cabin, breaks a handrail and lands on top of him. Joubert hears an enormous crack. There's water in the cabin and he thinks that either the planking is tearing or the deck is breaking open. 'My immediate thought was that we might be going to drown and we'd all have to get into the stupid life raft. My experience of life rafts wasn't healthy. I'd built a very large pump on the engine and my one thought was to get that connected. So I crawled up to the nav. area but I'd lost my glasses and couldn't see properly. My grandson threw the switch. The pump worked. It started throwing out bucketloads of water.' It's only then Joubert realises *Kingurra*'s real drama is going on above him, on deck.

Peter Meikle finds himself lying in the cockpit. He's alone. One of the three men who were on deck pops up from the water. Then Meikle sees the other two hanging off the back of the boat by their harnesses. One of them is his good friend John Campbell, from Seattle. Meikle screams for help and yells out to Campbell, but Campbell doesn't respond. Meikle tries to haul Campbell out of the water, but he's limp and unconscious and Meikle isn't strong enough to pull him back on board. The boat's navigator, Tony Vautin, comes up from below and he and Meikle tug together. But as they try to drag him up, Campbell slips out of his jacket. Campbell is wearing a new, top of the line, inflatable jacket that can be worn with a safety harness fitted between the jacket's lining and its outer shell. But the lining is slippery. One of Campbell's arms falls out of the jacket and Meikle grabs his friend's hand. Then Campbell's other arm slips out and the jacket turns inside out. Meikle recalls squeezing Campbell's hand as hard as he can, 'but there was a dreadful inevitability about it all. The hand was so lifeless.' Meikle knows he can't hold on much longer. He is already thinking, 'What next? Do I follow him in?'

A wave hits. Meikle's grasp breaks and John Campbell slips away. Even though Campbell is unconscious, Meikle thinks he hears a dull cry. But Campbell's already drifting away from the boat, face down. Meikle thinks about jumping in but stops when he realises it would only mean two people in trouble. Suddenly Campbell raises his head and looks at the boat. His boots and wet-weather pants float to the surface and everyone on deck thinks he's taking them off to swim. But he doesn't swim. The helmsman tries to turn the boat up into the wind but *Kingurra*'s storm jib is shredded from the knockdown. Someone throws an orange life buoy into the 70-knot wind. Anthony Schniders concentrates on keeping Campbell's head, bobbing up and down on the waves, in view. But Campbell disappears for longer and longer intervals until Schniders can only see him for about two seconds in every thirty. A part of Peter Meikle tells him that this can't really be happening. He wonders what he'll say to Campbell's parents in America.

Down below, Joubert rushes to the radio. Still without his glasses and needing his grandson to help him, he maydays that *Kingurra* has a man overboard and needs a helicopter. Lew Carter replies immediately, asks if *Kingurra* has turned on its EPIRB and suggests they throw it overboard after Campbell. 'Is he wearing a life jacket?' asks Carter. 'No,' says Joubert. 'What colour clothing?' asks Carter. 'Dark blue,' answers the horrified skipper, 'dark blue underwear.' 'I thought we had lost him,' says Joubert. Joubert has broken several ribs and punctured a lung. With no idea whether or not a helicopter is coming, he collapses into unconsciousness.

About half a kilometre away, tumbling through the furious seas, John Campbell opens his eyes. He can see *Kingurra* pulling away from him. The last thing he can remember is being on its deck, wearing his wet-weather gear. He knows he's in trouble and getting back to the boat is his only hope. He tries waving his arms, certain that if the others can only see him, they'll turn straight back. He tries swimming, knowing he can't make it to the yacht, but that he has to, somehow, keep it in sight. He doesn't know that his jaw, and the bones around his cheek and eye socket, are broken. He sees a flare being fired from the boat. He can't understand what his crewmates are doing.

THIRTY-ONE

> *In some sports, like mountain climbing, people are so
> driven they'll pass dead people halfway up mountains.
> The endeavour of getting to the top of Everest, or
> wherever, far outweighs the consequence of looking after
> other individuals. But sailing yachts is a little different
> from mountain climbing, in so much as the rules make
> provision for the time taken to help someone.*
> —Steve Kulmar, helmsman, Sword of Orion

The Bass Strait storm is an extreme event, but not an extraordinary one. Its freakishness lies not in severity, but timing. In 1979, just a few months after the Fastnet disaster, another such extreme storm struck south-eastern Australia. Back then, a yacht called *Charleston* was on its way to Sydney to compete in the 1979 Sydney to Hobart. *Charleston* was caught in the storm. The yacht and its five crew vanished without trace. Not a shred of wreckage was found. The storm that took *Charleston* hit Bass Strait in mid-December, about ten days before the start of the Sydney to Hobart. It could easily have blown up eleven or twelve days later.

Twenty years ago, *Charleston* was one of the new breed of ultra-light racers. After it disappeared, yacht designers warned that yachtsmen were sacrificing too much safety in the single-minded pursuit of speed. They were probably right. By 1998, ocean racing safety requirements are more stringent. Even so, in the first few days after the 1998 Sydney to Hobart, the debate resurfaced. This time the argument was soon abandoned. It wasn't the point. The 1998 storm didn't discriminate between light boats and heavier ones. It overpowered them all.

One yachtsman in the 1998 Sydney to Hobart will never forget the disappearance of *Charleston*. In the middle of December 1979, Richard Purcell was also in Bass Strait. He was delivering a boat, a yacht much heavier than *Charleston*, from Melbourne to Sydney. Richard Purcell is a tough bloke. But that night, caught in the same storm as *Charleston*, he readily admits he was truly frightened. Purcell remembers the forecast was for a 45- to 50-knot sou'wester. But as night fell, the boat's wind instruments started reading 60. In those days, the instruments didn't go any higher. For eight hours, the needle just sat still, jammed rock-hard at the far end of the windscale. Forced down to bare poles, and still doing 10 knots, Purcell didn't expect to survive till morning.

Nineteen years later Richard Purcell is a builder and a highly competitive yachtsman. He races to win, but he says he never takes chances. 'We weren't born to walk on water. You've got to know what racing's about. You've got to understand how unforgiving the ocean is.'

Purcell's boat, *Margaret Rintoul II*, is thirty years old. It's 14.6 metres, solid and heavy. But it is no holiday cruiser. In an earlier life, the boat was raced and owned by one of Australia's toughest and best known yachtsmen, Syd Fischer. Fischer's famous yachts have all been called *Ragamuffin*, and *Margaret Rintoul* was the first in the series. As *Ragamuffin*, *Margaret Rintoul* competed in at least two Fastnet races and won one of them.

Richard Purcell bought the yacht in the late 1980s. He's done five Sydney to Hobarts and skippered *Margaret Rintoul* in two. In 1994 Purcell came second in his division; in 1995 he won it. Part of his satisfaction is in beating yachts that are lighter and newer than his. In 1998, he aims high. Purcell thinks that if *Margaret Rintoul* gets the right conditions, he might pull off the big one and win the Sydney to Hobart. A big blow could give the old, heavy boat an advantage.

By Bass Strait, *Margaret Rintoul* is down to her storm jib. 'It was no picnic ride,' says Purcell later, 'but the Sydney to Hobart never is. I was concerned but I knew we'd get through if we stuck to our plan. As long as nothing broke.' The Bass Strait storm is in about the same place as the one he sailed through nineteen years earlier. But he doesn't think it's as bad. In 1979, he remembers, there were bigger seas and more breaking waves. But, even though he's taken some pills, Richard Purcell is seasick. 'Maybe,' he says later, 'I was more worried than I admitted.'

The rest of *Margaret Rintoul*'s crew isn't feeling too comfortable either. Colin Betts and Dick Norman are both in their late sixties. The two have sailed together since they were schoolboys and have endured more Hobarts than almost anyone else—sixty-nine races between them. Neither man can remember ever seeing the sea more dangerous than it is now. Afterwards, Betts says this race might be his last. Norman says he'll go back, but only on an older-style, heavy boat. Norman is a lucky man. This race, he was planning to sail on *Winston Churchill*. One of *Winston Churchill*'s crew, Bruce Gould, was to sail on *Margaret Rintoul*. But just before the race, Bruce Gould and Dick Norman swapped places.

At 6.00 p.m., Richard Purcell comes off his watch. Another of *Margaret Rintoul*'s eleven crew, Bill Riley, is steering. Purcell lies down in the cockpit on top of some sails, to plan for the night ahead. At about 6.30 p.m. he looks out to leeward. He can't believe his eyes. Someone is firing a red distress flare. He shouts out to Riley, 'There's a boat there, can you see it?' Purcell grabs a torch and flashes an acknowledgment. He can see that the other boat has no rig and there are two people in its cockpit.

Two or three hundred metres away, on *Sword of Orion*, Rob Kothe, a ligament torn in his knee, is still calling mayday. But he has only the emergency radio and no-one seems to hear him. Another crewman with an injured shoulder is lying on a bunk. It's about three hours since the boat rolled, and it's starting to get dark. The top of the yacht's coach-house has been ripped off. Its engine, thrown off its mountings, is floating loose. *Sword of Orion*'s crew is still reeling from losing a man overboard. Steve Kulmar is devastated by the loss of his friend. 'Conditions,' he says, 'were well and truly out of our control. The seas were still enormous, the boat had capsized and was seriously damaged. We'd lost the aerial on top of the mast. We had to cut the mast away from the boat. We'd thrown some sails overboard, attempted to force gear into some of the holes in the deck and bailed and bailed. We bailed for probably an hour to get the boat controlled. Eighty-five miles off the coast, you're left in a pretty fearful state.'

When *Sword of Orion* sees another boat to windward, it lets off four or five flares to get its attention. But Richard Purcell doesn't see them all. He only glimpses the one. He knows *Margaret Rintoul*'s motor isn't working, he's already tried turning it on earlier to recharge some batteries. But even if it worked, a motor wouldn't make much difference in these conditions. Purcell decides that it's too dangerous to turn downwind and that he can't get within a wave-length of the other boat without risking his own. He goes below. *Margaret Rintoul*'s navigator, Colin Betts, is lying on a bunk. 'Get on the radio!' Purcell yells to Betts. 'Say we've seen a dismasted yacht!' He continues, 'We can't turn around to stand by—that's my final decision.'

Betts turns on the radio. It's jammed with distress calls. He says later it takes him twenty minutes to break through. Neither Betts nor Purcell knows the name of the other yacht or what's happened to it. Because it hasn't had its radio on, no-one on *Margaret Rintoul* has heard Rob Kothe calling mayday earlier. By the time Betts finally reports the sighting, *Margaret Rintoul* has left *Sword of Orion* behind. The radio-relay boat thanks Betts for his report. But no-one asks the *Margaret Rintoul* whether it is standing by the dismasted yacht. And, though race directors in previous races have had a policy of directing yachts to help one another, no-one in this race directs *Margaret Rintoul* to help *Sword of Orion*. As a result, Richard Purcell doesn't have to consider what he would have done, had he been directed to help. After the race, he says he is glad he didn't have to decide. 'There's no room for heroism in those conditions,' he says. 'You've got to be practical. It's my job as skipper to make decisions. Ultimately the buck stops with me. Whether the crew appreciates it or not, I'm responsible for them.'

In reality, it's unlikely *Margaret Rintoul* could have done much to help *Sword of Orion*. But it's possible that if Purcell had stopped racing south, his boat could have at least made radio contact with the dismasted yacht. A few hours earlier, in similar conditions, another yacht, *Siena*, turned around to assist *Standaside*. *Margaret Rintoul* is a heavy boat, weighing about 25 tonnes. *Siena* is much smaller and weighs seven tonnes. 'That guy was crazy,' says Purcell after the race. 'He was knocked down and his crew were injured. He jeopardised his crew.'

'I don't know how other sports provide for assistance, but sailing does,' *Sword of Orion*'s Steve Kulmar says later. 'If that yacht had stood by us for two hours, he would have been given back two hours on his time.' So what would Kulmar have done if, in those conditions, the situation had been reversed and he'd seen the flare? 'Very simple. Get within 100 metres of the boat, stand by, talk to them on the radio and find out their condition. We probably wouldn't have come alongside because it was far too dangerous, but we would have certainly stood by them until they cut their rig away and tidied the boat up. Then we could have talked to them about what they needed.'

'I guess,' says Kulmar after the race, 'people may have spent months, even years, preparing for this race. It's a great endeavour, something they desperately want to achieve, to be able to say, "I did that tough 1998 Hobart and got there." There's a lot of self-esteem and I suppose satisfaction in that. But I don't think a sport like sailing has the right to endanger lives.'

Richard Purcell maintains that he might have endangered his own crew by stopping. 'Steve Kulmar's comment is hurtful but I know why he says that. He lost a mate. It wasn't that I wouldn't stop. It was that I couldn't. You have to be practical. If you get emotional, that's when you get in the shit.' He adds, 'I feel sorry for *Sword of Orion*. It would have been bloody frightening. You're there on your own, no matter who is trying to stand by you or not. But how would *Sword of Orion* have felt if I had lost one of my crew over the side trying to rescue them?'

On dry land, it's easier to be certain about right decisions and wrong ones. Richard Purcell says he had no idea how much drama was going on in the race. *Margaret Rintoul* reaches the finish without knowing that the yacht it has passed by has lost a man overboard and will eventually sink.

It isn't till after the race, in a Hobart pub, that the crew of *Sword of Orion* finds out that the boat that sailed past them was *Margaret Rintoul*. Richard Purcell admits he saw the distress flare, but says he wasn't able to do anything. But why, Rob Kothe, wants to know, did it take

Margaret Rintoul more than twenty minutes to get on the radio and report that it had seen a yacht fire a flare?

'He intimated it was because we didn't want to be asked to stand by,' Purcell says later.

That night in Hobart, emotions are already running high. There's a bit of a dust-up. Rob Kothe, still on crutches, breaks it up. 'It sounds like you're trying to be God,' Purcell remembers Kothe telling him. 'It sounds like *you* want to be God,' is the answer Purcell recalls giving.

Months after the race, when the issue becomes public, Purcell appears on television to defend himself. The wife of one of his crewmen is also interviewed, saying that she is glad Purcell acted out of concern for her husband's safety. But the club's post-race inquiry suggests that the delay between *Margaret Rintoul* seeing the flare and being able to break through on the radio to report it is about thirty-five minutes, even longer than Richard Purcell and his radio operator, Colin Betts, remember it. Rob Kothe tries to smooth matters over. The yacht club announces it will hold an inquiry into the incident, and then delays it.

In all the soul-searching that follows the 1998 Sydney to Hobart, no issue leaves yachtsmen as divided as this one. Richard Purcell gives it more thought than most: 'Ocean racing isn't for the faint-hearted. There is a lot of panic and poor seamanship in those situations. You have to be so exact. I have to live with my decision and I can. In the same conditions, I'd do it again.'

One man who isn't quite as comfortable is the gentle Colin Betts. 'What's past is past and what's done is done,' he says after the race. 'Physically there was nothing we could have done to help except give moral support. But maybe there's a lesson to be learnt.' Asked what it is, Betts says thoughtfully, 'That, whatever the circumstances are, you should at least try to give someone else aid.'

THIRTY-TWO

◄ ►

> [We] wrote down a list of things that had to go right
> for John to survive. We got to about fifteen of them,
> including the helicopter being out there on another call,
> the wind being strong enough to get them there quickly,
> the headwind on the way back just allowing them to
> get back before they ran out of fuel, how they hadn't
> seen us till we set off the flare. We figure John had
> about five minutes left.
>
> —Peter Meikle, crewman, Kingurra

Sunday, 27 December 1998
Early Evening

Diverted away from *Winston Churchill* by Search and Rescue, police pilot
Darryl Jones enters in his GPS the set of coordinates he's been given
for the helicopter's new job—the man overboard. His chopper reaches
the search area about fifteen or twenty minutes later, around 7.30 p.m.
The only word Jones can find for the conditions is 'incredible'. He's
never seen the sea wilder or more awful. The helicopter is buffeted by
relentless sheets of rain and sea spray. In places, the cloud base falls
below 200 metres above sea level. The water is a foam-streaked black.
Waves and swell fill the gap between dark clouds and dark water. He
estimates the waves are around 30 metres high with some rising to 35
metres. They look like huge dark platforms, their tops swept flat by the
wind and driving rain. The wind blasts a consistent 70 to 80 knots (135
to 155 kilometres an hour).

Jones knows he needs 110 per cent concentration. Helicopters and water don't mix. One small miscalculation and he'll collide with a wave or get caught downwind with no air-speed, lose lift and plummet into the maelstrom. Jones realises he is worried and afraid about winching in these conditions. He forces himself to overcome the fear and turn his full concentration to the job ahead: 'I noted that we were now 65 nautical miles out to sea to the south-east of Mallacoota, and I remember thinking that if we had any problems at all we were alone and would more than likely die before help could arrive.'

Darryl Jones can hardly see anything around him, let alone a yacht amid the waves. He starts an expanding search pattern, circling north, then turning south. Just as he turns, winch operator Barry Barclay sees a red flare flash ahead, slightly to the left. Jones still can't see a boat but he heads for the flare and Barclay tries raising *Kingurra* on the marine VHF emergency channel. *Kingurra* radios back that it fired a flare and that John Campbell was last seen somewhere about 300 metres to the left of the boat. But peering through the rain and spume, Barry Barclay's visibility is at times less than 100 metres. He can never see further than 500 metres in any direction. When finally he spots *Kingurra*, he realises it's tossing so wildly that Campbell could be anywhere in a 180-degree arc around it. Jones tracks upwind to the yacht. Suddenly David Key notices the orange life ring. At first he thinks someone is in it, but it's only a trick of the water and spray. Jones turns to get a better look at the life ring and as he does Barry Barclay notices something moving at the corner of his eye. Turning his head slowly so he won't lose it, Barclay sees Campbell waving his arms. It's incredible that Barclay spots him. Campbell is about 600 metres from the boat and about 400 metres away from the life ring. 'I've got him!' yells Barclay.

In nothing but his wet, dark blue thermal underwear, Campbell is a dark figure in a black ocean of 30-metre waves. 'Finding him was an absolute freak,' says David Key later. 'The proverbial needle in a haystack.' Looking down, Key can see that Campbell is floundering. He seems exhausted. Every few seconds he slips under a huge wave. Key knows that he is about to jump out of the warm helicopter and join him in the water.

Key and Barclay have been preparing for the winch on the trip out. As soon as Barclay spots Campbell, they are ready to go. Darryl Jones moves into a hover about 30 metres above the water. Jones has nothing he can use as a reference to keep the chopper in position. With one eye on Campbell, Barclay talks Jones into place—just above the man in the water. Then Jones hits the mission switch which powers the winch.

When he leaves the warm cocoon of the helicopter, David Key is hit by a freezing shock of wind and water slamming into his body. Rain and spray shoot into his face as if he is being showered by nails. Coming down on the winch, he covers his exposed cheeks with his hands. He can see Campbell going underwater, reappearing and trying to wave. Key hits the water and is immediately plunged deep below the surface. He struggles back up to find himself staring at the foot of a solid 30-metre wall of black water. Above, in the helicopter, Jones and Barclay see it too. Jones calls out to ask Barclay if there's enough cable out for a quick climb. Barclay pays out the cable and Jones jumps the chopper up another 15 metres from its 30-metre hover. The wave breaks just underneath it. The chopper's radio altimeter, which measures the distance to the nearest mass below, spins down to less than three metres. Jones sees spray from the breaking crest fly past him at eye level.

Underneath the chopper, the wave begins sucking Key up its side. Halfway up, buoyant in his wetsuit, he starts tumbling back down. Key is terrified. The rain and sea spray stab into his face like fork points. The wind is screaming in an unholy deafening shriek. Then the wall of dark greenish-black water dumps on top of him and pushes him under. He is thrown around like a rag doll. When he comes out the other side, about 20 metres and fifteen seconds later, he's swallowed litres of sea water. He plummets straight down into a 10-metre wave trough. Now completely disoriented, he can't see Campbell or the helicopter. He knows that his body-weight and the force of the wave could have pulled the chopper into the water. For the first time in his life, David Key thinks the helicopter must have punched him off (cut the cable), or crashed. He doesn't think he'll survive long on his own in the water. He's about to inflate his life jacket and set off his EPIRB. But there's no-one out there to rescue him anyway. He feels utterly alone.

Above, Barry Barclay is still trying to manoeuvre the winch to push Key closer to Campbell. He sees Key go under, and twice sees Campbell floating face-down before rolling over. He can tell they are both exhausted. In a last attempt to position Key, he pulls him out of the water, swings him on the end of the cable like a pendulum and dumps him back in the waves. Key is too confused to know what's happening. He feels himself hitting another wave and going underwater. But Barclay has timed the drop perfectly. When Key bobs to the surface, he looks three metres straight ahead and sees John Campbell. Campbell's face is ashen. For a moment he only stares blankly. Then he seems to wake up, see Key, and the two start swimming towards each other. Key grabs Campbell and holds him as hard as he can. Another wall of water hits. Both are pushed under. Campbell, totally exhausted and almost unconscious, is a dead weight. Key drags him to the surface and puts the rescue harness over his head. Campbell doesn't have any strength left to lift his arms. Key pushes the arms through. A wave hits and wraps the winch cable around Key's left leg. The wind is so loud, Key can't hear the chopper and he doesn't know whether he's still attached to it. But if the winch tightens now, his leg will be cut in two. He has to hold Campbell above the water and untangle himself. Campbell's face is badly injured. His body feels cold as ice.

Still not knowing whether anyone is there to see him, Key gives the signal that he's ready to be winched up. For what seems like an eternity, nothing happens. But, above, Barclay is 'conning' (talking) Jones into position overhead. Barclay starts winching. The cable tenses up. But half-way up, Campell's arms start lifting. He's slipping out of the strop. Barclay calls out to Jones, 'We're going to drop this bloke.' Then something happens that helicopter crews train for but that even Key, in all his years of flying, has never experienced. Just as Campbell and Key get to the door of the chopper, the winch freezes. The two men are stuck near the top of the cable outside the chopper. Key knows there is nothing he can do except hang there.

The only way Jones can reset the winch is to turn it off and back on again. It doesn't work. Jones tries it again, and again nothing happens. Campbell is about to slip out of the strop. Barclay leans as far as he can out of the chopper and grabs Campbell's thermal underpants. Realising it isn't enough, he leans out even further to wrap his arms around Campbell's chest in a bear hug. There's enough cable out to leave a little slack in the wire. With an almighty tug, Barclay hauls Campbell and the rescue harness half into the chopper and drags the rest of Campbell's body through the door. Just as he turns around to work out what to do with David Key, Darryl Jones recycles the winch for a fourth time and it hums back to life.

Back in the chopper David Key retches up sea water. In between his own spasms, Campbell is mouthing thanks. Key and Barclay cuddle up to Campbell on the floor and try to rub him warm. Judging by his facial injuries and severe hypothermia, Key is certain Campbell was only a few minutes from dying. After a short time Campbell collapses into shock. Watching from the sea, someone on *Kingurra* calls up the police chopper on the radio. 'How is he?' they ask. 'Alive and well,' comes the answer. The *Kingurra* crew, though still floundering in the storm, are ecstatic. Campbell has been in the water forty minutes. The rescuers took ten minutes to find him and pull him out.

The police helicopter radios in that it's rescued Campbell, and is directed to fly back to Merimbula airport, slightly north of Mallacoota. But Jones looks at his fuel levels and figures he won't make it. He'll have to head for Mallacoota, which the chopper's GPS tells him should take about forty-five minutes. He has eighty minutes of fuel. Thirty minutes later he does the calculations again. This time he has fifty minutes of fuel and, the GPS tells him, thirty minutes more flying. The figures don't add up and there's no land in sight. Jones is worried. He reduces engine power to a minimum. Just south of Gabo Island he turns right, to take advantage of the wind. By now he has ten minutes of fuel and twelve to fifteen minutes to Mallacoota. He finally sees land and flies along the coast, getting ready to put down whenever he has to. He makes it to Mallacoota with only a few minutes to spare.

At 8.15 p.m. John Campbell is transferred to an ambulance. Senior Constables David Key, Barry Barclay and Darryl Jones get out of the chopper and stare at each other in silence. The three men have never before done a rescue together as a team. That afternoon, if any one of them had made a single mistake, four people would have died.

THIRTY-THREE

*You can't expect other people and other vessels to
endanger themselves to help you. They have to look after
their own safety first. If they sink, they can't help you,
so you can't expect them to endanger themselves to help
you. I think, if they can, they can. If they can't, they
can't. Only they can make that decision. But if a boat
was in our vicinity and we could have offered help, we
would have attempted to stand by somehow. I don't
know how, but we would have attempted to do
something. It would have been dangerous, but I know
we would have tried.*

—*Steve Walker,* Business Post Naiad

Late that Sunday afternoon, safe in Eden harbour on *Trident IV*, Drew
Murray turns on his radio to find out what's going on in the Sydney to
Hobart. He can't believe what he hears. It sounds as if the race is in chaos.
Boats are in trouble everywhere. He crosses his fingers, hoping his friends
on *Business Post Naiad* aren't among them. He isn't too worried. They
know Bass Strait, and they know what they're doing. But a short time
later, to his horror Murray hears *Business Post Naiad*'s navigator, Peter
Keats, call up on the HF emergency frequency. *Business Post Naiad* is
sending out a mayday. What can have happened? Keats is a quiet and
unassuming man, but even on the crackling airwaves, Murray hears an
edge of panic in his voice. Shocked, Murray notes down the time in his
log-book. When he first hears his friends are in trouble it's 5.50 p.m.

Peter Keats's mayday isn't picked up by the radio-relay boat. But it is heard on Geoff Ross's yacht, *Yendys*. *Yendys* is thrashing around so violently that its navigator, Danny McConville, a policeman, can barely hold his pen still long enough to make notes. He scribbles down the mayday and notes *Business Post Naiad*'s position. McConville guesses it's about 25 nautical miles, or at least four hours sail, behind *Yendys*. McConville calls *Business Post Naiad* and says he'll pass on the mayday to Canberra.

On *Business Post Naiad*, Keats can't call Lew Carter directly but he can hear him talking. He also hears *Yendys* pass on the mayday. But the radio-relay boat is busy with other calls. Eventually *Business Post Naiad*'s mayday is acknowledged. But to Keats's surprise, there's no more than that. No message to be passed back, no questions about the nature of the mayday. He can only hope someone is trying to help, but he doesn't feel confident. 'The radio-relay boat was to some degree overwhelmed by the amount of radio traffic coming through,' he recalls later. 'Boats were calling for assistance, requesting information about getting back to Eden, and what the situation was. They were trying to organise a rescue for another boat at that stage. A fishing boat was out looking for another boat and they were trying to organise that.'

Keats feels helpless. Soon it will be dark. *Business Post Naiad*'s deck is cracked, its windows are broken, there's about half a metre of water in the hull and the waterlevel is rising. He has sent out the most urgent distress call possible and it's been barely acknowledged. The radio is jammed with traffic but none of it has anything to do with his mayday. Most of the talk seems to be about a fishing trawler, *Moira Elizabeth*, trying to find another yacht, *Team Jaguar*.

The search for *Team Jaguar* has been underway for hours. Every time *Moira Elizabeth* is given a position for the yacht, it goes there and finds nothing. Like many others that day, Tom Bibby, the trawler's skipper, is having trouble with his radio. He can hear what's going on but no-one can hear him. After a while Bibby picks up the trawler's phone and calls Lew Carter on *Young Endeavour*, the radio-relay boat, to find out what's happened to *Team Jaguar*. Carter passes messages between the trawler and the yacht, using the phone and the radio.

In Eden, listening to the chatter, Drew Murray is becoming anxious. Murray's own radio is receiving but not transmitting. He can't call in, but he can hear Carter on *Young Endeavour* talking about the yacht and the trawler, about the weather, and about boats pulling in to Eden. He can't hear anything about his friends on *Business Post Naiad*. Finally Murray hears Keats report that *Business Post Naiad*'s motor is working and the crew is trying to head back for shelter. *Young Endeavour* asks whether Keats can downgrade the mayday. But Keats, believing *Business Post Naiad* is still in imminent danger, refuses. Murray is certain Keats never downgrades the mayday; Keats certainly never intends to. But what neither of them knows at the time is that somehow, once Keats reports the motor is working, *Business Post Naiad*'s distress call loses its priority. In all the chaos, as Search and Rescue confirms later, *Business Post Naiad*'s mayday is effectively downgraded.

But even with its motor on, *Business Post Naiad* is making little progress. The storm seems to have worsened, and without the balance of its mast the yacht tosses more wildly than before. 'It was like you were sitting on the top of a car in the pouring rain, and being driven along the road at 160 kilometres an hour—that's how much wind there would have been,' says Steve Walker. 'Only, the car would be steady, but the boat was pitching and rolling as well.' The life rafts are ready, wedged in between the bottom of the companionway and a bulkhead. Walker thinks they might be needed any minute. So many waves break over the deck that, in one hour in the cockpit, Walker remembers being completely submerged at least three times. Each time, he has to hold his breath. Still clinging on inside the boat, he's almost swimming.

By now, three of the crew are injured. Walker has a deep cut across his nose, one man can't move his arm, and Keats has broken several ribs. Keats can still hear the radio-relay boat on the radio to *Team Jaguar* and *Moira Elizabeth*. At about 8.00 p.m., worried that *Business Post Naiad* won't make it through the night, he tries another relay through *Yendys*. This time Keats asks *Yendys* to pass on a request for a boat to stand by *Business Post Naiad* during the darkness and for a helicopter to take three men, two injured and one suffering hypothermia, off the boat. When Danny McConville on *Yendys* hears the request, he writes down the positions of a few boats he thinks may be nearby. The closest one he can find is *Loki*, probably about 18 kilometres from *Business Post Naiad*.

McConville calls *Loki* to ask if they can help. But *Loki*'s windows are broken and it's in difficulty itself. Another boat, *Tilting at Windmills*, also picks up *Business Post Naiad* on the radio. Its skipper, Thorry Gunnerson, remembers hearing *Business Post Naiad* ask if a couple of men could be lifted off the boat by a helicopter. *Tilting at Windmills* passes on the request for a chopper to the radio-relay boat *Young Endeavour*. *Tilting at Windmills* is also about 18 kilometres from *Business Post Naiad*. Looking out at the conditions, Gunnerson thinks it pretty unlikely that a helicopter would be able to rescue anyone. He doesn't recall hearing a request for a yacht to stand by.

Peter Keats doesn't know how many rescue helicopters there are, or whether any boats are available to stand by. He realises there probably isn't much that another boat can do. Even so, it would give them some security. But *Business Post Naiad*'s request for a boat to stand by is never answered, or even acknowledged. 'I know that in those conditions it would be virtually impossible for another boat to do anything,' Keats says later, 'but they might have been able to help if we sank. That was still a possibility, and it worried me. I thought that maybe if there was a boat there and we went down, they might at least have been able to pick us up.'

Shortly after Keats asks for a boat to stand by, *Young Endeavour* asks *Yendys* for a mobile phone number for *Business Post Naiad*. Peter Keats can't believe it is all he's asked. He already knows no-one's mobile is working so far out to sea. Frustrated, he passes on what he is certain is useless information. He hears nothing more. Not even an acknowledgment. After the race, Peter Keats is deliberately restrained. He won't say anything about what he really felt that afternoon and night in Bass Strait. But sitting at home, on the north coast of Tasmania, surrounded by tall trees and a well-tended garden, his voice shudders. 'I'd asked for assistance. I didn't see any point trying to push the issue when other boats were in trouble, I just took it that we would have to wait our turn. If there was no assistance available, we would have accepted that. It just would have been nice to have been advised and told.' Keats won't say any more.

≺ ≻

Steve Walker comes from a family of seamen. He's spent most of his life around sailboats. He knows that, in reality, *Business Post Naiad* is completely on its own. 'We thought we would always be found and helped,' says Walker. 'We thought we'd have to survive till equipment was available. We just didn't know if there were five boats, or ten boats, or twenty boats in the same situation as us. Only so many people can be helped at once. We obviously had to take our turn. We must have been a priority, but we didn't know what that priority was. We could only do what we were doing. We were between the devil and the deep blue sea. It just would have been reassuring to have heard something. It would have increased the comfort level to have known they knew where we were and what we were doing. I mean, we just felt that we probably weren't acknowledged all that well.'

Sometime after 8.00 p.m., after two hours of relaying messages from *Business Post Naiad*, and about twenty minutes after Peter Keats's request for a boat to stand by for the night, *Yendys* drops out of radio contact with *Business Post Naiad*. At 8.30 p.m. *Yendys*, still heading south, sends a message on Telstra's SatCom service to the Cruising Yacht Club in Sydney. 'There have been a lot of retirements and damage,' the message reads. '*Yendys* assisted in the coordination of assistance for the yacht *Business Post Naiad*, who was rolled over 360 degrees and three crew hurt when washed over the side ... We are about halfway across Bass Strait with a number four jib and two reefs in. Huge seas, but we are trying to get a warm meal going.'

Peter Keats, still listening to the radio, eventually gives up trying to broadcast. Sitting beside him, *Business Post Naiad*'s skipper, Bruce Guy, is very quiet. After the roll, Rob Matthews heard Bruce Guy say a couple of times, 'At least everyone's okay.' But now, as night falls, Guy is silent. He seems despondent. Later, Matthews wonders whether he was in pain. Over the next couple of hours, Bruce Guy takes over on the radio and relays messages through two other boats. One is *Midnight*

Special. At 8.45 p.m., listening in Eden, Drew Murray hears Bruce Guy tell *Midnight Special* he thinks *Business Post Naiad*'s fuel is running low. Guy is worried there may be water in the tank and that some of the fuel has been lost in the rollover. *Midnight Special* passes on *Business Post Naiad*'s position. Back in Eden harbour, Drew Murray, plotting *Business Post Naiad*'s course since its first mayday, notes it too. Murray knows *Business Post Naiad* is trying to steer north-west, but he can see it's drifting north. He looks at the positions given for *Business Post Naiad* and *Midnight Special*. The two boats are about 15 kilometres apart. Drew Murray guesses they are in the worst part of the storm. They both seem to be moving with it.

THIRTY-FOUR

The beginning of the rescue is a search in itself.
Anything to do with a beacon, we consider first off it's a
life-threatening situation. If people put a mayday out,
it's a life-threatening situation. It was very difficult
because all we usually had was a name. We didn't have
a position till we had an aircraft over each boat,
reporting its condition.
—David Gray, spokesman, Australian Maritime Search
and Rescue

You feel as though you're selling them short, because
you'd like to do more. You'd like to say, 'Yes, I'm here,
and I'm going to help you as well.' But all you can do
sometimes is reassure them that their mayday has been
answered and someone is out there. I suppose it's better
than nothing.
—Lt Phil 'Wacka' Payne, Royal Australian Navy

Sunday, 27 December 1998
Night

By nightfall, rescue coordinators in Canberra realise the Sydney to Hobart is on the brink of disaster. Search and Rescue, having declared a general mayday for the area south-east of Eden, is feeling the strain on resources. By night, most of the search aircraft will have to be grounded and the chances of pulling off rescues will be slim. Only one service, the Navy, is equipped for night rescues. Its choppers are on their way. But there are only two of them and the whiteboard in Canberra lists three yachts unaccounted for and thirteen yachts in trouble. The thirteen are: *Team Jaguar, Siena, Solandra, Atara, Renegade, Secret Men's Business, Pippin, Midnight Special, Business Post Naiad, Winston Churchill, Sword of Orion, Solo Globe Challenger* and *Miintinta*. Ultimately, half those yachts will limp to shelter. But four will sink. And three boats will, between them, lose the lives of six crewmen.

At Search and Rescue the maydays and EPIRBs rank equally. Without radio contact, the only way to prioritise the distress calls is to physically find each yacht and assess its situation. And that, during the night and at the height of the storm, is the proverbial search for a needle in a haystack.

In 1979 the storm that struck the Fastnet race was at its worst in the early hours of the morning. Yachtsmen reported winds over 60 knots and waves above 14 metres. The rescue operation began with the launching of lifeboats at about ten in the evening; the first helicopters were called in the next day, taking off at 5.30 in the morning. Flying one of them, a Sea King, was young Royal Air Force pilot Tanzi Lea. Nearly twenty years later, Commander Lea is on a Navy exchange program in Australia. He is stationed a few hours drive south of Sydney at what the Navy calls, rather poetically, HMAS *Albatross*.

The Navy gets its first call from Search and Rescue at 4.20 p.m. Within three hours the first Sea King has taken off. In the meantime, its crew, called in from holiday stand-by, has prepared the chopper, been briefed by Search and Rescue and organised a fuel drop and extra lighting at Merimbula airfield. A second Sea King, piloted by Tanzi Lea, takes off about two hours after the first. At first the crew on the first Sea King thinks only one yacht is in trouble. 'It didn't seem to be a huge problem,' recalls Lieutenant Phil 'Wacka' Payne. 'We had the night capability the civilian operators don't have. It sounded as though one boat was in distress and we were going in to help it.'

As it heads south, the first Sea King is briefed by Search and Rescue with the coordinates of an EPIRB signalling from *Business Post Naiad*. When the chopper hits the storm front, Payne estimates the wind is about 60 knots. 'Pretty breezy,' he describes it, 'hair-raising, actually. The sort of weather you're trained to avoid. We were operating the aircraft on its limits, the limits of the aircraft and probably the limits for the aircrew.' Soon more distress signals and maydays start flooding the airwaves. *Business Post Naiad* drops out of the picture. The Sea King is briefed to find another yacht, *B52*. As he turns away, Wacka Payne imagines that either someone else has found *Business Post Naiad* or it's no longer in trouble.

The Sea King's night capacity means it can hover over water in darkness with relative safety. But there's nothing magic about the rest of its equipment. Its radar gear is struggling in the storm and the crew has little more to search with than the naked eye. The cloud is low, it's pouring rain and Payne estimates the waves are on average around 10 metres. He isn't too hopeful about the chances of spotting a small yacht that, as he puts it, has just spent the last few hours in a washing machine.

Payne's image isn't far from the truth. As the Sea King is taking off from Nowra, *B52* is upside down in Bass Strait. For four or five minutes, eight of the ten crew are trapped in the upturned hull, standing on what used to be the cabin ceiling, and knee-deep in water. 'We even had time to go to the radio and try to send out a mayday,' skipper Wayne Millar told a reporter. The two men on deck, Mark Vickers and Russell Kingston, are trapped under the upturned hull. Vickers unhooks to swim out. A wave hits and Vickers is swept about 40 metres from the boat, without a life jacket. *B52* stays upside down long enough for him to swim back and check the keel and rudder for damage. Meanwhile, Kingston has managed to swim to the surface and cling onto a stanchion. When the yacht finally spins upright, its mast, engine and radio are broken. The only thing that might still be working is the EPIRB.

By the time Payne's chopper is redirected, one of the *B52*'s most experienced sailors, Don Buckley, has decided that this is definitely his last Sydney to Hobart. Buckley, a yacht repairer, was, until a few weeks earlier, planning a quiet Christmas holiday. But he'd raced with *B52* and grown to like its crew and its skipper, Wayne Millar. So when Millar called him, Buckley changed his mind.

From the very first Sydney to Hobart, when John Illingsworth recalled his stormy passage as 'uneventful', sailors describing the race have been perfecting the art of understatement. Talking about the start and the finish of the race is one thing. Describing the details of the long stretch in the middle is another. That's the part that's often known for being cold, wet and full of the smell of diesel and seasickness. The kind of conditions that can quickly build friendships or, just as quickly, break them.

Usually, Don Buckley isn't bothered by seasickness. But in this race he is. Severely. From early Sunday morning, everything he does or tries to do is overshadowed by nausea. Sometimes he blacks out completely. He isn't alone. Eight or nine boats pull out of the race because their crews are too sick to continue. Buckley feels guilty about being so ill, 'I was one of the most experienced people on board but I felt like I let the others down. No-one really talks about how seasickness affects crews but it's a big issue.' For the first time, Buckley also realises he doesn't really have a clue what to do in an emergency. He's never needed rescuing before. A little after *B52* flips back upright, a plane flies over it. 'Luckily,' he admits, 'two people on board had done a survival course and knew how to set off flares, because I didn't know how to.' The plane dips its wings, flashes its lights and flies away. The crew can only assume it's seen them. About an hour later, when Wacka Payne's Sea King turns up, Buckley has had enough. 'We were very relieved,' he says later. 'Some people were being very tough and saying they didn't mind not being rescued, but I know I had my hand up! I didn't care, I wanted out!'

Unfortunately for Buckley, Payne has no way of knowing any of that. At first, Payne thinks the Sea King will simply pull up the crew and fly them home. It seems straightforward. But he soon realises there's no way of communicating with the yacht to plan the rescue or find out if the crew really wants one. The Sea King keeps being swept away by the wind. It can barely hold nearby in a hover. The Navy crew decides to drop down a line with a message in a waterproof bag. 'Unfortunately,' says Payne, 'our waterproof bag wasn't as waterproof as it should have been.'

On deck the *B52* crew can see the chopper's having difficulty but they don't know what to do. They get the message but it's unreadable. Then the Sea King loses the line to the bag and has to back off. It fixes another, lighter, line and tries again. The yacht's bobbing wildly in the water, the helicopter is bouncing just as erratically in the air. Getting the bag on deck is like trying to thread a needle in a cyclone. It takes 40 minutes to land the second bag. The note Payne has written says they should wave their arms if they want to get off and flash their torches if they want to stay. Everyone waves their arms. Payne assumes they want to be rescued. But they may have been waving anyway. From what Buckley remembers, no-one can read the second message either.

The Sea King has to allow sixty minutes to get back to Merimbula. It's taken more than forty-five minutes to make contact and the helicopter has ninety minutes fuel remaining. It's too risky to try to winch the crew off the boat. To be rescued, they would have to jump in the water. The Sea King crew decide that's probably more dangerous than leaving them where they are. If Don Buckley thinks his ordeal is over, he's wrong. Looking down, Wacka Payne thinks B52 looks remarkably well organised. 'They looked very competent and safe. They mightn't have felt safe but as far as we could tell their boat wasn't holed. It was dismasted and riding very badly in the weather but they looked "together" and their life rafts were intact.' Down at sea level the B52 crew watches the Sea King turn around and disappear in the distance. 'We made the decision it was safer to leave them,' Payne says.

After a while, B52 gets its motor going and heads north. The wind seems to stop. Then it worsens. A few hours later the boat's on its side. 'There was water in the hold, water everywhere. It was very scary,' recalls Buckley. Then he blacks out. The next thing he knows, the navigator, Will Oxley, is shaking him. 'Land!' cheers Oxley, 'We can see land!'

Buckley doesn't know it at the time, but the Sea King has a second reason for suddenly leaving. Hovering near B52, it picks up a new mayday on the emergency frequency. Nearby another yacht has two injured crewmen and is taking on water. About 10 kilometres from B52, Sword of Orion has managed to get a light working and the Sea King only takes a few minutes to find it. If Buckley had known what was to happen during Sword of Orion's rescue, he might have been glad to be left behind.

THIRTY-FIVE

> The conditions could get pretty rough but [Phil] never got worried about it. He never got sick like some people do. He knew what to do. I thought he'd be able to swim and, being a diver, he'd know how to hold his breath underwater, but it was pretty treacherous and you've only got to get hit in the head and get tangled up in the line underneath and you're history in about half a minute.
>
> —Joseph Skeggs, father of Phil Skeggs

> My father knew everything in life was a challenge. You could win or lose, you could do it the right way or the wrong way. Dad always did it the right way and did it to win. He was joyful in victory and satisfied in defeat.
>
> Christmas time for my family is always a sailing time . . . years of happy memories will always come back at this time of year, and are now more precious to me than ever.
>
> —Karen Guy, daughter of Bruce Guy

In Eden, Drew Murray is still listening to the endless radio traffic. Now he can hear *Team Jaguar* being asked to release flares for *Moira Elizabeth*, and *Moira Elizabeth* announcing it's releasing flares for *Team Jaguar*. There is even a phone hook-up from Sydney, when someone from a company selling navigation systems is patched through to try to help

Team Jaguar fix its GPS. At one point Lew Carter calls for silence on the emergency frequency, to clear the airwaves for *Team Jaguar* and *Moira Elizabeth* to communicate clearly. But all Murray wants to know is what's happening to his friends on *Business Post Naiad*. He doesn't hear a word about them.

Out at sea, Peter Keats is also listening to the radio. Next to Keats, and knowing he'll soon have to go back on deck, Rob Matthews is lying on a bunk trying to get warm. He can hear the two men outside struggling to steer the boat in the darkness. Every so often, Steve Walker screams out, 'Hang on! Here comes another one.' Matthews and Keats hear the radio-relay boat call for silence on the emergency frequency. Matthews groans. Keats wonders why *Team Jaguar* isn't transferred to another radio or another frequency. He doesn't think that *Team Jaguar* has even sent out a mayday.

Keats is right about the fact that *Team Jaguar* never called mayday. The search by the trawler is part of a commercial arrangement. After the race, *Team Jaguar*'s skipper, Martin James, says he felt his boat was never in imminent danger. The crew only triggered an EPIRB earlier because the boat was out of radio contact before sked time. James says he could easily, the next day, have rigged up a sail on a spinnaker pole and limped into Eden. He says he never needed urgent assistance. But his boat just happens to be one of the first to get into trouble.

Around 9.00 p.m. Matthews staggers up from the wet bunk he's lying on. Incredibly, the locker he put his clothes in stayed watertight during the roll. He spends a fair bit of time putting on dry thermals, a dry set of clothes, his wet-weather gear and flotation jacket. He knows he will have a tough time ahead. Just as he finishes dressing, Walker calls out from above, 'I need a hand!'

At about 10.30 p.m., even Lew Carter decides the search for *Team Jaguar* is becoming ridiculous. Carter tells Tom Bibby on the trawler *Moira Elizabeth* that, if Bibby can't find the yacht, he can give up chasing it. *Team Jaguar* will sort out something else. By now Bibby assumes that *Team Jaguar* doesn't desperately need assistance. He's heard that a small cargo ship has already found the yacht and offered to pick up the crew but they have declined. But the *Moira Elizabeth* has already been out in the storm for more than six hours and Bibby decides to press on. After a while the search becomes a comedy of errors.

At one point, Drew Murray hears *Moira Elizabeth* report that it has found *Team Jaguar*. The trawler and the yacht are still talking to each other via Lew Carter on *Young Endeavour*. Bibby's crew is about to throw a line to *Team Jaguar*. Carter breathes a sigh of relief. 'The next thing,' says Carter, 'the skipper came down from the bridge and said, "Lew, we've got this bloody big trawler alongside us." I said, "Trawler? Is it far away?" "No," he said, "you could bloody near step on it!" The seas were really huge at this stage; it was rather precarious. So I immediately got on the radio and I said, "*Moira Elizabeth*, could you describe the vessel that you're about to throw a line to?" And he said, "Yeah. It's a lot bigger than I thought. It's got two masts. And it's got sails up." "*Moira Elizabeth*!" I said, "You're about to take a line to the *Young Endeavour*!" He said, in a typical Aussie way, "Christ Almighty! I thought it was strange. You told me that it had only one mast and that it had been lost. You said it was about 60 foot and it looks about twice that. You said it had no sails. This one's got two masts, plenty of sails and it's about 130 feet long. Christ Almighty, where is this bloody *Team Jaguar*?"'

Drew Murray hears it all. But he finds it less than amusing. What's happened to his friends? Murray looks at the chart he's been marking. He guesses *Business Post Naiad* is less than four kilometres from *Moira Elizabeth*. Both are quite close to the radio-relay boat, *Young Endeavour*. Why don't they send the trawler to find *Business Post Naiad*? Why don't they transfer *Team Jaguar* and the fishing boat to a radio frequency that isn't needed for emergencies?

Shortly before 11.00 p.m., bursting with frustration, Murray grabs his chart, jumps onto the jetty and runs up the hill from Eden harbour to Eden Police Station.

< >

Seventy kilometres out to sea, Murray's friend Rob Matthews is battling through the waves. Next to him, Phil Skeggs is leaning over the compass and shouting out bearings. 'The noise was so extreme he had to scream,' says Matthews. 'The wind and spume hit your face like bullets. You could only look up for a moment. You just try to steer up the waves by feeling where the wind is on your face. Then you crash through at the top of the wave, and thunder down its back, trying to set your course as you fall. Water was pouring in through the cabin roof. The motor was screaming its head off, revving like mad in the white water. Some of the waves went up, up, up—it seemed forever. And at the top of every one you would tumble and fall off. The boat was surfing sideways. Sometimes it would be dragged two or three hundred metres. Picture a wave on a surf beach and a small surfboat being hit, carted backward and spun around. Sometimes we'd go 30 or 40 metres backward.' Every time a wave hits, Rob Matthews grabs hold of the boom. Phil Skeggs clings onto a winch.

Mostly it's pitch black but a couple of times there's a brief glow of moonlight. For a moment Matthews can see where he's going. But he can also see how enormous the waves are. 'I could see for a bit, but I thought, Jesus, I don't really want to see this. It was mixed emotions.'

At about 11.00 p.m. Steve Walker is below deck, half dozing. Trying to keep out of the water, he's perched on one of the life rafts that's wedged in at the bottom of the companionway. He can hear the motor revving high. All of sudden, over the revs, he hears a crash of water. It sounds like a huge waterfall is heading for the boat. Before he knows what's happening, the boat is upside down and he's standing on the roof of the cabin. The motor cuts out. Seawater floods in through the broken windows. Everyone is thigh-deep in water. 'It was,' says Peter Keats, 'very scary. Very scary.'

Up on deck Matthews hasn't seen the wave coming. 'We just went up, up, up to the top. Then the wave slammed the bow to starboard and started casting us sideways. The wave was breaking over the whole length of the boat. The whole thing was awash. This time the boat seemed to go up on its side slowly, until the water pushed it on its roof. It was almost gentle when it tipped. My arm came off from where I was holding the boom and I was washed off.'

The wave pushes Matthews backward, over the lifelines. The boat is upside down. Underwater, he can feel the back section of the cockpit behind his head. 'The boat was surfing on its roof and I was under it, flapping and banging like a rag doll. I couldn't get my safety harness undone; it was being pulled as taut as a violin string. I just couldn't undo it. I got to the stage where I was right out of breath. And then the boat was picked up a bit by another wave. There was a shaft of air, about six inches wide. I took the biggest snout-full of air as soon as I could. The last bit of it was water. I kept thinking: "I'm not going to gag or cough or spit it out, I have to hold on and get myself loose."'

The deck slams back down on his head and once again Matthews is being dragged behind the inverted hull on the end of his lifeline. 'Finally, there was enough slack to get the harness free. I came up to the surface and hung onto the back of the boat. It was still thundering along on its roof at about a million miles an hour. I was hanging on like I was behind a giant surfboard.'

The seven men inside feel trapped. 'We wanted to make an escape route,' says Steve Walker. 'Bruce Guy and I tried to pull the main hatch back, which let more water in. Bruce was keen to push a life raft out, but I said, "Don't, Bruce, it's only going to get trapped in the cockpit." On deck it was a tangle of ropes and rigging where we'd secured the mast. I didn't want the raft getting stuck in that. I said to Bruce, "Just hang onto it. I think when we get hit by another wave, the boat will roll again and come upright."' Keats is wearing a bushwalker's head-lamp. He turns it on. Worried that the keel has come off, Steve Walker checks the bolts. The hull seems solid. For four or five minutes the boat stays upside down. The next big wave doesn't seem to be in a hurry. Everything seems unbearably quiet. Then, Walker hears Matthews outside the boat yelling: 'Phil, Phil!'

There's no reply.

Matthews can't see Phil Skeggs. He clings on to the back of the boat, trying to get his breath back and work out what to do next. 'I had two thoughts. The first was: I'm glad I didn't renew my subscription to *Cruising Helmsman*. Honestly. That's the first thing I thought of. The second was: I had this mental picture of Thierry Dubois, the solo yachtsman, hanging on for grim death to the rudder of his boat in the middle of nowhere. I looked up at the rudder and the keel and, even though the rudder was banging about pretty violently, I decided that was where I wanted to be if this thing was going to stay upside down.'

Matthews swims to the left and bangs into something sticking out from the side of the boat. Disoriented, he thinks it's the boom. Later he realises it's the mast, which had been dragged back on deck after the first roll. Sitting on it, he's up to his neck in water. He tries to grab onto the lifeline. He is still quite close to the back of the moving boat. He tries to launch himself up onto the keel. But he can't. A minute later, he tries again. He can't make it.

Suddenly a big wave arrives, washes over the keel and slams the boat upright. Below deck, as the boat flips upright, water gushes in through the windows and hatchway. There's so much water, Walker is certain the whole thing will sink any minute. Then, as the seven men below scramble to get up on deck, Bruce Guy seems to stumble on the companionway stairs. Walker sees him fall down in the water. He picks him up and holds onto him. Before he can do anything else, he realises his friend is having a massive heart attack. Hugging him, Walker drags Guy to a bunk and tries to clear his mouth. It's too late. Bruce Guy, who had wanted for so long to sail in the Sydney to Hobart, is lying dead in Steve Walker's arms.

Incredibly, when the boat bounces upright, the water picks up Matthews and flips him over too. He lands back in the cockpit, just past the lifelines. It's exactly the place he was trapped in when the boat turned upside down. 'I landed on my feet. Not exactly like a ballerina, but my harness was right there next to me. I clipped it back on and stepped back in over the lifelines. I know I am the luckiest man alive.'

But Matthews can see straight away that his friend Phil Skeggs isn't moving. 'He was back on the boat too. But he was lying in the cockpit, his feet up on the rails. He didn't have ropes wrapped around him, but they were stretched across his back. He was right at the end of his harness. I yelled out at the guys to come up and help.'

Shayne Hansen and Matthew Sherriff come up on deck. 'It took about a minute to get the ropes away,' says Matthews. 'We gave him mouth-to-mouth, cut off his life jacket and did CPR. There were still waves breaking over us the whole time. We kept working on him but it was too late. I'd spent a lot of time with him on that trip. We'd done a lot of miles. Had a lot of laughs. I sat down next to him and gave him a punch: "C'mon you bastard! Stop fooling around!" I just thought, things like this happen to other people. It couldn't be happening to us.' Matthews has no idea what is going on below deck. In hindsight, he isn't sure he would have been able to deal with it if he had known.

When *Business Post Naiad* rolls, Drew Murray is at Eden Police Station, trying to get the attention of the officer in charge, Sergeant Keith Tillman. Tillman is snowed under, fielding calls and trying to arrange rescues. The police station doesn't have a list of boats in the race, or names of crews. Finally, Tillman checks the record and tells Murray that *Business Post Naiad* is okay and motoring back to shelter. But Murray is sure his friends are in trouble. Pointing to the chart he's been marking, he starts telling a young officer from the Water Police what he's heard on the radio. The young man calls out to Tillman. 'You might want to listen to this guy,' he says, 'it sounds like he knows what he's talking about.' When Tillman hears the story, he asks Murray what he wants him to do. 'Ask Coastal Patrol to get Lew Carter to raise *Business Post Naiad* on the radio,' Murray answers. 'They've been forgotten.'

Murray and Tillman call Eden Coastal Patrol from the police station. They can hear Lew Carter on the radio-relay boat, still talking to *Team Jaguar* and *Moira Elizabeth*. The Eden operator calls up Telstra Control on the *Young Endeavour*.

'Coastal Patrol Eden to Telstra Control, do you copy?'

'This is Telstra Control.'

'What's the latest on *Business Post Naiad*?' asks Eden.

'I'm not sure,' comes the answer. 'I'll have to get back to you.'

By now it's clear that all the race communications are in chaos. The radio-relay team can't hear all the yachts directly and many yachts can't hear them. To add to the chaos, the main race frequency is also being used by another yacht race, from Sydney to Coffs Harbour, and by a private weather forecaster. With only one radio and few staff, Lew Carter and his team on *Young Endeavour* are overwhelmed. Only one person at a time can talk on the radio and relatively non-urgent arrangements like the *Team Jaguar* rescue are allowed to clog up the airwaves. On shore, it's even more of a shambles. No-one knows what's going on. Thousands of calls are coming in to race organisers from friends and relatives of sailors, and from the media. CYCA headquarters in Sydney can only find out what's happening by phoning Hobart or listening to the radio from a yacht in the club's marina. In Hobart, the Race Control Centre is inundated. There's no coordination and people in one centre come and go without telling others. Mobile phones have been diverted or turned off.

When the news of fatalities comes in, it's realised that there is no procedure for notifying families. No-one knows whether responsibility lies with the police, Search and Rescue or the race organisers. Some families first hear the news via the media.

In Eden Drew Murray waits impatiently for an answer from the radio-relay team. He hears more talk about *Team Jaguar* and the trawler but no-one calls back. Eden Coastal Patrol tries again. This time, someone on the radio-relay boat reads out *Business Post Naiad*'s last recorded position. But Murray knows it's hours old. He asks Coastal Patrol to request more information. For two or three minutes, he can hear the radio team scrambling through papers. Finally someone answers, '*Business Post Naiad*? We're hoping they'll come up on the next sked at 3.00 a.m.'

≺ ≻

Out at sea, the seven survivors on *Business Post Naiad* expect what is left of the yacht to soon be under water. 'We couldn't revive Phil and we couldn't revive Bruce, so we secured them as best we could,' says Walker. 'We were very close to sinking. Your survival instinct takes over. If you're ever in that situation, you haven't got time to think. You can either just sit back and wait to die or you can work to keep alive. Most people want to stay alive. We just did everything we could to keep the boat afloat.'

Rob Matthews also believes the boat is sinking. 'There was about a metre and a half of water in it. Water was rolling into the cockpit and going downstairs.' He has seen what the life rafts look like when they are inflated. He knows the last thing he wants to do is get into one.

But some of the crew put a life raft over the side. They throw in some blankets and supplies. As soon as they do, the raft turns over and everything falls out. They turn it over and try again. In all, it flips four times before they decide to leave it upside down till they need it. Steve Walker tries to work out what they will do if the boat sinks. They only have one EPIRB. Will they cram seven men into a six-man raft and take it with them, or will they split the crew and leave one raft without a beacon?

When the moon comes out for a moment, Matthews realises how low the boat is in the water. He remembers that a six-inch inspection port is open at the bow near the anchor. He goes below and wades through the water to try and block it up. He shines his torch around, thinking he'll never find the small plastic port cover but amazingly he finds it straight away. In all the chaos, it's sitting neatly on a bunk. 'I couldn't believe it. I whacked it in. As I was wading back, I noticed the toilet was two feet under water.' Matthews goes back on deck to where Phil Skeggs is lying. 'I thumped him again. I still wanted to think he might come back. It looked like he was resting. I tried to cover him up.'

The crew throw a storm jib and spinnaker over the bow to try to keep the boat heading into the waves. It doesn't work very well. Breaking waves keep pushing it side-on to the sea. Then they bail. They bail and bail. After three hours, the water is knee-high.

While they are bailing, sometime between midnight and 1.00 a.m., a few of the crew see a strong light reflected up onto the clouds, over to the east. They are certain it's a light from a fishing boat. And it isn't far away. They grab six flares and fire them. No-one answers. But there is a trawler nearby. Tom Bibby's trawler, *Moira Elizabeth*, is still looking for *Team Jaguar*. And Bibby is very close to *Business Post Naiad*. There are a lot of flares that night but one set of flares, just after midnight, sticks in Bibby's mind because *Team Jaguar* sees them too. The flares are fired off in between *Team Jaguar* and *Moira Elizabeth*. Bibby thinks someone else will respond to them. He has his hands full looking for *Team Jaguar*.

The crew on *Business Post Naiad* watch their flares shoot sideways in the wind. No-one responds and there's nothing more they can do to attract attention. Finally, they decide to leave some water in the boat to keep it more stable. The second life raft accidentally inflates so they tie it overboard, next to the first one. All of them freezing, exhausted and wet, and some of them injured, they close the hatch, leaving the EPIRB's antenna sticking out on deck. The red light is on and they can only hope the beacon is working. Below, the cabin is churning with water like a surf beach. With every wave, the stove, which broke free of its mounting hours earlier, hurtles from one side to the other. There's food and gear everywhere. Tubs of margarine, cartons of milk, charts, books and the debris of nine men's possessions slosh around in a greasy mix of seawater and diesel.

'If you're in a car crash,' says Rob Matthews, 'you skid, hit something and everything stops. You get out if you can. But this was like a car crash that went on and on. For twenty hours. You couldn't make it stop. You couldn't get out.' Matthews looks over at Bruce Guy, who's lying on a bunk. As the boat rolls, he moves a little. Earlier, Matthews asked Steve Walker where Bruce was. 'I put him in a bunk,' said Walker. Overwhelmed by all that has happened, Walker assumes that Matthews knows Bruce is dead. Similarly overwhelmed, Matthews assumes Bruce Guy is resting. He doesn't learn the truth till morning.

<   >

In Eden, Drew Murray spends the rest of the night trying to find a trawler to go out and rescue his friends. He calls everyone he knows and some people he doesn't. A qualified master seaman, he offers to take full responsibility—to be skipper, crewman, whatever. He writes a cash cheque for $10,000. But no-one will help him. The only fishermen ready or able to go out in the storm are already out there.

At about 3.00 a.m. Steve Walker hears another huge wave smash over *Business Post Naiad*. He's too exhausted to go up and see what's happened to the life rafts. 'At best,' he thinks, 'they're upside down, full of water. At worst, they've gone.' Two hours later, thinking the weather is improving, he goes on deck. 'Conditions had abated considerably by then,' he recalls. 'The seas were probably back to 6 or 7 metres and the wind was probably down around 50 or 55 knots. But there was still no way we could do anything except hang on the way we were.' He puts out a red sailbag, hoping that someone in a plane might see it. The life rafts have disappeared. All that's left are a few dangling ropes and the attachments they were tied to.

Back on his boat, Drew Murray listens to the radio. The *Moira Elizabeth* has *Team Jaguar* under tow and is on its way back to Eden. At 5.30 a.m. Murray turns off the radio. Defeated, he drops onto a bunk. Then he breaks down and cries.

≺ ≻

After the race, Lew Carter has trouble remembering any calls from *Business Post Naiad*. That night he spent about fifteen hours on the radio and talked to dozens of boats. Asked if he remembers hearing from *Business Post Naiad*, he says, 'Um, no. I think from memory *Business Post Naiad* might have been out of radio contact. I think, in a lot of cases, they've got a spare aerial, a whip aerial that they can mount at the back. But if you get rolled over and you get water into anything electrical, it creates a major problem. And I think they'd been rolled two or three times. So you know that boat would have been ... and I think now, having read about it since, they were actually rolled over and over for a matter of minutes. Well, you know, that would be the end of the radio for sure, it certainly would be useless after that.'

At 9.00 a.m., under tow from the *Moira Elizabeth*, the *Team Jaguar* crew sees Eden.

THIRTY-SIX

*It's a lot to ask. You have to have complete confidence
in the rescuers. Basically they are saying, 'We've never
met you before, we don't know who you are, but just grab
ahold of this line and jump off the boat in 30- to 40-
knot winds and 20-foot seas and just swim out there in
the middle of nowhere. And don't worry, somehow we'll
pick you up.'*

—Steve Kulmar, *chief helmsman*, Sword of Orion

When the Navy's Wacka Payne hears *Sword of Orion*'s mayday, he already
knows his Sea King helicopter doesn't have enough fuel left for a rescue.
All he can do is find the yacht, reassure the crew and report their position.
But by the time he does that and refuels in Merimbula, Payne's Sea King
is given another mission and the Navy's second Sea King, piloted by
Fastnet veteran Tanzi Lea, is sent to find *Sword of Orion*. Lea gets to the
yacht's last given position some time after 11.00 p.m.

'Visibility,' says Lea, 'was virtually non-existent. We haven't got any
night-vision aids so we were just using our own eyes. We have a radar
but that was pretty ineffective because the radar reflectors on yachts are
normally near the top of the mast and the yacht was dismasted. In the
sea state, the yacht was so low in the water the radar wasn't helping.
We had to use our searchlight, but it wasn't much good in the driving
rain. It just highlighted the sea state and the whitecaps. We just had to
go on positions we were given and hope there was a strobe light or
something flashing to attract our attention.'

Tanzi Lea spends an hour and a half searching, flying about 150 metres above sea level in a tight spiral. It seems futile. Trying another tactic, he flies downwind about 20 kilometres, turns back and heads for *Sword of Orion*'s last position. It works. The Sea King spots a strobe.

Dwarfed by waves and dismasted, *Sword of Orion* is floundering dangerously. Ropes and wires are strewn over the side. 'The skipper told us they were in need of rescue,' Lea says. 'They had injuries, they were taking water and they wanted rescue there and then.' But Lea's Sea King faces the same problems the first Sea King faced with *B52* a few hours earlier. 'Just winching someone down onto the boat sounds fairly straightforward,' says Lea, 'but if the platform he's going to be put on is moving up and down by eight or ten metres then he could get hit and seriously injured. We decided not to do it. We were hovering alongside at this stage and even that was virtually impossible.'

One of the main reasons the Sea Kings are called in that night is because they can auto-hover over water. But when Lea tries to hold position about 15 metres above the boat, even the automatic hover vacillates wildly. One minute the Sea King's down to about seven metres, the next it's up to 25. Sometimes the boat rides up to meet it, sometimes the two go in opposite directions. The wind is averaging 40 knots, gusting, Lea estimates, to 60. One of the air crew is leaning out the chopper door, trying to yell instructions. The Sea King tries to put down a steadying line. The line's designed to break if it looks like pulling the helicopter into the water. It does just that. The Sea King has only one line remaining.

Watching from below, the *Sword of Orion* crew starts to realise that the rescue is going to be extremely dangerous for anyone who is injured. They choose the youngest and fittest crewman to go first, Darren Senogles. 'They said they'd throw a line down,' says Steve Kulmar. 'The idea was you grabbed ahold of the line, jumped out of the boat, swum away so the line wouldn't catch onto the boat and pull the helicopter into the water, then, swimming away from the boat, you hop into the harness and they pull you up. Sounds nice and simple, doesn't it?' In fact, it's even more difficult than it sounds. 'Desperate measures,' Tanzi Lea says later, 'because if something happened to us, whoever is in the water would probably be another casualty.'

Even the young, fit Senogles spends ten minutes in the water, trying to struggle into the harness. The second-fittest crewman takes about eight minutes to get out of the water. By now, *Sword of Orion* isn't flush with volunteers for rescue. 'No-one was keen to go,' says Kulmar. 'It was 2.30 in the morning, still pretty windy, but they wanted a third person.' Reluctantly, Kulmar comes on deck. The line's already there. In the darkness, about 20 metres from the boat, the harness is bouncing up and down on the waves. Terrified, he grabs the line, jumps off the deck and pushes himself away from the boat. He doesn't really need to push. The yacht's moving away fast enough anyway. By the time he reaches the harness, he's 30 metres from the boat. 'All of a sudden,' he says, 'you realise it's a long way back to the boat if you don't get into the harness. Even before I hopped off the boat, I remember thinking being rescued was more dangerous than staying where I was.'

The harness is tricky. Even though the aircrew tries to shine a light on him, the chopper's being blown around so much that Kulmar is left fumbling in the darkness. All he knows is that he's supposed to pull the harness over his head, put his arms through, grab the wire and be pulled up. But the harness is heavy and he is wearing about 20 kilograms of wet-weather gear, as well as an old-fashioned, bulky, life vest. The wind's blowing the harness around and he can't fit it on over the life vest. He manages to get his left arm in when the harness jerks upward. 'I think they thought I was in, and they raised it. They have to raise it pretty quickly to get you out of the water, because all the time you're going up the crests of waves and falling into troughs. Anyway, they raised it quickly and I fell out of it. So by then I had no line. I'd let go of the line from the boat to the harness. The harness had gone up and I had nothing. So then I spent the next, gee whiz, it felt like a lifetime but it was probably six or eight minutes swimming around the ocean in these 20-foot seas in all my wet-weather gear and this life vest, trying to find the line again.'

Eventually Kulmar finds the line and struggles with the harness a second time. Once again, it's enormously difficult to get it over the back of his life vest. The same thing happens. The harness goes up, leaving him in the water. By now, he's been swimming around for more than fifteen minutes. He's starting to run out of energy. 'By the time I had dropped out of it twice,' he says, 'I think they realised I was struggling. And I was struggling. The wind had been building the whole time and a lot of waves were coming through and breaking. Every ten or twelve seconds there'd be white water everywhere. My lungs were full of salt water and I was feeling pretty exhausted. I'd swum around and around trying to get hold of this line. I'd swim this way and all of a sudden the line would go that way. It was hard work. They lost me under the light because they had to move so far beyond me in the wind. Finally, I think they realised I was really struggling.'

In fact, Tanzi Lea is worried about running out of fuel. He asks the crew frogman, who's already wearing a wetsuit, to go down and help. Lowered into the water, the frogman swims to Kulmar and Kulmar swims to him. 'I can honestly say that by that stage I was almost gone,' says Kulmar. 'By then, I didn't think I could get into the harness by myself. All the ligaments in my right arm were pulled. I was only swimming with my left. He came down and realised pretty quickly that I couldn't get the harness over the back of my life vest. So he pulled and shoved and tugged on it and got me into it, which was a great help, and pulled me out of the water. I can honestly say that I was in a complete and utter state of exhaustion. All I remember doing is looking up at these two white lights shining down on me, and I wasn't sure if I was alive or dead. All I knew was I was heading toward these two white lights. That's all I knew.'

Kulmar lands in the helicopter. He can feel his pulse pounding. His brain feels like it's about to ooze out his ears. 'It was a defining moment,' he says later, 'I knew that if I was still alive I would never do another Sydney to Hobart. My wife, my childen, family and friends meant too much to me. Nothing else mattered.' Kulmar realises that his new sea boots and wet-weather gear are still on *Sword of Orion*. He doesn't care. He won't be needing them for a long time.

The Sea King flies back to Merimbula. Tanzi Lea thinks Kulmar must have had so much trouble because he was one of the injured crewmen. By then, he almost is. The Sea King doesn't attempt another rescue that night.

At 4.00 a.m. another Navy helicopter makes contact with *Sword of Orion*. In the early light it takes just about half an hour to lift off the remaining six crew. *Sword of Orion* is abandoned. It has never been found.

Three months after the race Rob Kothe takes the helicopter crew that rescued him for a sail in his new boat. Like the last one, it's called *Sword of Orion*. By mid-year Kothe and his new *Sword of Orion* are racing again.

THIRTY-SEVEN

*It's a wonderful race. You're mixing with really
talented people. It's as good as going to the Olympics.
We were unlucky. But turning back wasn't the wrong
thing to do.* Midnight Special *turned back to go north.
The wind was coming from the west. It was a logical
conclusion. We'd do the same thing again.*
—Kevin Foran, crewman, Midnight Special

*There should be a big sign at Sydney Heads saying 'No
Right Turn'. But if the opportunity was right and we
had a crew like last time, I'd go again. I mean, it
would never be that bad again, would it?*
—Peter Baynes, co-owner, Midnight Special

At about the same time *Sword of Orion* turned around, *Midnight Special*
was turning around too. By the time it gets dark *Midnight Special* is
only about 25 kilometres from Gabo Island. Peter Baynes guesses the
wind is up around 80 knots, but he can't be sure; all the instruments
have been blown away. At the tiller, steering by feel, Peter Carter doesn't
see the huge wave coming towards him until it is too late. The boat
rises up and does a complete roll. Harnessed on, Carter is thrown against
the boom.

Below deck, lying on the floor near the galley, Peter Baynes hears
water smashing onto the cabin roof. He's flung across the floor. Neil
Dickson is still partially concussed from an earlier knockdown. 'There

was just a huge crash, everything just fell out of everywhere. Torrents of water poured in. I was only semi-conscious but it certainly woke me up in a hurry.' When *Midnight Special* bounces upright, there's a metre of water inside it.

On deck, Carter can feel that he has hurt his back. He can see that the mast has smashed. Dragging himself out from under a pile of rigging, he goes down and starts working the bilge pump. Months later, Carter will still be wearing a back brace. He has two smashed vertebrae and broken ribs. After the race he spends three weeks, flat on his back, in a hospital spinal unit. But now he doesn't have time to think about the pain. 'When your life depends on it, you just get going,' he says later. 'As long as the boat is floating, you've still got a chance.' After the race, another of the crew, Kevin Foran, describes Carter as 'probably the bravest of us all'. 'He was as tough as boots,' says Foran. 'I will admire him forever.'

Midnight Special's cabin top and windows are smashed. There is a one-metre hole where the front window was. The crew cuts away the rigging and the remains of the mast. Up on deck the wind is still howling. 'It sounded like a train,' says Baynes. 'While we were cutting the mast away, waves were washing over the boat.'

All the electronics are out, including the radio, so they turn on the EPIRB. They get the motor going to recharge batteries and rig up some lighting. 'We were a bit limited with steering,' says Carter. 'The tiller had broken off. We decided to let the boat sit with the bow going into the waves. The boat was in the best situation it could be in.' The crew lash the tiller and stuff a spinnaker and sleeping bags into the holes in the cabin. It takes about two hours to pump and bail out most of the water.

For a while they keep up a watch system, but eventually everyone goes below. They are all freezing and wet. There is food and gear everywhere. The food that is left in the fridge is swimming in salt water. No-one has eaten since breakfast. They all know they have little chance of being rescued before morning. They just have to sit it out.

'My life didn't flash before me,' says Peter Carter. 'You just keep going. Even during the night, there wasn't really any panic. Everyone is shit-scared. I know I was. But that emotion doesn't come through.' But Carter says that getting through the night was the hardest part. At one stage he thinks at least an hour has gone by, but when he looks at his watch, it's only been ten minutes. He decides not to look at the time any more. He tries to sleep. 'I was woken up a lot, taking a bit of a bath.'

'You're not confident you'll get out of it,' says Kevin Foran. 'You're in the present. You can't think about the future. You can't think, "In two or three hours, are we still going to be floating?" because right now you are still floating. You are just trying to keep things steady. If the thing keeps floating, in the end you will be all right. You've just got to accept reality as it is. I really don't think any of the guys sat down and thought "Jesus! I'm going to die."'

During the night *Midnight Special* is repeatedly rolled on its side. A few times it tips to 90 degrees. Some people are ill. 'It was a combination,' says Peter Baynes, 'of fear, exhaustion, hypothermia and cold.' 'Some guys did funny things in the night,' says Foran. In one roll, the kettle flies across the boat—he notices later that someone has found it and put it neatly back on the stove.

At about 4.30 a.m., just on first light, they hear the sound of a plane above the roar of the wind and the sea. The crew fires flares and the plane flies over, dips its wings to let them know it has seen them and flies away.

Half an hour later, a helicopter appears on the horizon. It is carrying one of the two crews from SouthCare: pilot Simon Lovell, paramedics David Dutton and Steve Mitchell, and crewman Matt Smith. When the chopper arrives, most of the yacht's crew are below deck. Three are on deck.

As the helicopter hovers above, Mitchell leans out the door and tries to use hand signals to explain he wants each man to climb into the life raft before getting into the water. 'Next thing,' he says, 'instead of deploying the life raft, one of the men jumped off the yacht into the water.' Within thirty seconds, the crewman, David Leslie, is about 100 metres from the boat. 'He was off to New Zealand unless we got him,' says Mitchell. Steve Mitchell and David Dutton plan to alternate winches so that whoever does a rescue has time to treat the survivor for injuries. Dutton is closest to the winch so he goes first. It takes Dutton about five minutes to pick up David Leslie. But during the rescue another huge wave rears up and hits *Midnight Special*.

Waiting below deck for his turn to be rescued, Neil Dickson feels the wave pick the boat up and dump it upside down. It stays there. Dickson finds his feet and stands up on the cabin roof. He is chest-deep in water. It's dark. All he can see is the pale green glow of the ocean coming through the hatchway. Dickson's first thought is to get out of the boat to help the two men on deck. He dives towards the light. But halfway through the hatch he gets caught in a tangle of ropes. 'I remember thinking how bloody stupid I was,' he says.

As Dickson heads for the hatch, Peter Baynes is also worrying about the two men still on deck. 'This isn't meant to happen in boats like this,' he thinks, 'they are meant to come back up again.'

Peter Carter thinks this might be the finish. 'First of all I thought, this is it, we're all going to drown. Then I realised there was still an air-pocket. But I thought things weren't going too well. The chopper is out there to rescue us and we were all trapped in the boat.'

Midnight Special seems to stay upside down for an eternity. Later the crew estimates it is about thirty seconds. Eventually, another wave hits and rolls the boat back upright.

The men below rush up to help the others. Soon everyone is wearing their life jacket. They keep their harnesses on but unclip them from the boat. They're worried the boat might go down and there won't be time to unclip them. 'The guys all decided,' says Carter, 'it's time to get out of here.' They prepare the life rafts.

Above them paramedic Steve Mitchell is about to take his turn on the winch. It's his first ocean rescue. Sitting anxiously on the edge of the helicopter, he wonders if he really wants to go ahead with it. But he has to. He just hopes he can manage it successfully.

By now, the next man to be rescued, Peter Carter, knows the boat he is standing on is sinking. Despite his injuries, he jumps in the water and swims. He knows from seeing the first rescue that if he isn't picked up, he probably won't make it back to the boat. Steve Mitchell hits the water near him. Swamped by a wave, Mitchell loses sight of Carter, then spots him, grabs him and doesn't let him go. Mitchell tries taking off his snorkel to talk but he only swallows seawater. Finally Mitchell signals the helicopter that he's ready to be lifted. Overall the rescue takes about ten minutes. During it another helicopter has arrived and hovers overhead. It's Gary Ticehurst in the ABC-TV chopper. That night Carter's family will see him on the evening news being pulled out of the water. 'I think I've seen myself being rescued 400 times,' he laughs later.

At first the SouthCare crew think there are only three sailors to be rescued. When they find out there are nine, they know they won't have room for all of them. Battling the wind, pilot Simon Lovell is concerned about running out of fuel. Between them David Dutton and Steve Mitchell pull five men to safety. Then Lovell hits what pilots call 'bingo' fuel. If he doesn't leave now, he won't make it back to shore. Peter Carter is lying on the floor of the helicopter, a drip in his arm and an oxygen mask over his face. He can feel the chopper bucking in the wind. He starts hoping it won't crash. But what he's really worried about is his four friends left below on the water.

By now *Midnight Special* is filling with water. The four men left behind realise that trying to bail it out is futile. 'The boat was a wreck,' says Kevin Foran. Peter Baynes finds the EPIRB and puts it in the life raft. Then he sees the rescue helicopter is going. Even the television helicopter has left them. None of the four men on the boat has any way of knowing that the two helicopters are running out of fuel. 'We were saying,' Neil Dickson recalls, with some restraint, '"There must be another one on the way." We didn't think they would forget us.'

Inside the SouthCare helicopter, Carter can hear the crew talking on the radio. To his relief, someone tells them that another chopper is about twenty minutes away.

THIRTY-EIGHT

◄ ►

Well, hindsight's a marvellous thing, but the storm warning was up near the start of the race, and I think in most sporting organisations there are administrators who will make a decision to cancel or postpone an event in the interests of safety. The yacht club feels that it's the responsibility of the skipper and it is to some extent. But they have a responsibility too. The Melbourne race was postponed in the interests of safety.
—Locky Marshall, Eden fisherman, owner of
Josephine Jean

We were the fortunate ones, and the loss of a fine ship is insignificant in comparison with the loss of life and other injuries suffered during this race. The thoughts, prayers and condolences of my crew and myself go out to the loved ones of those six fine seamen who lost their lives doing what they loved and did so well.
—Brian Emerson, skipper, Miintinta

It's about 10.00 p.m. when Brian Emerson calls back the *Union Roetigen* to see if it's still close enough to stand by his yacht *Miintinta*. Emerson knows a trawler is on its way from Eden, but it's three hours away and he isn't sure *Miintinta* will last the distance. The *Union Roetigen* returns. A couple of hours later Emerson hears that the trawler *Josephine Jean* is close by.

By about 2.00 a.m. the *Josephine Jean* has found *Miintinta*. Even though his boat is filling with water Emerson is still convinced he will save it. 'With a good strong boat between us and the sea, I thought we'd be able to get a tow on it and continue to bail,' he says later. 'I hadn't really realised we were in dire peril. It was still blowing about 60 knots. Goodness knows how high the seas were.'

It takes some time to attach the towline. The *Josephine Jean* throws a light line across. Then for about half an hour Emerson struggles to loop the heavy towline over a bollard. Finally he turns on the motor, which has cooled down by now and is working again. With a bit of slack, he secures the rope. 'Immediately we hooked it on I said, "We're saved—we'll be okay." But that wasn't to be the case.'

Fighting the wind and the sea, the trawler can only tow the boat at about one kilometre an hour. After about two hours the bollard holding the towline snaps off. Emerson doesn't think he'll be able to re-attach the towline. But the *Josephine Jean*'s skipper, Ollie Hreinisson, circles *Miintinta* and backs the trawler up till it's almost on top of the yacht. 'Ollie just put that boat in the most amazing positions,' says Emerson. One of the *Miintinta* crew is standing at the front of the yacht. As the boat rises and falls 10 or 12 metres on the waves, the crewman on the trawler passes him the towrope. The next time *Miintinta* goes down on a wave, the two men shake hands as they pass.

Back in Eden, Locky Marshall is pacing the floor, worrying about *Josephine Jean* and her crew. Every half hour he phones up Ollie Hreinisson.

The second tow from the fishing boat holds for a few hours. But *Miintinta* is filling with water and getting heavier. Brian Emerson is having a nap when someone wakes him. The towline has broken again. This time Emerson knows it really is over. It's dawn. He grabs his camera and takes some last photographs of his boat. The seas have gone down but there are still four- to six-metre waves and the wind is blowing about 50 knots. To get onto the trawler, the crew will have to either jump into the water or climb down to the life raft. They choose the raft. Brian Emerson is the last to jump from *Miintinta*. The raft is already pulling away. He leaps and lands on top of someone. When the crew of the *Josephine Jean* pulls him onto the trawler, he couldn't be more grateful. 'I couldn't have clambered up onto that trawler for love or money, if it wasn't for the good strong arms of those two professional fishermen who were deckies on the trawler,' he says later. 'I was exhausted. But they pulled us up. And their lives were at stake. I mean, they're just leaning over the rails, dragging people like us up. It's amazing. Very professional.'

Brian Emerson watches *Miintinta* drift away. He never sees his boat again. His only souvenir is the remains of the bollard that snapped off during the tow. The following day *Josephine Jean* pulls into Eden. The rescue has taken thirty-two hours. Locky Marshall meets the trawler and the yacht crew at the wharf. After the race, Marshall and Emerson stay in touch. 'The six people from *Miintinta* were very grateful and appreciated what we were able to do for them,' says Marshall later. 'But that's not the case with some of the others.' *Josephine Jean*'s Ollie Hreinisson was happy to help with the rescue. But next Christmas, he says, he might stay out of town during the Sydney to Hobart.

THIRTY-NINE

*We weren't heroic. We lost the boat. That's probably
the biggest disgrace you can have. It was a bit unlucky
but, at the end of the day, we sunk it. The only people
who were heroes were the rescuers. None of us could say
we would honestly be game enough to jump out of the
helicopter.*

—*Kevin Foran, crewman,* Midnight Special

*The big thing I remember is the looks on people's faces
when we were rescuing them. It was like we were their
last resort. They'd been through so much, I don't think
they thought they were going to make it. There was just
a look of despair until I got them into the helicopter.
And then it was, 'Thank heavens!'*

—*David Key, Victoria Police Air Wing*

Monday, 28 December 1998
Early Morning

During the night, the Victoria Police rescue crew don't get much rest.
After saving John Campbell they work till nearly midnight. Early the following morning, David Key, Barry Barclay and Darryl Jones are being
briefed for the next day's search. By now the target area is spread over
8000 square kilometres and the search involves thirty-eight aircraft, five
helicopters, several cargo boats and a Navy frigate. A SouthCare helicopter
is sent to look for *Winston Churchill* and the police helicopter is sent to

find *B52*. Both are thought to be about 120 kilometres south-east of Mallacoota. The emergency beacons from both boats have stopped working.
It's possible they might already be too deep under water.

When the police helicopter takes off, conditions are only slightly
better than the day before. Pilot Darryl Jones measures 60- to 65-knot
winds. The waves look 12 to 15 metres high. The only improvement is
that the cloud has risen to about 500 metres and it's no longer raining.
On the way out winch operator Barry Barclay has time to think about
the job ahead: 'After the previous night, and seeing that conditions were
almost as bad, I had deep reservations about whether I had the skill
necessary to complete the winches. It's one thing performing water
winches off the back of a police boat in St Kilda, and another doing
live winches off a sinking vessel in Bass Strait.'

Less than an hour after take-off the police helicopter is redirected. On
the radio, SouthCare tells the police that it has lifted five men from a
yacht and another four men are still on board needing rescue. By
8.00 a.m. the police helicopter has found *Midnight Special*. It's wallow-
ing low in the water, surrounded by floating sails and ropes. Once again,
David Key realises it's far too dangerous to winch from the boat itself.
He will have to go down into the water.

At first, when the four men see the helicopter coming they worry it's
only another TV crew. As it gets closer, the first thing they look for is a
winch. They find one. Without wasting time, Barclay drops Key about
10 metres behind the yacht. As soon as he is in the water Key sees the
waves are higher than he thought. He estimates some are up to 20 metres.
The first of the remaining men to jump off the boat is Neil Dickson. 'I
don't know how we worked it out. It was a bit of a lottery who was going
last,' says Dickson. 'But no-one wanted to jump the queue.'

Just as Dickson jumps overboard a large wave hits Key. He's pushed
under the water and winded. Surfacing, he grabs Dickson and throws
the rescue harness over his head. But Dickson, like many other sailors,
has an old-fashioned, foam life jacket. It's so bulky that Key can't
connect the safety strap around his chest. He'll just have to hold him.
Waiting to be lifted up, Key looks over to *Midnight Special*. He can see
that it's sinking.

In the helicopter, Darryl Jones is finding it almost impossible to maintain a hover and Barclay constantly has to 'conn' him back into position. Barclay waits till the two men below rise to the top of a wave crest. Then he tightens the cable. Wrapped in Key's bear hug, Neil Dickson feels himself fly out of the water. Dickson doesn't realise Key has to hold him because he isn't properly strapped in. 'I've never cuddled a 16-stone man before in my life,' he laughs later. 'It all just happens. You leave the water very quickly. The water just seems to drop away beneath you and the next thing you know, you're hanging under a helicopter. You're actually wrapped in this winchman and he just hangs onto you. When you get to the helicopter door they turn you around so you are facing outward. The winchman inside grabs you by the back of your neck and you're in. There's nothing aesthetic about it, you're just in.' Dickson knows it's only a matter of time till the boat goes down. He realises how much safer he feels to be off it. Then he realises it's the first time he's been in a helicopter.

By now Barclay's anxiety has worn off and his experience kicks in. Considering the conditions, the first winch has gone as routinely as possible. Immediately, Key goes back down. The second man jumps overboard almost as soon as Key hits the water. Key is about 15 metres from the boat and hasn't had time to get ready for him. The yachtsman, wearing a life jacket, is swept past him by a wave. Barclay has to lift Key again and drop him closer. Key can see the man is panicking. He seems to calm down when Key puts the harness over his head. But as the two are being lifted, a wave hits and the man panics again. Key has to struggle to hold him.

The last two men on the boat are Peter Baynes and Kevin Foran. Somehow they work out that Foran will go last. 'My mate Kev is a better fighter than me!' says Baynes later. David Key winches Baynes up fairly routinely. 'Now I know why helicopter rescuers wear big helmets and face shields,' adds Baynes. 'It's to stop the victims from kissing them!'

By now David Key is exhausted. He lies on the floor of the helicopter, vomiting up seawater. Barry Barclay can see that he needs a break. He tells Jones to fly around for a minute. Jones needs a break too. He is starting to cramp from the struggle of holding the helicopter in position. Jones does a circuit and flies back, and Key goes down the winch for the fourth time. When he's ready, he gives the signal and Kevin Foran jumps in the water. Swimming to Foran, Key notices seawater is flowing out of the yacht's cabin, over the deck and into the ocean. As Key and Foran are pulled upward, Key looks down at the yacht again. He sees *Midnight Special* sinking into Bass Strait. By the time Key and Foran reach the helicopter the yacht has disappeared without trace. The four rescues have taken about twenty minutes.

Just before 8.30 a.m. the Victoria Police helicopter lands back at Mallacoota. An ambulance picks up the four yachtsmen. Less than two hours later the chopper is back in the air searching for the beacon from *B52*. About 80 kilometres offshore, the helicopter's homing instruments pick up a signal. The indicator shows the beacon is under the water. The crew search but can't see anything. By now Key is too ill to do any more rescues. He's still vomiting up straight seawater. The Victoria Police turn back to Mallacoota. A few minutes before they arrive, they hear that *B52* has been found safe about 80 kilometres from the area they were searching, and is limping back to shore.

While David Key stays to help out at Mallacoota, Darryl Jones and Barry Barclay head out again with a replacement crewman. They start searching south-east of Eden at the last position given for *Winston Churchill*. All they find are a couple of other boats and a shredded life raft with no-one in it.

By midday, the waves are down to 10 metres, the wind has dropped to about 30 knots and the sun is shining. The helicopter searches until early afternoon without finding anything. On their way back to Mallacoota, the Victoria Police crew are told that they can stand down. They refuel, pack up and return to Essendon airport.

'I found this experience to be very moving and yet terrifying,' Darryl Jones says later. 'At times I was concerned for our own safety and in fear of losing our lives on some occasions.' A couple of times, after the Sydney to Hobart, Jones says he wakes up at night from dreams about the rescues. The memory and impact of those two days won't leave him. In 1987 he was a crewman on the helicopter hit by a high-powered rifle during a massacre in Hoddle Street, Melbourne. The image of that night returns to him regularly. Now there are two events to haunt him.

'We've been through a few sleepless nights,' says David Key later. 'The problem is you don't show your emotion. If you start to crumble, people take it as a sign of weakness. But you don't have things like that happen to you every day of the week. In a split second, it could have gone any way.'

'But,' he adds, 'that's our job. We're just policemen and this is another role we do. Sometimes you have to work beyond your capabilities to do it.'

In all, fifty-five sailors are lifted off yachts in the Sydney to Hobart and more than twenty are towed ashore. If rescuers hadn't risked their own lives the toll would certainly have been higher. After the race the helicopter crews are jointly presented with an award in America, and the Victoria Police rescuers are given an award in Canada. But not until seven months later is there official recognition in Australia.

FORTY

*It's made me more aware of the power of the sea, just
how strong it is when it's at its worst, in a tempest of
its own. And just how fragile yachts and people are.*
—*Steve Walker,* Business Post Naiad

Just before dawn on Monday morning Rob Matthews learns that Bruce
Guy is dead. He goes on deck, and sits in the cockpit, his head in his
hands. He sits there for a long time. He doesn't know what to do. Then
he stays on deck to keep a look-out for planes. 'If I yell out for a flare,
pass me one bloody quick,' he says to the others. After a while, he does
see a plane. It's about two or three kilometres in front of the boat. He
screams for a flare. But it's a parachute flare and the wind is still blowing
hard enough to blow it sideways almost immediately. He screams for a
smoke flare.

But the first flare works. The plane flies downwind and dips its wings.
'Relieved?' says Matthews. 'Hugely! We weren't even sure after the night
if anyone would be looking for us.'

At first, everyone is afraid to get too excited. 'We didn't know if they
were going to be able to do anything for us,' explains Walker. 'We were
elated that someone knew where we were. We were even more elated
when they circled and were obviously trying to identify and position us.'
The twin-engined Cessna stays circling for about half an hour. Then a
helicopter appears. The men below still don't dare get their hopes up.
They don't know whether it's there to rescue them or take pictures.

The Bell helicopter is Careflight One, based at Westmead Hospital in Sydney. On board are pilot Dan Tyler, winchman Graeme Fromberg and paramedic Murray Traynor. Dan Tyler is a Nebraska farm boy and a veteran of more than a thousand helicopter sorties in Vietnam. He's been a search-and-rescue pilot for nearly twenty years, but this is only his second winch at sea. It's only when he flies down to 20 metres that he realises how bad the conditions are. A 10-metre wave roars up beneath him. A 50-knot wind is battering the helicopter. There's still so much spume and spray in the air that Tyler is virtually flying blind.

Leaning out the hatch, Fromberg directs Tyler through the head-phones. Fromberg can see a man stretched out on the deck below him. He can't tell whether the sailor is dead or injured. The rescuers decide it's too dangerous to winch from the boat. Traynor will have to go down the wire.

Traynor and Fromberg try to explain with hand signals what they want the men to do. 'They pointed at me,' says Matthews, 'and then at the water. I pointed at Jim Rogers and the water and they shook their heads. I figured they'd been watching me walk around and thought I was the most able-bodied.' Matthews finds the longest rope he can and hooks it through his harness. 'I didn't know how good they were and I guess they didn't know how good we were. I thought that at least with a rope the others might be able to winch me back.'

Above Matthews, Traynor jumps out of the helicopter. As soon as the wind hits him, he spins around. Paddling with his swimming flip-pers, he steadies himself. Matthews takes a breath and jumps into the sea. Traynor drops down and Matthews swims. 'I got to within a metre of the frogman and I thought, I'm there!'

But as Traynor reaches Matthews a wave drives them both under-water. In the helicopter, Fromberg desperately pays out cable. A few seconds later, as the two men come out the other side of the wave, he winds it back in again. Twice the cable tangles in Traynor's legs and he has to dive down to free it. Matthews holds his arms in the air and Traynor slips the harness over his head. Traynor has to dive down to fasten the rescue strop. Eventually Traynor gives Fromberg the thumbs up.

'Next thing,' says Matthews, 'we bungee-jumped backwards out of the water. It looks gentle on television but there's an initial jerk as it rips you out. I thought the cable would snap in half. Then you swing through a huge pendulum.'

Matthews and Traynor drop into the helicopter. Traynor is already clearly exhausted, but he doesn't unhook the cable. A few moments later he goes back into the water. Matthews is given a helmet with headphones in it. The rescuers start asking questions. How many on the boat? How many are injured? At one point Matthews hears the rescue crew saying they only have enough fuel for four winches. Graeme Fromberg says later that Matthews, in no uncertain terms, convinces them to try to do them all. They do—Traynor manages to go down the winch seven times in a row. In thirty-five minutes all seven survivors of *Business Post Naiad* are safe in the helicopter. Steve Walker is last to be lifted. He closes up the boat and lashes an EPIRB into the hull. There is no way of taking Bruce Guy and Phil Skeggs in the helicopter. Eventually the boat, with the two men in it, will be towed into Eden.

When the *Business Post Naiad* crew reaches shore Drew Murray is there to meet them. The first person he sees is Walker. As Murray throws his arms around him, Walker tells him what has happened to Bruce Guy and Phil Skeggs. Drew Murray dials Bruce Guy's home number on his mobile and passes it to Walker. Guy's son answers the phone. Almost as soon as Walker hangs up, the phone in Bruce Guy's Launceston home rings again. It's a local TV reporter, wanting to know the family's reaction.

Rob Matthews makes a reverse-charge call to his wife, Carmel. When she hears the automated voice say his name, she passes out.

Later, in Eden, Drew Murray identifies the bodies of Bruce Guy and Phil Skeggs. When *Business Post Naiad*'s hull is towed into Eden harbour, he goes on board. 'That boat,' he says later, 'didn't look like it had been in a yacht race. It looked like it had been in a war.' A week later the boat's insurers declare it a write-off. *Business Post Naiad* is cut up and dumped on the Eden rubbish tip.

FORTY-ONE

It looks like he has got his wish. At least he died doing something he loved.
        —Peter Dean, son of John Dean

I let that man be the man he was and I would never have had it any different. He was doing what he loved. I married for better or sailing. I could understand his love of sailing, he was a wonderful man . . . I'm going to miss him terribly.
        —Shirley Bannister, wife of Mike Bannister

Jim Lawler was truly a man of the sea. A veteran of many blue-water cruises, he commanded a quiet respect and a genuine affection.
        —spokesman for the family of Jim Lawler

I just thought to myself—God, I was lucky. I really could feel for those other boys, and I could only hope and pray that they could hang on long enough. What else can you do? It's life. It's hard to take when it happens. You've still got to fight for your own life and if you've got someone with you, help them. Prior to that wave, we were all helping each other.
        —John Stanley, chief helmsman, Winston Churchill

By Monday most crews have been found and rescued. But five heli-copters and a number of fixed-wing planes are still looking for *Winston Churchill*. No-one has heard from the boat since its one mayday on Sunday afternoon.

There are two problems with the search for *Winston Churchill*. The first is that the initial position of the yacht, given from memory by skipper Richard Winning, is vague. The second is that early in the search the yacht is mistakenly reported to be elsewhere.

On Sunday afternoon, when Rupert Lamming at Search and Rescue headquarters makes a split-second decision to direct a helicopter to rescue the man overboard from *Kingurra*, he sends a fixed-wing plane to continue the helicopter's search for *Winston Churchill*. At the time, the closest plane is circling near the yacht *Standaside*. Its pilot, Neil Boag, is a flying instructor and pilot trainer with Search and Rescue. When Boag is sent to find *Winston Churchill* all he knows is that two yachts are in trouble. He's seen one—*Standaside*. When he sees another dis-masted yacht he comes in as low as he can, flying at about 150 metres, but can't see the boat's name. He assumes it's *Winston Churchill*, and reports its position to headquarters in Canberra.

But at the time Neil Boag isn't the only pilot searching for *Winston Churchill*. At least two others are doing the same. One is John Klopper in the Lifesaver Rescue helicopter. The other is ABC-TV's Gary Tice-hurst. Ticehurst, after first hearing the *Winston Churchill*'s desperate mayday, has refuelled and headed back out to sea to try to find the boat himself. When Ticehurst hears Neil Boag radio in a position for *Winston Churchill* he's surprised. Boag reports seeing the yacht about 40 kilometres from the original position estimated by Winning in his mayday. Ticehurst knows Winning might have made a mistake, but he searches near both locations and can't find the yacht in either. Nor can John Klopper, who does the same.

Late Sunday night, back on shore, Klopper and Ticehurst play *Winston Churchill*'s taped mayday call over and over, trying to work out what might have happened. Finally, Ticehurst tells Search and Rescue he thinks the second position for the yacht could be wrong. It's only later, in a debrief, that a Search and Rescue official tells pilot Neil Boag that *Winston Churchill* is an old-style wooden yacht. Boag is startled. He has no idea what *Winston Churchill* looks like. The boat he reported seeing was modern. His confusion is understandable. Usually he would be given a search brief, but there hasn't been time for that.

$$\prec \quad \succ$$

At first, when their boat sinks and the nine men take to *Winston Churchill*'s life rafts, each of the rafts is relatively stable. Both put out drogues. But the lines to the drogues aren't strong enough. Within about half an hour both drogues break away. Sometime after 8.30 p.m. the smaller, four-man life raft carrying Richard Winning, Bruce Gould, Paul Lumtin and Michael Rynan overturns. Winning decides he will have to go outside the raft and push it back over. But it's impossible to undo the small nylon ties on the canopy flap and he has to cut them. He takes off his life jacket, climbs out into the storm, and turns the lip of the raft into the wind so that it's blown upright. The trouble now is that the open flap is letting in water.

Looking for something to bail with, the four men realise that most of the gear in the raft's emergency bag must have fallen overboard when it flipped over. All they can find to scoop out water with is a plastic bag and a sea boot. It isn't long until the raft overturns again. 'The damn thing capsized twice on these great seas at night, which is bloody frightening, let me tell you,' says Winning. 'You have got four of us underneath this little canopy and the next thing is, you are upside down. So one poor bastard has got to go out and right it while the other three are inside. That happened twice, and it was twice too many.' What Winning doesn't say is that both times he is the poor bastard who goes outside to do it.

'You're sitting upright, arse in the water,' says Bruce Gould. 'Any rest we had between bailing I wouldn't call sleep. We were fairly confident we'd stay afloat, but we were getting a bit worried about whether anyone would find us.'

'We were all trying to keep each other's spirits up,' says Paul Lumtin, a young accountant. 'It's a funny thing. You drag lots of courage from all little places you don't expect.' Lumtin thinks frequently about his wife and two small children. 'I told them I would be back for our holiday. I said, whatever it takes, I will make it. And we all said, that's what we'll do. You can't lay down and die.'

Bouncing in the darkness, there's little any of the men can do except hope to survive till the morning. John Stanley, John Gibson, Mike Bannister, Jim Lawler and John Dean are in the second, bigger raft. 'When it gets dark,' says Stanley, 'and it's blowing a gale and raining and there's a lot of water out there, yeah, it's pretty scary. When there's a big broken wave, you can hear the surf coming. You tense up, hang on and hope it's not going to throw you upside down. We went very close a couple of times.'

Then it happens. One big wave tosses Stanley's raft upside down, too. Suddenly the five men inside find themselves standing on the roof frame. Stanley remembers it as relatively comfortable. 'In fact, as we all started to talk about it, we all thought that we were better off upside down, because we were more stable. But the problem then was oxygen. So we had to decide what to do. At that time it was really howling. To go outside and try to work out how to right this thing was going to be awkward and dangerous. Jimmy Lawler was alongside the opening and he could feel it. He said, "Well, if I have to go out, first I'd have to take my life vest off to get through this opening." We said, "Well, that's dangerous." And if one or two people went out there, there was no guarantee that you weren't going to get hit by another wave, get thrown back the other way and in that space of time, lose the one or two people. So, feeling better upside down anyway, we decided to cut a hole in the floor which is now the roof. It was a team decision which we all agreed to. You could already feel the air tightening up and getting clammy due to the oxygen being used. So we just made a four-inch cut in the roof. We could get oxygen and it felt good. A big wave would crash over us and the roof would come down, but we'd all just put our hands up, shed the water off and away we'd go again.'

For some time, it works. 'It was comfortable,' says Stanley, 'even though we were immersed in water. We were immersed in water either way, because the rain was coming in and we were continuously bailing. So you're sitting in water the whole time. We continued on like that until we got another big wave—they seemed to come every twenty minutes or so, maybe half an hour. We got this big one again and up we went again and back over again, right side up. And then it was a case of body-weight on the floor. It slowly started to disintegrate where we had cut it; it just got bigger and bigger till you end up hanging onto the edges, tucking your feet around the edges of it.'

Then, around midnight another big wave flips the raft again. 'Now,' says Stanley, 'we're standing on the roof frame, just hanging on to the inside of the raft. That was all you could do at that stage. Then, I don't know what time it was—but I'd put it at 2.30 a.m., 3.00 a.m.—this one big wave came along. We didn't hear any surf on this one. My recollection was that we tended to go up the face of this wave and it broke as we got to the top.'

John Gibson is the only person in the larger life raft who is wearing a safety harness. John Dean, who was caught around the backstay when *Winston Churchill* was knocked over, took his harness off, possibly to put on a life vest. The others, resting below when the yacht is first hit, have rushed on deck too quickly to put their harnesses on. But Gibson, who is doing the Sydney to Hobart for the first time, is extra cautious. He wears his harness and attaches himself to the raft, putting the rope around the frame and clipping himself on. It probably saves his life.

'And this one particular big wave just took off,' says Stanley. 'It really had a lot, a *lot* of power. I had my arm around the roof frame and I hung on. It just seemed to be forever. Finally it stopped and I was on the outside of the raft with my arm still around the roof frame, and I came up and got air and I yelled out, "Are you all out there?" I only got one reply. And I looked back and it was white water for about 300 metres, and I could see two people in the water with their life vests on. I couldn't see the third. And I dived underneath, back on the inside of it where John was, and I said to him, "We're by ourselves here. We can't help those guys. This wind's just gonna blow us faster than they can swim. We can only hope they can hang on till daybreak and there's gonna be a chopper in the air."' But as he says it Stanley knows it's going to be very hard for his friends to last the distance, 'You have got to be pretty realistic. Can you survive going under and just coming up for air all the time? How long can you do it?'

Jim Lawler, Mike Bannister and John Dean are lost. John Gibson and John Stanley cling on to the remains of the life raft. They're flipped over several more times in the darkness. It was Stanley who invited Gibson to sail on *Winston Churchill* in the Sydney to Hobart. 'This is a nice mess you've got me into here,' Gibson tells him as the pair hang on grimly. 'Gibbo wanted to go into conversation all the time because he's a barrister,' Stanley says later, 'I didn't have a great deal to say.' Gibson is wearing full wet-weather gear. Stanley is wearing shorts and a spray jacket.

When it gets light, Stanley expects that they'll see someone by mid-morning—earlier, he hopes, for the sake of the three other men. 'But we didn't see anyone,' he says, 'We just had to hang in there. I mean it was okay for us, but time was getting pretty desperate for the other three. The conditions started to die off after lunch. We still got flipped over every now and again, but we had a sort of system where you would flip over and take up a position on the roof frame, either back to back or facing each other, depending on which way up it was.' Gibson says later that it was, 'like going in an inner-tube down Niagara Falls'.

At first light Richard Winning and the other three men in the smaller raft notice that one of its rings is deflating. They realise that the EPIRB has broken free and disappeared and that part of its aerial seems to have punctured the raft. The repair kit has gone too. With some difficulty they re-inflate the ring and cover the holes as best they can with a bailing sponge and by sitting on them. The raft is still constantly filling up with water. They keep on bailing with the sea boot.

At about 4.00 p.m. on Monday, Winning and the others see a plane heading south. It turns west. They fire a flare but nothing happens. Then about twenty minutes later they see another aircraft. They fire their last flare and the plane signals it has seen them. 'I tell you, you had four blokes very happy to see that plane flash its lights at us,' says Bruce Gould. At about 6.00 p.m. a crew from the Victorian Ambulance Sevice, Heli-Med, arrives. The team paramedic, Cam Robertson, drops into the water and pulls up each of the four survivors.

At about the same time the four men in the smaller raft first spot a plane, Stanley, clinging to the remains of the larger raft, sees one too.

'I believe it was three or four o'clock in the afternoon,' he says. 'It was a light plane and he was travelling from east to west, probably about a half a mile away, possibly more. I waved, but there was no response. And then he came back some time later, but he was on the same line as when he went down, which I thought was a bit strange. I would have thought he'd be a bit more north or south. But then he didn't see us again. So I said to John, "Bad luck, missed that one." Then we kept going for some time and I was facing east, and it was about five in the afternoon and I'm not 100 per cent sure whether they saw us. I *thought* they saw us because I saw this big plane coming at us, low over the water, right on our path. But I was pretty aware that the raft was black— we'd lost the floor and the roof—so we were really a black ring in the water on a black background. We had our life vests there, which were yellow, and I had a white parka on. When they got near us I waved this life vest pretty furiously. Then when he went past I thought he actually blinked the light on the end of his wing. I thought he saw us because I thought: he's put his light on and he's indicating that he saw us. I said to John, "We've been spotted, we'll be right!" And then he kept on going. Then, about three-quarters of an hour, maybe an hour, later a helicopter came and went past us. They kept going east. I assumed then they were going to pick up Richard and the other raft. It was the only reason I could think of that they kept on going because I thought they had seen us. I thought Richard would be out further, that if he still had the floor in his raft he had to be travelling a lot faster.'

Stanley estimates at this point he and Gibson have travelled about 90 kilometres. In fact they have been blown about 130. Richard Winning and the men in the other raft are blown more than 160 kilometres.

The plane and the helicopter disappear. 'Sometime—it seemed forever—they came back,' says Stanley. 'It was getting dark and John had a strobe light and I had a Maglite and I could see them coming, so we put the lights on.' In the fading light a P-3C Orion, on its way back to Merimbula after a search mission, sees a torch flashing on the water. It starts circling at 150 metres and spots two men clinging to the remains of a life raft. 'They circled and buzzed us, probably about ten times. I guess it was around six or seven o'clock,' says Stanley. 'And then, finally, around nine o'clock, the chopper arrived.' The two men have spent eighteen hours clinging to the shredded remains of the life raft.

'They're here, mate,' Stanley says, as the helicopter hovers overhead, 'we might be lucky.' 'I'll buy you a beer at the fisho when I see you again,' promises Gibson.

By now it's pitch dark. The helicopter is a Sea Hawk, flying off the Navy frigate HMAS *Newcastle*. On board are Lieutenant Commander Rick Neville, Lieutenant Nick Trimmer, Lieutenant Aaron Abbott and Petty Officer Shane Pashley. The Sea Hawk, like the Sea King, is able to hover over the ocean in the darkness. Its Radalt (radar altimeter) can automatically adjust the distance between the helicopter and the water. Now the Sea Hawk flies away, swings back to the raft and moves into a hover about 20 metres above the sea. The Radalt tosses it up and down with the waves.

Pashley, who a few years earlier rescued solo yachtswoman Isabelle Autissier from the Southern Ocean, drops down the wire. He lands near the raft, swims over, climbs in, and falls back in the water. The raft has no bottom. Pashley puts the rescue harness around Gibson. Above, Abbott starts to haul Pashley and Gibson up to the helicopter. Suddenly there's a huge gust of wind. It's too much for the Radalt. The Sea Hawk is blown sideways and down. For a few seconds, Pashley and Gibson are dragged across the waves. Neville resets the Radalt and pulls up the chopper. This time it works. Pashley and Gibson are lifted into the helicopter.

But by now the Radalt is failing more often. Rick Neville has to weigh up the risks. He decides it's too dangerous to send Pashley back down the cable. Stanley will have to get into the rescue strop on his own. Incredibly, in the darkness and the gale, Neville manoeuvres the Sea Hawk over Stanley, and Pashley drops the rescue strop into the raft. After all he has been through, John Stanley's life depends on whether he can make one final, but phenomenal, effort.

Stanley climbs into the strop and signals. But as the helicopter lifts him, he feels a weight around his ankles. He realises he is tangled in the life raft and pulling it up with him. With extraordinary courage, he releases the strop and drops about 10 metres, back into the water. He unhooks the raft, gets back into the strop and is, finally lifted up into the helicopter.

Stanley, his leg broken, is taken to Pambula Hospital. John Gibson is rushed to Canberra for microsurgery to a deep cut on his hand.

At the end of the next day the bodies of Jim Lawler and Mike Bannister are found in the Tasman Sea, about 90 kilometres east of Eden. Around the same time, the search for John Dean's body is finally called off. He is presumed drowned.

FORTY-TWO

◄ ➤

*The whole town was out. Mallacoota's a pretty close
town when it comes to things like this. Some of those
men were tragically traumatised. Your heart broke for
them.*
    —Pat Peel, Red Cross volunteer, Mallacoota

It could have been you. You know what it's like.
    —Geoff Ross, skipper, Yendys

Even the people who live in the tiny resort town of Mallacoota call it
'the end of the line'. The road ends at the beach. From there, just off
the tip of a point, you can see Gabo Island. Mallacoota's population is
eleven hundred. It's a laid-back place. In local vernacular, to 'Malla-
cooterise' is to put something off till tomorrow.

Mallacoota has a police station with one policeman and a fire station
with no firemen. When there's an emergency the town's volunteers come
to the rescue. One of them is Pat Peel—a local shopkeeper, mother of
four and grandmother of ten. It's Sunday evening when Pat Peel gets
her first phone call from the local policeman. A crew has been rescued
from a sinking yacht. They need clothes, showers, food and accommo-
dation. Can she help them?

Pat Peel runs down to the trailer where the Red Cross volunteers keep
a supply of paper plates and spare blankets. She calls a friend who runs
the op-shop, opens up her own small clothing store and grabs a selection
of shirts and trousers. She collects extra towels from the neighbours. The

local radio station puts out a call for sheets and pillows. By eleven o'clock that night Pat, her daughters and two other women have the nine men from *Standaside* warmed, fed and tucked up in bed. 'They got lots of kisses and cuddles from all the ladies,' she says.

The next morning, Monday, Pat Peel is turning on bacon and eggs for dozens of rescuers and survivors. She and other volunteers wait at the airfield to meet the survivors as they're flown in. Three of the new arrivals are from *Midnight Special*. 'That place is one of the few fair dinkum communities left. They are wonderful people,' says Kevin Foran. 'We stepped out of the helicopter and a lady grabbed each one of us. They pointed to a phone and told us to use it without limit. Someone went down to the local store and bought each one of us a pair of shoes. Those Red Cross ladies were unbelievable.'

'They were older guys, the men from *Midnight Special*,' recalls Pat Peel. 'Three lovely men, but very traumatised. They perked up after a while.'

But later that evening nothing can relieve the agony of the next group of survivors. It is the four men rescued from the first of the two *Winston Churchill* life rafts to be found. 'They didn't know where their mates were,' says Peel. 'They thought their mates would be okay because they had the good life raft.' That night the four survivors hear that a search plane has found the second life raft. It's only much later they find out that three men are missing from it. 'It was devastating to see their faces. They were all just silent, sitting with their heads in their hands. I have never seen anyone in distress like those men were. They were so beaten up. The boat's owner was just staring. He didn't come good the whole time. He said, "Pat, I'll never go to sea again."'

A few days later, Mega, the former navy diver, remembers noticing the caulking on the waterline near *Winston Churchill*'s bow, just before the boat left Sydney. And, though he doesn't know who he spoke to, he remembers warning three men on the boat about a possible problem. Eventually, the police interview Mega and the *Winston Churchill* survivors about what happened on the morning of the race. 'It's irrelevant anyway,' says Richard Winning, when asked about a possible warning.

'That boat was damaged amidships. Even if he did see something near the bow, it wouldn't have made any difference.'

In the months after the race, sailors, sailors' mothers and sailors' mates write to Pat Peel or drive out to Mallacoota to find her and thank her. Nine years earlier, Pat's husband was lost from a fishing boat during a storm. 'I knew what these men were going through,' she says. 'I know if anyone had found my husband I would have wanted them to do the same thing.'

By mid-morning on Monday the low-pressure system picks up speed, loses intensity and the storm blows away to the south-west. As the conditions improve, a SouthCare crew finds Tony Mowbray's *Solo Globe Challenger*. No-one has heard from the yacht for more than sixteen hours. SouthCare winches up three men, David Cook, Tony Purkiss and David Marshall, and flies them to Mallacoota.

On Tuesday morning, Mowbray sees the frigate HMAS *Newcastle*. 'Two sailors came across on an inflatable and said: "Good morning, sir, how are you today? We have instructions to remove all people from this vessel."' But Tony Mowbray won't give up. 'We sent two off with them and that left three of us on board.' Mowbray sets up a makeshift sail with the spinnaker pole and heads north. He sails on for another day till a trawler turns up with written instructions from his insurer to tow the boat back to Eden. 'I've got to admit that in my heart I wanted to get back under my own effort,' he says later, 'but in the face of that we went along with the trawler. And, also, I was very relieved.'

By then the race was won. At just after 8.00 a.m. on Tuesday morning, 29 December, the first yacht cruises over the finish line in Hobart. It's Larry Ellison's *Sayonara*. *Morning Glory*'s race record remained unbeaten. *Sayonara* took a little over two days and nineteen hours to sail the course. During the race the big yacht damaged a mainsail, which its crew repaired, and pulled the end out of a spinnaker pole. One crewman fractured his foot in the storm.

'I had never experienced this; if I had, I would never have gone back to sea,' the Oracle software billionaire tells a reporter. 'We are a big boat and a professional crew. This is the best crew in the world and there were a lot of little boats out there, guys who don't go sailing for a living, so we were very, very concerned about other boats that were going to be following us through the track we went through. It was just awful. We just wanted to make it through ourselves and we were very worried about them. There were weekend yachties out there. It's crazy. We were horrified.' Ellison's leading crewman, Graeme 'Frizzle' Freeman, isn't so alarmed. 'It was not the toughest race I have been in,' he says. 'I have done tougher ones, that's for sure.'

The morning he arrives in Hobart, Larry Ellison says he won't do the race again. Later that day he is already wavering: 'My first reaction was that I would not do this race again if I lived to be 1000, but who knows?'

Ellison isn't as tasteless as his American friend, media tycoon Ted Turner. Turner sailed the Fastnet race in his yacht *Tenacious* the year fifteen sailors died. At the end of the race a much smaller boat was mistakenly listed as winning. Asked by a reporter what had been his worst moment during the Fastnet, Turner replied, 'When I was told that some little boat was the winner. I had four hours of bitter disappointment before it was straightened out. It was a big sea all right,' he went on, 'but we pressed on and never thought about stopping racing. One or two were seasick, but at the height of the storm we had a steak dinner.' After the Sydney to Hobart, Larry Ellison says he wants to talk to Ted Turner, because Turner 'didn't race much' after the Fastnet. 'It is going to take a lot of time to place this in perspective,' adds Ellison. 'Turner and I are doing the Fastnet [in 1999], the twentieth anniversary of the tragedy.'

The race winner on handicap is the smallest yacht to win for ten years, the 10.5-metre *AFR Midnight Rambler*. 'It's so hard to believe,' says the yacht's owner and skipper, Sydney chartered accountant Ed Psaltis. 'It seems wrong to be having a drink and celebrating after so many lives have been lost, but I hope they wouldn't hold it against us.' The race holds mixed emotions for Psaltis's father, a veteran of nineteen

Sydney to Hobarts. 'My father,' says Psaltis, 'lost a close friend in the race. Jim Lawler off the *Winston Churchill*. He was in tears [on the phone]. I've never heard him in tears in my life.'

'I wanted to do the Hobart when I was a kid of fifteen,' says Psaltis. 'My father made me wait till I was eighteen. You need experienced people.' Psaltis puts much of his success down to teamwork. He and his crew have sailed together for about ten years. 'We ended up going further west than other boats and it paid off. It wasn't a tactical thing. We were really surviving in the storm like any other boat. We heaved to and we stayed our course and we had phenomenal speeds to Tasman Island.'

Geoff Ross's *Yendys* and Gary Shanks's *DocTel Rager* cross the Battery Point finish-line early Wednesday morning. *Yendys* wins its division; *DocTel Rager* is placed fifth.

It's only as *Yendys* sails up the Derwent River that Geoff Ross finds out six men are missing. 'You know you're on the edge a bit, you know you can be lucky or unlucky for whatever reason,' he says later. 'But I'm going next year. It was a tragic race for some of the people I know and some of the boats I know. But from our personal point of view, we actually enjoyed it. It was hard, we sailed well, we got a good result. So, notwithstanding the tragedy, it was a deeply satisfying race for us. Albeit we could have lost one person, albeit we did a lot of damage to the boat on the way down. A lot of damage. And it was very difficult.' A month after the race *Yendys* is still in Hobart. Its inside is described as resembling a 'pile of matchsticks'.

On *Rager*, the radio is broken and Gary Shanks knows nothing of the tragedies. He's shocked to see the flags over Constitution Dock flying at half-mast. It isn't the usual jubilant welcome. Journalists shove cameras and mikes in his face and ask how he feels about lost boats and lost lives. 'I felt embarassed and humbled,' he says later, 'that we had made it through the race from hell, and yachties more credentialled than us were dead.'

A few hours after *Rager* and *Yendys*, Richard Purcell's yacht *Margaret Rintoul* reaches the finish. Purcell wins his division.

FORTY-THREE

> I have noticed since this last race there has been a bit
> of negativity and whingeing about various matters
> relating to it. I believe this negativity is born out of
> ignorance of what the sport is all about. Because it is a
> tough sport it needs tough people to cope with it. There
> is certainly no use complaining after the event about
> anything that happened. Each skipper knows full well
> that he is in charge of his own boat and has to make
> decisions on the boat at the critical time.
>
> All in all, the Sydney Hobart race is not a fun race.
> It is a competitive and dangerous race. It needs to be
> taken seriously and not treated as a 'jolly' or for social
> purposes or the so-called 'glory' of doing a Hobart.
>
> —*Syd Fischer, skipper,* Ragamuffin

In the months after the race, the Bureau of Meteorology conducts an inquiry into its weather forecasts and clears itself of any responsibility for the disaster. The highest wind speeds the bureau forecast for the race were 45 to 55 knots, well down on what many sailors reported. Fending off criticism, the bureau argues that its forecasts were for average winds over ten-minute periods and that sailors should have expected they would include wind gusts up to forty per cent higher than forecast. In other words, according to the bureau, its forecast of 55-knot winds means gusts up to 77 knots should have been expected. But few of even the most experienced yachtsmen say they understood the weather

forecasts that way. Most say they expected the winds to be as they were
forecast by the bureau; some expected they might be a little stronger.

The bureau claims that the highest average wind speeds during the
race were probably between 55 and 60 knots, considerably lower than
the speeds reported by many sailors. It argues that yachtsmen who
reported 70- to 80-knot winds weren't measuring average speeds but
regular gusts. To support that argument the bureau uses wind reports
from an oil rig, Kingfish B, and the radio-relay boat *Young Endeavour*.
According to the bureau, on the second day of the race the highest
average winds picked up by the oil rig were 55 knots and the highest
average winds recorded by *Young Endeavour* were 56 knots. But neither
the radio-relay boat nor the oil rig was in the worst of the storm. Kingfish B lies west of the race course. And *Young Endeavour*, moving more
slowly than yachts at the front of the fleet, didn't reach the worst area
until some hours after most of the yachts struck trouble.

So how high were the winds really? Many sailors who measured more
than 70 knots claim their wind instruments were the most accurate
available. Rob Kothe, the skipper of *Sword of Orion*, says he could turn
his boat full circle without altering its wind reading. But Roger 'Clouds'
Badham says most yachts don't have the equipment to measure such
strong winds accurately and, since wind instruments are usually fixed to
the masthead, many would have been affected by the violent rocking.
'True wind speeds,' he says, 'may have been less than those measured
due to the fact that the boats were moving.' Conservatively, Clouds
estimates that the winds during the Sydney to Hobart averaged 60 to
65 knots, with gusts up to 80. Even so, more than a third of the fleet
reported average wind speeds greater than 60 knots. And a dozen yachts
reported gusts of 80 knots or more.

The Bureau of Meteorology is just as skeptical about waves as it is
about wind speeds. It explains that waves are measured in two ways: by
their 'significant' height and by their 'maximum' height. Significant
height is an average of the biggest third of all the waves visible.
Maximum height includes the rogue waves, which can be expected to
be much higher. So, according to the bureau, its forecast for seas of five
to seven metres meant some waves should have been expected to be up

to 13 metres high, more than 80 per cent higher than the height stated in the forecast. As with the wind speeds, few yachtsmen understood the wave forecasts in the same way as the bureau.

But given the bureau's own wind forecasts, Roger 'Clouds' Badham says the bureau's sea forecasts were 'ultra' conservative: 'A wind speed of 50 knots for nine hours theoretically produces a maximum wave height of at least nine to 10 metres, without taking into account the shallowness, the "in phase" development or the opposing currents.' Clouds argues that even according to its own wind forecasts, the bureau should have expected 10-metre seas in Bass Strait during the race. He says the waves could easily have been higher because the storm's worst winds moved at about the same speed and in the same direction as the building seas. 'That,' says Clouds, 'makes for a really nasty "Bass Strait-type sea" where large wave trains or sets of five- to ten-minute periods develop. In a chaotic sea, those wave trains can easily double up on each other.'

It's extremely difficult to accurately estimate wave heights. The bureau points out that its forecasts measure vertical heights, not the length of wave faces, which can be much greater. But television pictures of rescues show seas about 15 metres high, and many sailors and rescuers reported seeing many waves that were at least 20 metres high. Some helicopter pilots estimated them as closer to 30 metres. Several boat crews say the waves that did them most damage were over 25 metres.

'The Bureau of Meteorology,' says Clouds, 'has no marine weather section, though they have been proposing such a section for at least ten to fifteen years. The quality of the [bureau] marine forecasts suffers as a result, for it often comes down to the quality of the individual that is on the shift. I frequently read coastal waters forecasts that are either wrong [or] poor and often at odds with their other forecasts.'

Before the storm hit, Clouds was able to forecast its timing, worst area and, to a large extent, its severity. But the bureau's forecasts, intended to be relied on by more than a hundred yachts, had none of that detail. Clouds is particularly critical of the forecasts compiled at midday on the Sunday: 'The observations available show that the winds were already in excess of what those forecasts reference. Why then did they reference less? The bureau appears to fail to understand the difference in wind speeds here; 40 to 50 knots is "hard" but manageable by most yachts and crews, whereas 55 to 60 knots is much more severe.'

Clouds argues that with the information available on Sunday morning, the bureau could have compiled a much more accurate forecast. It could have predicted 50- to 60-knot winds, with gusts of 70 to 80 knots. And it could have predicted 12-metre waves, with much larger waves (up to 20 metres) in areas where the current was opposing the sea.

'I feel confident,' says Clouds, 'that if this last forecast was read to the fleet that afternoon, it would have put much more doubt in the minds of many of the skippers and crew.'

'I'm also sure that many or most of the yachts would still have continued in the race,' he adds. 'For such is the nature of yacht racing and sailors.'

Like the Bureau of Meteorology, the Cruising Yacht Club of Australia also conducts an inquiry after the race. The club finds no single cause for the disaster. But it does make a great many recommendations for changes to future races. Among them are plans for all yachts to check in before they enter Bass Strait and for improvements to the club's administration, race communications, safety training and weather forecasting. Some of the same recommendations were made after an inquiry into the 1993 race. Back then, some changes were implemented. But others went by the wayside. 'Lessons like this get forgotten,' says yacht designer Peter Joubert. 'Committees change in the yacht club. Attitudes change. The crews who are in the race won't still be there in ten years time. So history will repeat itself, you'll find.'

Whatever yacht clubs or weather forecasters do in the future, there will be more storms. And some of them will be fatal. 'Shit happens,' says Richard Winning, skipper of the ill-fated *Winston Churchill*. 'One day, God might decide to put a cyclone off the top of Australia. Or He might decide to put it in Bass Strait. There's nothing we can do about it.'

FORTY-FOUR

*We will miss you; we will remember you always; we
will learn from the tragic circumstances of your passing.
  May the everlasting voyage you have now embarked
on be blessed with calm seas and gentle breezes. May
you never have to reef or change a headsail in the
night. May your bunk always be warm and dry.*
  —*Hugo van Kretschmar, commodore, Cruising Yacht
Club of Australia*

Friday, 1 January 1999

A few days after the first yacht crossed the finish line, the first day of
the new year is warm and sunny. In the afternoon a gentle breeze blows
up the Derwent River to Constitution Dock. The strains of the Christopher Cross song 'Sailing' echo over the water. As 5000 people gather
to farewell six sailors, nearby yachts, in an unrehearsed tribute, lower
their race flags in unison. A red plane turns away from the sea to the
mountain, in the symbolic 'missing man' manoeuvre. A lone helicopter,
signifying search and rescue missions, hovers at a distance.

  The CYCA's Commodore, Hugo van Kretschmar, delivers an emotional eulogy. Sailors, their friends and families weep openly. Bruce
Guy's children speak bravely about their father, Steve Kulmar talks of
his mate Glyn Charles, and Richard Winning pays tribute to John Dean,
Mike Bannister and Jim Lawler. The tragedy, says Winning, has shown
that 'man and anything made by man are finite and have their limits in
the face of natural forces'.

Muted bells ring out from Hobart's St David Cathedral. The crowd is silent as six wreaths, each a circle of white daisies and a single red rose, are cast into the still waters of the dock.

AFTER THE STORM

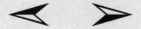

> *So how did this tragedy occur? How was it that many of the fleet sailed on past 'the corner' into such perilous waters? There is, of course, no single answer.*
> —*John Abernethy, NSW State Coroner*

The Sydney to Hobart is notoriously unpredictable. But one thing about it can usually be relied on: when the race finishes, the drinking begins.

Most years during the Quiet Little Drink, one pub alone, the Customs House, expects to sell at least one full bottle of rum for each one of the eight hundred or so sailors who make it to Hobart. Some years, there has been a craving for liqueurs as well. Then, on top of the rum every pub anywhere near the waterfront has been drunk dry of benedictine, cointreau, drambuie or all three.

But 1998 was different. According to the manager of the Customs House, drinking and celebrating were 'virtually nonexistent'. 'I think,' says Paul Jubb, 'it just frightened the shit out of everyone.'

There was little to celebrate. Even before the radio-relay boat Young Endeavour *pulled into port, a police launch met it, and log books and tape recordings of race communications were taken into custody. A few days later, police investigators began taking the first statements from survivors. At the time, no-one could foresee the extent or complexity of the resulting inquiry. Or that it would be nearly two years before the Coroner handed down his completed report and the 1998 tragedy could, finally, begin to be laid to rest.*

FORTY-FIVE

I guess it's a case of confronting the demons.
      —Rob Kothe, skipper, Sword of Orion

*I've done a lot of racing on boats around the world and
I was lucky enough to represent my country. So I don't
have this desperate need to prove myself, whereas a lot
of our crew members are going back and doing it
again.*
      —Steve Kulmar, ex-helmsman, Sword of Orion

*Yacht racing isn't my all-consuming passion. My true
passion is work. This sailing is only a subset of that.*
      —Geoff Ross, skipper, Yendys

A few months after the 1998 Sydney to Hobart, Geoff Ross was in
Hong Kong; his yacht, *Yendys*, was in Hobart; and his company was
going gangbusters on the Australian stock exchange. In 1998, Ross's goal
had been to win his division. And he did. By 1999, he was looking for
the big one—a win overall.

'I decided,' says Ross, 'that I needed a proper race boat. So I went
to the best designer in the world, Bruce Farr, and commissioned him
to build a boat and optimise it for the Sydney to Hobart.'

The new *Yendys* hit the water in December, a few weeks before the
1999 race. Geoff Ross had set some of the specifications himself. 'It's
built with Bass Strait in mind,' he says. 'It can spend twelve hours falling

off waves there if it has to. I don't want to be out there on a boat that might break up, or be worrying that it might.'

But Geoff Ross needn't have worried. On 26 December 1999, in his final pre-race message to clients, Roger 'Clouds' Badham wrote: 'This is the most exciting Hobart race forecast that I have ever prepared—fast and downhill for much of the way ... with strong NE-NNE winds ahead of a deepening trough with developing low pressure centre.' It was a forecast for the kind of conditions that hadn't been seen since *Kialoa* set its race record in 1975 and as Clouds predicted, 1999 was a record year. The wind started out in the north-east and stayed there long enough to push the fastest boats on a 'downhill' run the whole way to Tasmania. Before long, *Yendys* was up with the leaders.

'We were surfing these huge waves; running and pushing the boat to the limit,' says Geoff Ross. 'But we had the wrong spinnaker up and I was talking to the helmsman about changing it. Then we hit this 40-knot gust and it exploded. I saw it disintegrate on the pole. We were up with *Ragamuffin* but it's a much bigger boat so we would have been winning on handicap. It was just near the beginning of Bass Strait. At that moment the guy trimming the main let go and the boat went to windward. Suddenly, the boat was submerged on the windward side; the mast's in the water. We were within an ace of doing the mast.'

Thanks to 1998 and also, no doubt, to his reconvened safety committee, Ross was clipped on. 'A wave picked me up and threw me into the superstructure—that was one of the things I had had specially strengthened. I just thought, "I hope this bloody tether holds." Then I saw the boat listing at an angle and I thought, "Shit. It's sinking."'

But the new *Yendys* had the same luck that blessed the old one in 1998 when crewman Peter Seary was washed overboard and almost immediately swept back by another wave. The yacht bounced back upright. Half an hour later Ross and his crew were charging past *Ragamuffin*. *Yendys* crossed the finish-line nine hours ahead of the race record. And Geoff Ross, with three broken ribs, pulled off his overall win on handicap. On corrected time, *Yendys* came in almost seven minutes ahead of the maxi and race favourite *Brindabella*.

< >

By the time the 1999 race began, two New South Wales policemen, Detective Sergeant Stewart Gray and Senior Constable David Upston, had been investigating the 1998 disaster for nearly twelve months. Race organisers, who had spent most of that time deflecting criticism, couldn't afford to wait for the police inquiry to finish. They had to take steps to improve safety before the next race began. And they did. In 1999, crews had to meet stricter training requirements, competitors had to be at least eighteen years old and a satellite system was set up to keep track of every yacht's position to within 15 metres. The satellite tracking, it seemed, signalled an end to the old days of competitive secrecy.

Most radically, and thanks to *Sword of Orion*'s weather warning in 1998, it became compulsory for yachts to report any winds over 40 knots to other competitors. How well that rule might work in practice isn't clear. 'I wouldn't call in 40 knots myself,' says Geoff Ross, with typical candour. 'Up to 50 knots, you should be expecting it. If you can't stand 40 knots, you shouldn't be out there.'

In 1998, yachtsmen were fighting for their lives. A year later, it seemed to be the race organisers who were fighting for survival. In 1999, race entries were down by more than a quarter and more skippers than usual signed up for a rival race north from Sydney to Coffs Harbour. Looking for new sponsors and hoping to promote a new Sydney to Hobart class of 'super-stretch' yachts, the CYCA allowed a 44.7 metre giant, *Mari-Cha III*, to set out five minutes ahead of the fleet and sail to Hobart as a so-called 'demonstration' entry. Owned by American television shopping channel billionaire Bob Miller, *Mari-Cha III* featured a mahogany staircase, queen size bed, lounge room with timber columns and a collection of paintings of Spanish galleons. Since it was also about twice the size of some of its rivals for line honours, no-one was surprised when the so-called 'five-star hotel' finished an hour and twenty minutes ahead of the official race winner. Along the way, *Mari-Cha III* loitered around Sydney Heads, attracted plenty of TV coverage and got in the way of at least one serious racer.

The CYCA called the $45 million *Mari-Cha III* the 'future of yachting'. Some sailors, already outpriced by increased insurance premiums and more expensive safety precautions, wondered whether the club was predicting a future for billionaires only.

Others, like Geoff Ross, accepted the trade-off. 'The *Mari-Cha* is just a gin palace,' he says. 'The Sydney to Hobart is the Wimbledon of sailing. I want to see it survive and if that means they have to put a puffing billy in it, then they can.'

But *Mari-Cha III* wasn't the only controversy. *Nokia* took line honours, with a time of 19 hours, 48 minutes and 2 seconds, cutting a massive 18 hours and 19 minutes off the race record. But while most yachts rely on human ballast—the weight of their crew—to go faster, *Nokia* was designed to carry water which can be shifted between tanks in the hull and used as ballast. In downwind conditions, such as those in 1999, the extra weight of the water can give a yacht a considerable advantage. Before the race, the CYCA, hoping to attract more water-ballast yachts in the future, had changed the race rules to allow *Nokia* to compete against conventional boats. As it turned out, *Nokia* didn't just compete, it snared the prize.

Few competitors complained openly. They didn't dare. Race organisers made it clear that yachtsmen could be disqualified for talking to the media without permission.

One competitor unafraid of speaking out about *Nokia* is Gary Shanks, the skipper of *DocTel Rager*. 'If they're going to have water ballast, they should have a separate division,' he says. Like others, Shanks believes that sooner or later, the water-ballast boats will come unstuck. 'To me, it doesn't make sense to put two and a half tonnes of water *inside* the boat. It defies logic,' he says. 'They're a disaster waiting to happen.'

Though the new age limit meant that Gary Shanks' children, Catherine and David, were now ruled too young to sail with him, Shanks enjoyed the 1999 race. It helped that *DocTel Rager* came third in its division. Comparing the 1999 race to the one before it, Shanks says, 'Shit happens. 1999 blew 1998 out of the water.'

≺ ≻

In 1999, the seventh boat in on handicap was Rob Kothe's new *Sword of Orion*. Kothe only had one of his 1998 crew, Adam Brown, with him. Darren Senogles, voted Crewman of the Year by the CYCA, sailed on *Nokia*. Steve Kulmar, keeping the promise he made as he was hauled out of Bass Strait by rescuers, stayed on shore with his family.

One year on, Kulmar still hadn't come to terms with the death of his friend Glyn Charles. He says he is not sure he ever will. Before the 1999 race, Steve Kulmar and Rob Kothe agreed that at 5 p.m. on 27 December, the time the original *Sword of Orion* rolled, each would raise a glass of rum in a toast—one of them on land, the other at sea.

Like Steve Kulmar, John Stanley and John Gibson, the only two survivors from *Winston Churchill*'s five-man life raft, followed the 1999 race from the shore. Since his rescue, John Stanley had been outspoken about the inadequacies of most life rafts. 'I've come back and there's been a lot of attention on how I survived and why I survived,' he says. 'Something inside me has said, "Well, what are you here for? You should have a purpose."'

John Gibson found a purpose too. 'I have to be circumspect,' he says. 'There is guilt about being a survivor; there is fear that you are going to be seen as a bore; there's a real concern of self-aggrandisement. For me personally, it's given me an opportunity. When I feel emotional, I now feel at liberty to let people see that I'm being emotional and the response ... it's quite beautiful. I guess after Hobart, when you are down, you can really let go and cry, and when you are really happy you can have a huge laugh and perhaps even shed a few tears.'

In Tasmania, Steve Walker and Rob Matthews, two survivors from *Business Post Naiad*, spent the first anniversary of the storm on their boats with their wives, Helen and Carmel. The Matthews were on the river outside Hobart. 'We were in a beautiful sheltered area between Bruny Island and Tasmania,' remembers Rob. 'That night I just ended up sitting quietly with Carmel. At about eleven o'clock we had a drink to Phil and Bruce.'

The next morning, very early, he weighed anchor and headed off out of the river channel. The sky was turning grey and stormy. As Rob Matthews left the channel, he saw *Mari-Cha III* rounding Iron Pot, heading for the Hobart finish-line. A little later, *Nokia* followed. Matthews, motoring, tried to keep up with the race leaders but couldn't.

Rob Matthews dropped his wife Carmel off to do a day's work in Hobart. Then he turned his boat around and headed, alone, back up the river into the growing southerly. 'I felt glad,' he says, 'that I wasn't out at sea.'

Later that day, with less than one-third of the race's seventy-nine starters safely in Hobart, that same southerly smashed into the yachts that were still at sea. By the end of the race thirty boats had retired and eleven yachtsmen had been taken to hospitals in Tasmania. But unlike 1998, very few yachts pulled in to shelter in Eden and none of the town's fishing boats was needed for rescues. For the first time in its short history, Eden's 'Nautical Night' was a wash-out. 'It was wet and miserable,' says Locky Marshall. 'People didn't show up and a lot of the things that were planned didn't go ahead.' He adds: 'It was a real let down from all the hype of the year before.'

FORTY-SIX

> *If people want boats to be bulletproof, it just won't
> happen. You can't totally take the risk out of it, but
> you can certainly minimise it.*
> —*Ed Psaltis, skipper,* AFR Midnight Rambler

> *I realise that the cost of any changes recommended will
> ultimately be borne by the yacht owners and the crews.
> However, when one considers the cost of rescue to the
> community, not just in monetary terms, nor in the risk
> of damage to aircraft and vessels, but in the very real
> risk of injury to the rescuers, then such costs to the
> yachting community are not great. When these costs are
> considered, society, which never hesitates to aid those in
> distress, has the right to ask of the yachting community
> that it also plays its role in such efforts and adopts these
> recommendations.*
> —*John Abernethy, NSW State Coroner*

Sydney, 12 December 2000

On the last day of the inquest into the 1998 Sydney to Hobart race,
Sydney was sweltering in a heatwave and the courts were just about to
shut down for Christmas. Outside the courthouse, an endless stream of
traffic thundered past on the main road, and reporters and photographers jostled one another in the sun. It all seemed a long way from the
terrors of Bass Strait nearly two years earlier.

Inside, the courtroom was packed and waiting. Shortly after 10 a.m., the Coroner, John Abernethy, began reading out his formal findings and a summary of his recommendations. Five men had died of 'immersion' and one man of heart disease. The hearing was over in minutes. It was deceptively brief. The police investigation had taken more than sixteen months, there had been eight weeks of hearings and the inquiry had amassed thirty large volumes of evidence. John Abernethy's report was so detailed and long—340 pages—that he couldn't read it out aloud. It would have taken all day.

One of the first men to leave the court was engulfed by reporters and cameras. He stopped to speak, but few could hear him over the roar of the traffic. 'Who was that?' asked one reporter. 'No idea,' said another.

The next day, the kind face of John Gibson appeared in a newspaper. A tape recorder had picked up his words: 'The sea is always boss and when you go out there, you go out on its terms. Life is beautiful.'

Stephanie Skeggs, whose husband Phil died during the race, didn't hear the Coroner's findings or any of the evidence. She would have liked to. But since she wasn't a witness, no-one paid to fly her up from Tasmania and she couldn't afford to pay for it herself. She found being so far away frustrating.

'All along I wanted to know everything about what happened to Phil,' she says. 'I even had to get hold of the autopsy report. I wanted my doctor to tell me what it meant. I hated to think of Phil drowning, spending his last moments gasping for air. Everyone says drowning is a peaceful way to die—the thing is, how do they know?'

Stephanie Skeggs says the police handling the investigation did all they could to help her. The 1998 race was the first time her husband had ever been to Sydney. He'd missed his family in Launceston and phoned them often, filling them in on the things he'd been doing and seeing. In one call, he said he'd seen a boat with a helicopter on it and had taken a photo to show his son Josh. But in all that happened later, Phil's camera disappeared.

During the investigation, one of the policemen, David Upston, asked Stephanie if there was anything he could do to help her and she told him about the photo of the boat with a chopper on it. Upston found the boat and contacted its owner, Sydney stockbroker Rene Rivkin.

Rivkin paid for Stephanie and her two children to fly from Launceston and stay in Sydney and arranged for the family to be taken out sailing. 'All along,' says Stephanie, 'the police couldn't have been more helpful.' Her experience with the CYCA was a different story.

≺ ≻

From the start, like other bereaved family members in Tasmania, Stephanie Skeggs felt she was almost the last to know what was happening. During the crisis, the CYCA had been chaotic. 'Even on the day *Naiad* was found, they were saying the boat was okay,' says Stephanie. 'Then they said they couldn't give us any information because there were deaths involved and it was up to the police. Then finally the next day or so someone from the club rang me and said something like, "I guess you've heard the news."'

Apart from one trip to Sydney for a memorial dinner and a bunch of flowers on the first anniversary of the race, for a long time Stephanie Skeggs heard virtually nothing from the CYCA. Nor did she hear from the organisers of a trust fund that was set up after the race and had attracted more than $200,000 in donations. She had lost her only form of income. She had two children to support, no qualifications and was unemployed in a part of Australia where jobs are notoriously scarce. Even so, more than sixteen months after the race, the trust fund officials hadn't contacted her. In fact, they hadn't distributed any money to anyone. At the time the CYCA claimed there were tax and administrative difficulties.

'Friends said they would have rather given me the money than put it into a trust fund if they had known,' says Stephanie. 'I know I'd never give money to a trust fund now. I'd just give it directly.' For the sake of her children, Stephanie went public for the first time since the race, and revealed her plight in a TV interview. The next day, her phone rang. It was Martin James, the skipper of *Team Jaguar* in the 1998 race, and later, the lawyer in charge of the trust fund. James told her the trust happened to be meeting that night. Shortly afterwards, Stephanie was sent some forms and, in her words, asked to 'justify why I needed the money'.

She wrote back angrily, 'I have been through so much in the past 16 months—a tragedy that I had no part in, and having to fill out forms to prove that I need help is another stressful thing. Friends and other caring people believed that by donating money to this fund that I and other victims would receive help, not be subjected to this interrogation.' A little later, and not long before the opening of the inquest, Stephanie received about $5,000 from the trust. She was told she would get approximately $27,000 spread out over three years. (By coincidence, it's the same sum as the amount raised from donations in Tasmania.)

'You feel like you're just left out and forgotten,' says Stephanie. 'I think they would prefer if we just disappeared down here in Tasmania.'

If Stephanie Skeggs is scathing about the CYCA, the New South Wales Coroner, John Abernethy, was far more damning. Among his findings: that weather forecasters tried to warn race organisers about the storm 'but were unable to speak with anyone who understood the urgency of their telephone calls'; that the CYCA sailing office was unattended during a crucial four-hour period on the first day of the race; and that the race manager's failure to understand the formula used by forecasters to predict wind speed and wave heights was 'inexcusable'.

The club, wrote Abernethy, 'had no emergency or crisis plan from which guidance could have been obtained'; the roles of individual organisers were 'practically useless'; and the whole management team 'was organised in such a way that at the time of crisis it was to all intents and purposes, valueless to the race fleet'.

He found that the high wind readings at Wilsons Promontory were important and that the radio-relay boat could have contacted the fleet on any hour or half hour rather than wait for the skeds. The Wilsons Promontory weather report 'should have been conveyed to the race fleet as soon as it was known'.

'It is clear to me,' wrote Abernethy, 'that the Race Fleet required information on the weather conditions from the early morning of the 27th December. The Race Management Team failed to provide this.'

Stephanie Skeggs says that, at first, she didn't think she was angry about what had happened during the race. 'But then I did something that a counsellor suggested to the kids,' she says. 'I got a book and wrote letters to Phil in it. When I look back on what I wrote I can see that I was angry. Then later, things began to come out about what happened that really did make me very angry.'

One of those things concerned *Business Post Naiad*'s first mayday. According to Drew Murray, who heard the race communications on his radio in Eden, the mayday was acknowledged by the radio-relay boat and then seemed to be forgotten. One member of the rescue team said later that he had the impression the mayday had been downgraded. The inquest, however, was told that the mayday had been passed on to rescuers immediately. It was also told that several other transmissions concerning *Business Post Naiad* were recorded and monitored by race headquarters in Hobart. The Coroner made no specific finding about the mayday but he was critical about evidence from the club's race manager, Phil Thompson, as to what happened later that evening.

'We were advised that *Business Post Naiad* was running out of fuel,' Thompson told the inquest. 'At that point we discussed what we would do if they ran out of fuel and decided to just wait and see what happened.'

Not long after reporting that it could run out of fuel, *Business Post Naiad* was rolled a second time. It was then that Phil Skeggs drowned and Bruce Guy suffered a heart attack. After that, *Naiad* lost the use of its radio and was close to sinking. In Eden, Drew Murray tried to get the radio-relay boat to check on his friends on *Naiad* but was told that the yacht was okay and motoring to Eden. As Murray suspected at the time, that information was many hours old.

Stephanie Skeggs says she realises that the storm and other emergencies may have made an early rescue of the *Naiad* crew impossible. But she feels that some help could have been provided later. 'Maybe they couldn't have done anything the first time they rolled, but maybe if they'd had someone nearby when it rolled again, it might have been different.'

Referring to the club's failure to set up a rescue plan for *Business Post Naiad* if it did run out of fuel, as well as to other examples of inaction, John Abernethy wrote: 'These are not the actions of those who are managing or controlling. The only conclusion that can be drawn is that during this critical period, the race management team did no more than adopt a "wait and see" approach and effectively abdicated their responsibility to manage the race.'

Stephanie Skeggs was even more angry to discover that *Business Post Naiad* had been accepted to race in the Sydney to Hobart even though, according to a certificate submitted to the CYCA with the boat's entry form, *Naiad* didn't comply with the CYCA's own requirements for stability. 'The yacht club accepted the boat for the race when they shouldn't have,' says Skeggs. 'Why have these rules and regulations if they don't take any notice of them?'

Though, during the race inquest, the race manager, Phil Thompson, tried to blame junior staff in the CYCA office, Abernethy found Thompson solely responsible for the mistake. But because after the race, *Business Post Naiad* had been cut up and thrown on the Eden rubbish tip, the significance of the bungle was difficult to determine. After extensive evidence from experts, Abernethy concluded that *Naiad*'s entry certificate was most likely incorrect itself and that 'the limit of Positive Stability of *Naiad* was, in all probability, 109.5 degrees'—only slightly less than the 110 degree limit required for the race. And although the Coroner found that 'the lower a vessel's limit of Positive Stability the more susceptible it is to being knocked down and being inverted', he also noted that it was unclear whether Phil Skeggs died entangled in ropes or because he couldn't release his harness or because of a combination of the two. In short, the Coroner found that the extent to which *Naiad*'s positive stability contributed to the yacht's tragedy could be impossible to determine. All that would be little comfort to Stephanie Skeggs. As she puts it, 'All I can say is that if the CYCA hadn't accepted it for the race, it wouldn't have been there.'

Overall, the CYCA's race manager Phil Thompson drew severe criticism from the Coroner. John Abernethy concluded: 'Mr Thompson's inability to appreciate the problems when they arose and his inability to appreciate them when giving his evidence causes me concern that Mr Thompson may not appreciate such problems if they arise in the future.'

Phil Thompson had been race manager since 1995. At first, when the Coroner released his report, the CYCA made no comment. But the next day, just two weeks before the 2000 race, the club announced Thompson's resignation.

< >

After dealing with race organisation, John Abernethy investigated the three boats from which lives were lost: *Business Post Naiad*, *Sword of Orion* and *Winston Churchill*.

In the case of *Winston Churchill*, two boat builders gave evidence about the likely significance of the missing caulking that the diver, Geoff Bascombe, had noticed on the yacht's hull before the race started. One builder suggested that it may have been that putty was missing as the result of a slight impact, the other said that missing caulking may have caused a slow leak. The Coroner said he didn't need to decide whether it was caulking or putty that had come away. Either way, it was the huge sea that caused the most 'serious damage' to *Winston Churchill* and ultimately sank it. Bascombe's evidence, though never disproved, was considered immaterial in the light of what happened later in Bass Strait. Geoff Bascombe's pre-race warning about a problem with *Winston Churchill* was never clarified and investigators never discovered the identities of the three men whom Bascombe saw and spoke to near the boat that morning.

Another imponderable was the confusion during the search for *Winston Churchill* after its mayday. To begin with, *Young Endeavour* had not been far from *Winston Churchill*'s position, as guessed by the yacht's skipper, Richard Winning. In fact, *Young Endeavour* had initially set off to find the yacht where Winning estimated it was. But later *Young Endeavour* was directed to a different position. The second position came from a rescue plane that had mistakenly identified another yacht as the *Winston Churchill*.

The Coroner noted that had *Young Endeavour* continued on its first course, it would have reached the first position before dark and would have been well placed to search for survivors. But would it have found the life rafts and saved the lives of the three men who were later swept away? Taking into account the appalling weather and the enormous demands on the rescue effort, John Abernethy concluded that it was impossible to say.

Abernethy was careful not to lay blame on the rescue team. He quoted evidence from Brian Willey, a senior rescue officer at the Hobart race control centre. 'There's only a certain number of helicopters available, there's only a certain number capable of operating at night and they're the Navy helicopters. In the rescue coordination centre itself I think we had about twenty people there at the time and all of us were flat out doing various tasks. So it was the resources available to us in the rescue centre and it was certainly the physical assets, helicopters and vessels at sea, who we could call on to help. We felt they were stretched and we didn't know if it got worse if we were going to be able to cope with it.' Willey said he spoke with two or three of his colleagues about what they should do. 'I felt it was quite reasonable to ask for the race to be called off, to relieve the pressure on us. I guess that was the ultimate objective.'

John Abernethy made no specific finding that the race should have been called off. But he made it clear that from 1995 to 1998—the period Phil Thompson had been running the race—the administration of the Sydney to Hobart 'had deteriorated and led to problems'.

After hearing evidence from Greg Halls, the oceanographer who directed the race from 1986 to 1994, the Coroner pointed out that Halls and the former race Secretary, Robert Brenac, had established a system that would have avoided many of the problems of 1998. In particular, he noted that, in the past, race applications had been systematically vetted, the sailing office had been staffed properly, information had been discussed and passed on to the fleet and volunteers had been briefed on the race and what to do if help were needed. From 1995, said John Abernethy, this organisation had ceased. 'Why this occurred,' he added, 'has not been explained.'

≺ ≻

It was the plight of the men in the *Winston Churchill*'s two life rafts that led to some of the Coroner's most significant and detailed recommendations. 'It was abundantly clear to me,' he wrote, 'that these rafts were not fit for the purpose for which they were intended.'

During the inquest, *Winston Churchill*'s John Stanley said he believed a better raft could have saved the lives of his friends John Dean, Michael Bannister and James Lawler.

'Those three blokes would be here today if that raft had been ten or twenty per cent better and as far as I'm concerned, that's not on,' he told the court. 'It wasn't worth two bob.'

John Stanley and his fellow survivor, John Gibson, listed a number of recommendations to improve raft safety. The Coroner adopted most of them and went further, recommending that life rafts used in the Sydney to Hobart comply with the world's highest standard, the *International Convention for the Safety of Lives at Sea* (SOLAS).

Most significantly, SOLAS requires that the floor of a raft must not only be waterproof, but also insulated against cold to protect occupants from hypothermia, a condition which leads to hallucinations, helplessness and ultimately unconsciousness and was experienced to some extent by all the men in both *Winston Churchill* life rafts.

Abernethy accepted that SOLAS-compliant life rafts would be heavier and more expensive than most used by racing yachts: 'However, when safety is sacrificed for the sake of lightness the whole purpose of the life raft is subverted. It has to be remembered that the life raft will more probably than not be required during heavy seaways such as those experienced by the crew of the *Winston Churchill*. It must therefore be adequate for its task in such seaways.' In short, if a yacht has already been damaged in a storm, a flimsy life raft will be even more vulnerable. Finally, Abernethy provided a long list of equipment rafts should carry— from effective sea anchors and sun cream to hand pumps that don't require complicated assembly.

Some of the most moving evidence at the inquest came from John Gibson, who described how the larger of the two rafts flipped over, leaving the five men inside without fresh air. Together, they decided to cut a small hole in the floor, which had become the roof.

'Jim Lawler made the cut. But it was like being at a wedding and everyone putting their hands on the knife to cut the cake. Jim made the cut, but we all did it,' said Gibson. Later when the raft turned over again, the cut expanded and soon afterward, the raft disintegrated.

Was cutting the hole the right decision? According to respiratory specialist Dr Iven Young, within ten minutes of the raft overturning the men inside would have risked drowning due to 'becoming disorientated, confused, distressed' from the lack of oxygen. The doctor concluded that it would 'seem a very reasonable strategy to open the roof of this space within the first five or ten minutes of confinement'.

As to the smaller raft, which also flipped over, the Coroner noted the bravery of *Winston Churchill*'s skipper, Richard Winning, who twice went outside to right it.

'In doing this there can be little doubt that Mr Winning risked his life on both occasions,' said John Abernethy. 'Had he lost his grip at any stage then without his life jacket, which he had to remove to get outside the raft, he would have stood little, if any, chance of survival in the sea.'

During the inquiry, when Abernethy commented on the risk he took, Richard Winning said, 'It illustrates luck. If I had been swept away, people would have said, "Why did he do that?"' On the decision to turn the raft himself, Winning said that, to him, it was simple: 'You can't send another bloke out to do a job like that.'

≺ ≻

Of all the incidents in the 1998 Sydney to Hobart, the experiences of one yacht led to more speculation and controversy than any other. That yacht was *Sword of Orion*. It was *Sword of Orion* that, during the 2 p.m. race sked, alerted the rest of the fleet to the severe weather conditions it was experiencing, details of which were re-broadcast by Telstra Control. Later that afternoon, after *Sword of Orion* turned around, heading, unknowingly, back into the worst of the storm, a huge wave swept the yacht's helmsman, Glyn Charles, overboard. About an hour and a half after Charles was lost, another boat, *Margaret Rintoul II* saw the disabled *Sword of Orion* fire a distress flare. But *Margaret Rintoul* continued sailing to Hobart.

Sword of Orion had been a state-of-the-art yacht, sailed by a first-rate crew. It had warned the rest of the fleet about the conditions it was experiencing. So how did it get into so much trouble? Had the crew been in agreement about the course they had taken? Ever since the race, rumours had abounded that some on board had been too gung-ho and that others had been paralysed by fear and seasickness. It's likely that only the crew themselves will ever know the truth. But the Coroner revealed at least part of the story.

In his report, John Abernethy was critical of *Sword of Orion*'s skipper, Rob Kothe. He noted that Kothe believed he knew more about meteorology than the rest of his crew. Yet Abernethy pointed out that Kothe wasn't aware of what the Bureau of Meteorology emphasised after the race: that its forecasts should be understood to include wind gusts forty per cent higher than stated and wave heights more than eighty per cent higher. To be fair, Kothe wasn't the only one. After the race, a CYCA questionnaire found that even the most experienced yachtsmen had no idea that weather forecasts were supposed to be interpreted in that way.

During the inquest, *Sword of Orion*'s most senior helmsman, Steve Kulmar, said that some time between eleven in the morning and noon, after an 82-knot gust hit the boat, he suggested to Rob Kothe that they 'should be thinking about retiring'. But Kothe had replied that he was 'puzzled about the weather', wanted a better idea of the position of the low pressure system and needed to wait until the official forecast at midday. Kulmar had agreed to wait. But later, when the forecast came through, it was too vague to be helpful.

According to the Coroner, even though the forecast was vague about the low pressure system, the bureau's storm warning alone should have been enough. 'If one accepts that a storm warning is the highest grade of warning which can be issued for those waters it concerns me that such importance was placed by Mr Kothe on locating the low pressure system alone,' he wrote.

Abernethy quoted evidence from the Royal Australian Navy's Captain Crispin George that storm warnings indicate the kind of weather the navy is 'trained to avoid'. Even in a large vessel like a frigate, said Captain George, 'there's a call for you to assure your survival by taking specific actions regarding where you're heading, the aspect to the weather, how long you're going to remain in the weather, because you don't have the option of carrying on at the speed that you are generally. You must take very specific action to assure your survival, you're talking survival in storms. And most ships just cannot sustain storms, no matter how big they are, without suffering some form of structural damage.'

Rob Kothe was not, of course, the only skipper who heard the storm warning and continued his course to Hobart. But he was probably unluckier than most. After the vague noon forecast, Kothe had contacted Eden Coastal Patrol for more information. He told the inquiry that the information he got seemed 'inconsistent with the forecast'.

But Kothe's own evidence was confusing. In his first police interview, only six days after the storm, he had claimed to have had no shortage of information: 'I had the oil rig information, I had the barometric pressure, I had the wind temperatures, everywhere, you know, I had the whole thing plotted, so I did have a pretty good idea. And so we, the weather we got didn't surprise us.'

According to Steve Kulmar, at one o'clock in the afternoon, Glyn Charles said he wanted to pull out of the race. As Kulmar put it, 'Glyn expressed to me in no uncertain terms about his concern about the weather conditions and he did ask me to try—endeavour to convince Rob to retire.'

But Rob Kothe told the inquest he took little notice when Kulmar said that Charles was worried. 'Well to be honest I didn't give a lot of credence to the reporting that Glyn Charles felt we should turn around because he had at no time had a weather briefing in the intervening three or four hours. So what I knew was that he was probably being leant on . . . but I hadn't had the opportunity to talk to him.'

At that point, the third senior helmsman, after Kulmar and Charles, Adam Brown, was steering. Shortly after one o'clock Glyn Charles took over from Brown, whom Kothe described as 'trembling with exhaustion'.

Steve Kulmar said in his evidence that he then had asked Brown about pulling out of the race. 'I went and spoke to Brownie, he was below deck in one of the bunks. Rob had agreed that the decision should be made by the helmsmen and I went and spoke to Adam at that time, and Adam said that he did not consider his experience to be such that he should be making the decision so he deferred to me.'

Rob Kothe said he 'was not in disagreement with changing course, I was just concerned that if we changed course that we went the right way.' For that reason, he said, he overruled his helmsmen and decided to wait until the next weather forecast at 2 p.m. When that forecast was no different from the one two hours earlier, it was decided that during the sked, *Sword of Orion* would tell the rest of the fleet about the conditions it was experiencing in the hope that other boats further ahead would do the same. The sked took about fifty minutes. Only one boat, *Yendys*, which was too close to *Sword of Orion* to be helpful, reported its conditions.

Kothe told the inquiry that at the end of the sked he intended to go on deck to talk to Glyn Charles about the weather. Instead he got caught on the radio for almost another hour, relaying messages for other boats which needed help. A little later, the weather improved and the wind dropped. Thinking that they had passed through the eye of the storm, Rob Kothe said he then decided that if the wind went back up above 65 knots, they would 'go home'. He didn't speak to Charles about the weather. Shortly afterward, when the wind did pick up to 60 knots, Kothe finally gave the order to turn around but not to retire from the race. Once the boat was turned, Charles was at the helm. About fifteen minutes later, *Sword of Orion* was hit by a huge wave and rolled and Charles was lost overboard.

A year after the storm, both Rob Kothe and Steve Kulmar were adamant there was no bad blood between them. But since the race, they have met only rarely. Kulmar says that shortly before he was swept overboard, his friend Charles had been extremely worried: 'His words to me were, "Don't people realise, these are the conditions that people die in."'

John Abernethy made no specific findings on the adequacy of forecasting or seamanship in relation to *Sword of Orion*. He didn't need to. The inquest revealed other matters that were found to lead directly to the death of Glyn Charles.

When *Sword of Orion* rolled, its boom was either thrown or fell across the deck, smashing into the wheel that Charles had been holding. Charles, who was wearing a harness, had been clipped onto the boat by a lanyard, or line of webbing. When the yacht righted itself, Darren Senogles, the other crewman on deck at the time, saw Glyn Charles' lanyard hanging loose and Charles behind the boat in the water. The stitching that held the clip connecting Charles' lanyard to the harness had come apart.

It is thought that when the boat turned over, Charles was either hit by the boom swinging upwards or was thrown into the boom or other parts of the boat. Medical evidence at the inquest suggested that Charles would have suffered major injuries to his chest and, probably, his spine. It was found that he died immediately, or shortly after, he was last seen in the water.

In his report, the Coroner found that though the lanyard Charles was wearing had been labelled as meeting the Australian Standard, it probably did not comply. He wrote that he had 'grave doubts' that the lanyard would have met the standard even when it was first manufactured. He recommended a review of the relevant standard and a recall of all harnesses and lanyards of the brand 'Tuff Marine Australia'.

The final issue dealt with by the Coroner's report was the sighting, and passing, of the disabled *Sword of Orion* by the yacht, *Margaret Rintoul II*.

Should *Margaret Rintoul*'s skipper, Richard Purcell, have stopped or turned around when he saw a boat that was clearly in distress? Should he have tried to help, though, in the conditions, there might have been little he could have done? Should he at the very least have attempted to make radio contact with the stricken *Sword of Orion* after he saw it fire a flare?

Ever since the 1998 race, no dilemma had proven more controversial and divisive among both yachtsmen and laymen than this one. On one side of the argument is the law of the sea, which makes it a legal as well as a moral duty to help others in distress. On the other side, the perilous conditions, the fact that *Margaret Rintoul*'s engine was not working and the principle that no skipper should knowingly endanger his crew. And last, but not least, is the belief held paramount by many yachtsmen: that since each skipper is responsible for his own crew and his own boat, no-one else should tell a skipper what to do.

At least part of the controversy about *Margaret Rintoul* was fuelled by the CYCA. In June 1999, at a press conference for the release of its report into the 1998 race, the CYCA announced it was taking disciplinary action against *Margaret Rintoul*'s skipper, Richard Purcell, charging him with gross misconduct. If found guilty, Purcell would be banned from racing anywhere in the world. Purcell says the club gave him only one day's notice of the charge and the public release of its details.

But having announced that it would charge Purcell, the CYCA almost immediately stated that a hearing into the charge would have to be suspended due to the Coroner's inquiry. When the Coroner made it clear that Purcell would not be called as a witness to the inquest, lawyers said there was nothing to stop the misconduct hearing going ahead. But it didn't. A year later, as the Coroner took evidence on the death of Glyn Charles, the charge was still unheard and Richard Purcell was still trying to clear his name.

Ultimately, the Coroner's report did vindicate Richard Purcell. John Abernethy found that a search for Glyn Charles by *Margaret Rintoul* 'would have been futile', given that Charles had died soon after he was last seen in the water and that *Margaret Rintoul* only saw *Sword of Orion* one and a half hours later. That finding would have been the end of the matter, had Richard Purcell not made his own, further submissions to the coronial inquiry.

Richard Purcell said that trying to assist *Sword of Orion* without an engine would have endangered his own boat and his crew. The Coroner agreed saying that, 'under the circumstances, as stated by Mr Purcell, his decision to consider the safety of his own vessel and crew above any obligation to *Sword of Orion* was justified.'

Abernethy compared the actions of *Margaret Rintoul* with those of *Siena*. At the height of the storm, *Siena* had turned around to assist the stricken *VC Offshore Standaside*. *Siena* had stayed nearby until it was clear that *Standaside*'s crew would be rescued. But the Coroner found the two situations differed on one key point—*Siena*'s engine had been working at the time and *Margaret Rintoul*'s had not.

But Purcell's submissions to the inquiry went further, raising the issue of whether *Margaret Rintoul* and its radio operator, Colin Betts, a veteran of thirty-three Sydney to Hobarts, should have done more to assist *Sword of Orion* via radio.

Richard Purcell said that after he saw the hand-held orange flare he flashed a torch back and 'yelled out to Col ... to get a fix on where we were, then I, I'd sighted a yacht ... and I said, he asked me what sort of yacht it was, I said I thought it was a Farr 37, it was laying at an angle ... I think it must have had drogues because otherwise ... his stern would have been facing us. I could see men on deck in the cockpit, how many I can't remember ... I did say to Col when he got through to advise Telstra [Control] that we could not render assistance, that we did not have a motor and I felt that it was too dangerous to make an, attempt to, to turn the boat in those conditions.'

Purcell agreed that even though *Margaret Rintoul* had a VHF radio, he didn't try himself, and didn't ask Colin Betts to try, to use the emergency radio channel to contact the yacht that had fired the flare.

At twenty past seven that night, Telstra Control logged *Margaret Rintoul*'s report of a flare seen thirty-five minutes earlier. Colin Betts recalled there was a lot of radio traffic and said it took him fifteen minutes to get through to Lew Carter: 'I said, "Lew, it's Colin Betts on *Margaret Rintoul II*, we have just sighted one red flare, its bearing 090 from our position, approximately half a mile", and I gave him the lat. and long., and he repeated that to make sure he had it down right and to the best of my knowledge that was, he said "thanks for that". And ... I think that was the end of our conversation, I listened for quite a while, there was no, I didn't volunteer any information as to whether we were going down to see if we could see them and what their problem was. There was nothing back from *Young Endeavour* as, asking us were we going to stand-by or asking us to do so. And I left the radio on for a while, but I didn't hear any more, so I turned the radio off and we carried on.'

During the inquest, Colin Betts said he told Telstra Control not only about a flare but also that there was a 'dismasted yacht'. This contradicted evidence from Lew Carter, who said: 'No information was supplied as to whether the vessel which sent the red flare had been sighted or identified or the location of that vessel.' Carter said he assumed that if *Margaret Rintoul* had any more information about the boat which fired the flare, it would have passed it on.

The Coroner noted that the words 'dismasted yacht' were not recorded in the Telstra Control radio log. 'Also of concern,' wrote John Abernethy, was that 'Colin Betts did not volunteer ... details of the decision by Richard Purcell not to render assistance to *Sword of Orion*'; that 'no attempt was made by Colin Betts to try to contact *Sword of Orion* either on HF or VHF radio'; that at the time the flare was seen, Colin Betts did not have *Margaret Rintoul*'s 'VHF radio switched on and was not listening to Channel 16 (being the International Distress Frequency)'; and that 'after Mr Betts was not contacted by Telstra Control with further instructions he simply turned the HF radio off'.

Colin Betts told the inquest that he assumed that the boat firing the flare, having lost its mast, had probably also lost its aerial.

'If this was in fact his belief,' wrote the Coroner, 'then without radio communications the stricken yacht was in grave peril. If no more than an answering flare had been used to acknowledge the distress flares that had been seen this would have at least allayed any fears of the stricken yacht crew that they had not been seen. That someone knew of their plight and would alert rescuers. I am concerned that a man with the experience of sailing, as Colin Betts has, could consider this conduct, adequate under the circumstances.'

But despite his criticism of Colin Betts, the Coroner laid most blame for poor radio work on Richard Purcell. John Abernethy's view was that, as skipper, Purcell was 'completely responsible' for the running of *Margaret Rintoul* and for its communications.

'Richard Purcell did not communicate with Colin Betts for some three and a half hours after his initial instructions to contact Telstra Control. For that amount of time, Betts was left to his own devices without any instructions from Richard Purcell.

'It was during that time that Richard Purcell should have ordered and controlled the attempt to communicate with *Sword of Orion*, if by no more than an acknowledging flare, and displayed the conduct reasonably expected by Masters of vessels.'

'I accept the criticism,' says Purcell. 'There's wisdom in the criticism. I wasn't thinking about the radio. Now, I'll be more attuned. But as to firing a flare, it isn't a simple thing on a boat. No-one thinks of just firing a flare.'

For many of those touched by the tragedy of the 1998 Sydney to Hobart, the Coroner's report helped bring some kind of resolution. But Richard Purcell was not among them. More than two years after the race, Purcell was still accusing the CYCA of using him as a scapegoat, publicising the misconduct charge against him to deflect attention from itself. He challenged the charge on procedural grounds, failed, appealed and failed again. Arguing that he had lost a valuable contract to sell safety equipment because of the damage to his reputation, he launched defamation actions against two CYCA directors and the club itself. Months after the handing down of the Coroner's report, Richard Purcell was still fighting his battle for a full public apology from the CYCA and for damages for his lost business. His legal fees, already more than $200,000, were still mounting.

'My reputation as a man and as a sportsman is at stake here,' he says. 'I'm not going to let them get away with it. And why should I? They have said I could be barred for the rest of my life. I've been sailing since I was twelve and I've never had anything like this. They took on the wrong bloke when they took on me. I'm tougher than all those blokes put together.'

FORTY-SEVEN

*If we hadn't been rolled, we'd be gung-ho too. But
we're proud of the way all the guys worked together.*
—*Rob Matthews,* Business Post Naiad

*It's made me think about what's important in life. And
do it. Some lessons can't be forgotten.*
—*Steve Walker,* Business Post Naiad

When Gary Shanks first heard about the new safety requirements for
the Sydney to Hobart, he had been skeptical. Shanks and his yacht
DocTel Rager had crashed through 1998's seas and sped south in the
winds of 1999. But in March 2000, on his way home from a race
between Adelaide and Port Lincoln, Gary Shanks had his first encounter
with a rescue helicopter. And he didn't enjoy it.

'We'd won the race on handicap,' says Shanks. 'It was about seven
o'clock at night, and I was about to go down and get changed. Suddenly—scrunch, scrunch, scrunch. We had about thirty seconds—the
boat flipped, bounced across this reef and wedged the mast in on
the other side. There were six people inside and six outside.'

Shanks, who hadn't been wearing a harness or jacket, was thrown
about five metres from the yacht. He managed to get back on board.
DocTel Rager was jammed between the reef and a rocky headland. The
boat's port side was smashed in and its keel bulb ripped out. It was
dark, raining and there was a 35-knot wind.

Luckily, Shanks had fitted one of the newer, more expensive and more accurate 406 MHz distress beacons made compulsory, since 1998, for the Sydney to Hobart. Even more luckily, a Sikorsky rescue helicopter, usually based thousands of kilometres away, happened to be at Adelaide airport for repairs. The helicopter's new parts had just been put in and tested when *DocTel Rager*'s distress signal was picked up. Four and a half hours after his boat hit the reef, Shanks saw the Sikorsky arriving. But even a Sikorsky can't carry twelve people plus its air crew.

'It took five and pissed off,' says Shanks. 'It was gone for an hour and a half, so we spent six hours in the freezing cold.' Shanks, who is a doctor, could feel himself becoming hypothermic. 'I was looking at the pages of the textbook in my head. It was weird. You try to think clearly and do things like clench your fist and you can't. You shiver like shit. Then, when your body temperature drops to about 34 degrees, you stop shivering and you really get worried. The skinny ones went first.' When the helicopter returned, three people were taken to hospital with hypothermia.

Later, *DocTel Rager* was salvaged by a fishing trawler. 'For about a week I wasn't interested in seeing it again,' says Shanks. But he recovered. By November 2000, the reborn *Rager* was back in the water and Shanks was getting ready for the next Sydney to Hobart. His views about safety equipment had changed. 'In the beginning I said the rule about the 406 MHz beacons was overkill,' he says. 'No longer. Now I think, have as many as you like!'

≺ ≻

Around the time Gary Shanks was trying out his rebuilt yacht, Launceston was sweltering in an early heatwave. November is the beginning of the summer yacht racing season. But 2000, said locals, was the quietest year they could remember. For the first time in a long while, not one boat from northern Tasmania was preparing for the Sydney to Hobart. Rural Tasmania was in recession and yacht racing was more expensive than ever. There was also the memory of what had happened two years earlier. As one sailor put it, 'Since Bruce Guy died, the heart's gone out of our yacht club.'

Ros Guy, Bruce Guy's widow, found the two years after the 1998 race very painful. That first Sunday night of the storm, she says, she *knew* something was wrong. Bruce had always phoned her, wherever he was and as soon as he could. But that time when the sun rose on Monday, no call had come. A few hours later, when Steve Walker stepped out of the rescue helicopter, the first thing he had done was grab a mobile phone and dial the Guys' number in Launceston. Ros had already known what he was about to say. 'I suppose I just thought it must have been meant to be,' she says.

Ros and Bruce Guy had been together thirty-five years and spent some of their happiest times on the water. Most of the *Business Post Naiad* crew and their families had been close friends. 'We used to have a lot of fun,' says Ros Guy. 'We spent a lot of time together. Wherever they were racing to we'd all be there to meet them at the end. We all got on well.'

Two years after losing her husband, Ros Guy still couldn't bring herself to step back on board a yacht. 'These days I just try to live in the present. If someone tells me they'd like to do this or that, I say, "Go ahead and do it now. You never know what may happen tomorrow."'

≺ ≻

Stephanie Skeggs doesn't even have a proper photo of her husband Phil. The two of them had planned to have a family portrait taken at a photo studio. But they had put it off.

Years ago, says Stephanie, a fortune teller said that someone she loved would be lost at sea. 'Phil and I used to talk about it. But we never thought it would be him.' Even when the first reports had come through that two of the *Naiad* crew were dead, Stephanie thought that Phil would be okay. 'He was one of the youngest and fittest. I thought that if anyone was going to make it through, it would be him.'

Stephanie and Phil Skeggs were together thirteen years. Looking back, she says she doesn't know how she survived the first year without him. 'It was hell. I couldn't sleep. I remember being up all night, doing jigsaw puzzles, doing anything. But there are big parts of the time I can't remember at all. Like what I felt just after I heard.'

Two years after the race, Stephanie says she still has trouble believing that Phil won't come back. But, not long after his death, a throw-away comment to a friend that one day she'd like a ride on a Harley turned her life around. 'A couple of months later, this guy, Tim, just called and asked if I'd like to go for a ride.' The two had met once, some years before. 'He rang just at the right time. Any earlier would have been too soon. But he came just when I needed someone the most. It's uncanny. I feel as if Phil must have sent him. If you'd told me a year ago how I'd be feeling now, I never would have believed you.' By the time the 2000 Sydney to Hobart started, Stephanie Skeggs had sold her house and she and her children had moved to a new house with Tim Bowden. For the first time since her father died, twelve-year-old Kirsty Skeggs slept peacefully all through the night.

'I'm just beginning to get over this thing, to come out of the tunnel,' says Stephanie. 'I still often feel Phil is here with us. One day I was in the garden, cutting something down. This bee was buzzing around me all the time. Phil used to hate me cutting things down, I'm sure it was him.'

A wind chime hangs outside the Skeggs' new kitchen window. When the wind moves it, eight-year-old Josh Skeggs says he feels as if his father has come to visit.

≺ ≻

November 20 is the birthday of Rob Matthews' youngest daughter, Ange. Since 1998, life for Ange and her family has changed so much she says she can hardly remember the way it was before. 'My birthday was always around the time of some big race weekend and my Dad usually wasn't there,' she explains. 'From when I was about twelve for the next ten years he just wasn't around much for the big things like my birthday and Christmas. He'd be doing a race or taking a boat up to Sydney. I remember I always used to cry when he left. Sometimes if there was enough money he'd fly back but usually it was just me, my Mum and my sister Lynda opening the presents together.'

In 1998, Ange Matthews hadn't known about the storm until her mother had phoned her. 'I'd been away and when I got back, Mum called and said, "Dad's in trouble." She'd heard from Drew Murray in Eden. I went round to Mum's house and we just sat there with the TV on but there was no news. Everyone was ringing but no-one knew any-thing. It was quite terrifying. Mum and I just sat and cried. The last call we had late that night, someone told us the weather was better and everything should be okay. But I had this aching feeling, a real pain in the chest. I could remember Dad saying when we were kids that you never know what can happen on a boat, especially in the dark. I cried all night, I couldn't sleep.'

Ange Matthews says that what upset her most was realising that she and her father hadn't been close. 'I'd always been the one in the family who seemed to be in trouble. I felt left out of things. I don't think I even really knew my father. He never seemed to take much notice of me. Then that night I thought about how much he loved me and how much he'd done for me and all I could think of was that I hadn't even told him that I loved him. Then we heard on the news there were two confirmed dead and I was sure that one of them was Dad.'

For a long time after the race, says Ange, everyone in her family was too afraid to talk about what had happened. 'I wanted to know what he was thinking when he was under water but I was too scared to ask him. Then one day I couldn't wait any more. I asked him and he said, "I always knew I was coming home." But I said, "The trouble was, I didn't know you were."'

Now, Ange says, she knows how lucky she is. 'I got my Dad back and I'm going to make the most of him. I stopped and looked at my life and my parents' lives and I realised that I took them for granted. I appreciate them both more every day now and I have a lot of fun with them. My Dad's my best friend. We talk a lot and cuddle a lot and send each other e-mails all the time.'

In the two years since the race, Ange moved ahead at work, began a Master's degree and bought her own house near her parents' home in Launceston. 'I always wanted to go to university but I never had the confidence. I think what my Dad went through taught me that you can do the impossible. Now I want to make him proud. And he's much more supportive of me than he used to be. I think that now he just lives one day at a time. When I bought my house he cried, he was so happy for me.'

After the storm, it was sixteen months until Ange's father made another yacht trip across Bass Strait. 'Going past Gabo was pretty emotional,' says Rob. 'It was a cold rainy night and I felt I just didn't want to be there.'

Rob Matthews and Steve Walker both say they will never be able to forget that they were the last men to see their friends Phil Skeggs and Bruce Guy alive. 'It makes you change your priorities,' says Walker. 'Now I try to do the things that really matter.'

Matthews says he has good days and bad days. He says that sometimes, like Stephanie Skeggs, he feels as if Phil is right beside him. Sometimes he suddenly remembers forgotten details. And sometimes he realises that whole passages of time have disappeared from memory. Matthews is a big man known as one of the State's toughest sailors— he says he never used to cry: 'I feel like I never had emotions before. Since that race I cry at anything. You realise how fragile life is and how people get attached to one another and what it means to lose them. My father died when I was really young and I had never really pondered on what that meant till this happened.'

After the 1998 race, Rob Matthews had done nine and a half Sydney to Hobarts. In the year 2000, he couldn't help thinking that he'd like to make it ten. He made a few phone calls, and asked about places on boats. Then he called them all back and said he wasn't ready.

Matthews says he doesn't know what changed his mind. But whatever it was, that year he stayed near home all through November and December. And on his daughter Ange's twenty-fourth birthday, the whole Matthews family was together in Launceston.

SOURCES

◄ ►

Newspapers, magazines and media releases

Bresnehan, James. 'The floating palace', *The Daily Telegraph*, 22 December 1999.

Brown, Malcolm. 'Symbol of family taken by the sea', *The Age*, 29 December 1998.

Burrough, Bryan. 'Storm warning', *Vanity Fair Magazine*, May 1999.

Button, Doug. 'Sailing close to the 80 knot winds', *The Daily Telegraph*, 18 September 1998.

Campbell, Peter (Media Director, Cruising Yacht Club of Australia). 'History of the Sydney Hobart Yacht Race: 1945 to 1997'. Media release.

Chulov, Martin. 'Two men of the sea', *The Australian*, 24 December 1999.

Cornford, Philip. 'Deliverance', *Sydney Morning Herald*, 1 February 1999.

Gibson, Rachel. 'We were too busy to be frightened', *The Age*, 29 December 1998.

Green, Penelope & others. 'Proud family farewells a soulmate', *The Australian*, 30 December 1998.

Keenan, Amanda. 'Hopes smashed by just one wave', *The Australian*, 30 December 1998.

Kennedy, Alan & others. 'Sydney crew lost at sea', *Sydney Morning Herald*, 29 December 1998.

Kennedy, Alan. 'Storming home on a course for glory', *Sydney Morning Herald*, 27 December 1999.

Kennedy, Alan. 'Stunts and gags: has the CYCA lost the plot?', *Sydney Morning Herald*, 29 December 1999.

Kennedy, Alan. 'A tale of grace', *Sydney Morning Herald*, 13 December 2000.

Kogoy, Peter & Darby, Andrew. 'I should be dead now', *Sun Herald*, 3 January 1999.

Lagan, Bernard. 'The last wave', *Sydney Morning Herald*, 18 December 1999.

Lagan, Bernard & Connolly, Ellen. 'Memories of a night of terror', *The Age*, 29 December 1998.

Leggett, George R. 'A history of Bass Strait', *The Victorian Historical Magazine*, Vol. XXV, No. 2, June 1953.

McCabe, Melissa. 'The most dire strait', *Who Weekly*, 11 January 1999.

Marshman, Michael. 'Questions of life and death', *The Australian*, 2 January 1999.

Mellish, Morgan. 'Home are the sailors', *Sydney Morning Herald*, 31 December 1999.

Montgomery, Bruce. 'Control is the key says old man of the sea', *The Australian*, 30 December 1998.

Montgomery, Bruce. 'Ellison horrified for those in his wake', *The Australian*, 30 December 1998.

Montgomery, Bruce. 'Thousands gather to say goodbye', *The Australian*, 2 January 1999.

'Now the search for answers', *The Australian*, 30 December 1998.

Offshore (Magazine of the Cruising Yacht Club of Australia), Dec/Jan 1999; Feb/March 1999; April/May 1999; June/July 1999.

Saltau, Cloe. 'Yacht race pounded', *The Age*, 28 December 1998.

Saltau, Cloe. 'A very fit fellow', *Sydney Morning Herald*, 29 December 1998.

Simonds, John. 'Stout hearts go down to the sea again', *Australian Financial Review*, 24–28 December 1999.

Simpson, Lindsay. 'Hobart hails heroic *AFR Rambler*', *Australian Financial Review*, 31 December 1998.

Stapleton, John. 'Seven year hitch', *Sydney Morning Herald*, 26 December, 1991.

Stevenson, Andrew. 'Life and death adrift in two rafts', *The Daily Telegraph*, 30 December 1998.

Whittaker, Mark. 'The howling', *The Australian Magazine*, 6 March 1999.

Reports

Badham, Roger. 'Sydney Hobart 1998 Weather Notes', Marine Weather Services.

'Inquest into the deaths of John William Dean, Michael Bannister, James Michael Lawler, Glyn Roderick Charles, Phillip Raymond Charles Skeggs, Bruce Raymond Guy during the 1998 Sydney to Hobart Race', 12 December 2000.

'Preliminary Report on Meteorological Aspects of the 1998 Sydney to Hobart Yacht Race', Bureau of Meteorology, February 1999.

'Report of the 1998 Sydney Hobart Race Review Committee', Cruising Yacht Club of Australia, May 1999.

'1979 Fastnet Race Inquiry', Royal Yachting Association and Royal Ocean Racing Club (UK).

Books

Conrad, Joseph. *'Typhoon' and Other Stories*. William Heinemann, London, 1927.

d'Alpuget, Lou. *Yachting in Australia: From Colonial Skiffs to America's Cup Defence*. Collins, Sydney, 1986.

Davidson, Donald. 'Davidson of Kiah' (150-year family history of the Eden district).

Davis, Murray. *Australian Ocean Racing*. Angus & Robertson, Sydney, 1967.

Dunbabin, Thomas. *Sailing the World's Edge: Sea Stories from Old Sydney*. Newnes, London, 1937.

Gleick, James. *Chaos*. Cardinal, London, 1987.

Laughlin, Greg. *The User's Guide to the Australian Coast*. New Holland Publishers, Sydney, 1997.

Lawrence, Larry. *Marine Meteorology: Supplementary Notes.* Training Publications, Perth, 1981.

Loney, J. K. *Victorian Shipwrecks.* Hawthorn Press, Melbourne, 1971.

New South Wales Safe Boating Handbook. NSW Waterways Authority, Sydney, July 1998.

Racing Rules of Sailing for 1997–2000. Australian Yachting Federation, Sydney.

Rousmaniere, John. *Fastnet Force Ten.* W. W. Norton & Co., New York, 1980.

Scott, Ernest. *Australian Discovery by Sea.* J. M. Dent & Sons, London, 1929.

Slocum, Joshua. *Sailing Alone Around the World.* Phoenix Paperback (Orion), London, 1996.

Stephenson, P. R. *Sydney Sails: The Story of the Royal Sydney Yacht Squadron's First 100 Years.* Angus & Robertson, Sydney, 1962.

Wellings, H. P. *Eden and Twofold Bay: 1797–1965*, Eden Killer Whale Museum, Eden, NSW, 1996.

Zebrowski, Ernest, Jr. *Perils of a Restless Planet.* Cambridge University Press, Cambridge, 1997.